Explaining Hitler's Germany

# Explaining Hitler's Germany

## Historians and the Third Reich

SECOND EDITION

*John Hiden and John Farquharson*



Batsford Academic and Educational Ltd
London

First published 1983
Second edition 1989



Typeset by Progress Filmsetting
and printed in Great Britain by
Billings & Son Ltd
Worcester

Published by B T Batsford Ltd
4 Fitzhardinge Street, London W1H 0AH

A CIP catalogue record for this book is available from the British Library

ISBN 0 7134 6257 4

# Contents

# Preface

Historians have been trying to explain both Hitler's rise and how Germany was subsequently governed ever since the National Socialist accession to power took place fifty years ago. During the intervening timespan a vast amount of empirical data has been assembled about the Third Reich and this has been accompanied by the proliferation of explanatory models of the whole era of National Socialist rule. It is the latter above all with which we are concerned in our attempt to take stock of the historiography of National Socialism, particularly as it existed as a system of government after 1933. As any specialist will be aware, such an undertaking is a fearsome task in view of the sheer weight of material published on the subject in the last five decades. The increasing difficulty, for non-specialists, of keeping track of this crucial era of European history threatens to leave a serious gap in their knowledge. Whatever we think of Hitler and National Socialism our century bears its impress to an extent which is scarcely paralleled by any other doctrine except Marxism.

The volume of literature on our theme in itself precludes a fully comprehensive treatment of historical writings on the Third Reich. This is one reason why we have rejected a purely chronological approach and have decided to concentrate instead on the historical treatment of certain major issues which have figured most prominently in academic debate, and therefore constitute the more controversial areas in the historiography of Hitler's Germany. For reasons of space there are inevitably certain themes which do not figure prominently in our treatment. Our emphasis has been throughout on the ideology and development of National Socialism and government as practised by the NSDAP, and therefore by definition excludes for fuller consideration those areas of German life which either remained relatively unpenetrated by the doctrine or even engaged in active resistance against it. In other words the book does not pretend to be the complete story of Germany under Hitler.

In no sense, however, is our book a mere compilation of historical views on Hitler's Germany since 1933. It is, rather, the outcome of a critical debate between ourselves and the relevant published material. In that connection it is for us a happy coincidence that two historians whose main research interests lie in modern Germany should have come together in the same department in the same university. This has given us the perfect opportunity to pool the fruits of our individual research and background knowledge: in that respect it has made our project seem less daunting than it actually is. The book is in every sense a joint work, and this is equally and literally true of each individual chapter. We can only hope that the finished product bears out our conviction that in this particular undertaking two heads are better than one.

Although we wanted to confront rather than to describe historical writing on the Third Reich, we did feel that it was important to include a solid foundation of information about Hitler's Germany, without which some of the problems being debated would scarcely be intelligible to those who are not specialists in the field. The book can therefore be used on two levels. It offers on the one hand, with its bibliography, a critical review and guide to the various explanatory models which historians have offered since 1933. At the same time it does contain a good deal of the empirical information which has accumulated on the National Socialist era in the last 50 years. Here our approach was reinforced by our own combined experience of trying to teach the history of National Socialism to university students and by our respective contacts with sixth form historians. It is our fervent hope that our efforts will convince our readers that the history of the Third Reich, like that of any other time, is a matter of continuous debate. At a more general level we have also therefore tried to make a small contribution towards closing the gap which exists between popular perceptions of Germany in the 1930s and the views of specialists. The gap is of greater concern precisely because of the enormous and still growing public interest in the Third Reich; an interest which is unfortunately, at least in the United Kingdom, accompanied by cuts in both school and higher education which make it increasingly difficult for students to obtain reliable information. In addition, the fact that our study is based very extensively on foreign language material should render it more valuable to those unable to read French or German. Ignorance of the latter is a particular obstacle to the general reader. Although in the immediate postwar era the field of Third Reich studies was dominated by Anglo-Saxon historians, by the mid-1960s the revival of interest in their own immediate past led Germans to re-enter the field of research and thereafter increasingly to dominate it. Most new works on the Third Reich are now written in German and the majority of these never find their way into the English language. Ignorance of German is now proving to be a greater handicap than ever to the serious English-speaking student.

The only task which remains is the pleasant one of acknowledging those who helped us in the preparation of this work. Our grateful thanks are therefore due to the *Institut für Europäische Geschichte* in Mainz, which placed its excellent library at our disposal during our period of joint research in that city in the summer of 1981. We are particularly indebted to Claus Scharf and to Hugo Lacher and his library staff. These did everything in their power to cope with our inordinate and pressing demands for books and periodicals during our stay in Mainz. Financial help was extended to us by the School of European Studies in the University of Bradford and part of the research was generously financed by the British Academy. In the present economic climate such aid was absolutely crucial to the successful completion of this book.

University of Bradford — John Hiden
June 1982 — John Farquharson

**Preface to the Second Edition**

This new edition includes references to the development of controversies since 1983, and the original bibliography is extensively updated to take account of the developments in studies of the Third Reich between 1983 and the close of 1988.

J.H.
September 1988 — J.F.

# 1 The personality of Adolf Hitler

> His hair is brown, not black, his eyes blue, his expression rather disagreeable, especially in repose, and altogether he looks entirely undistinguished. You would never notice him in a crowd, and would take him for the house painter he once was.[1]

The actual personality of Hitler, even the state of his health, must always be of crucial importance in any overall assessment of the Third Reich. The interest in this topic is certainly both wide and of long standing although even serious historical research, let alone journalism, has not yet been able to locate Hitler in a wholly convincing perspective. Earlier attempts to do so centred around the biographical approach, notably in the work of Konrad Heiden in the early 1930s.[2] The preoccupation with the Führer continued to manifest itself even in books purporting to deal with broader issues of National Socialism appearing later in the decade, as in Roberts's *The House that Hitler built,* with its clear implication in the title.[3] Contemporary analyses of fascism did little to counter an already developing trend since they were invariably interested in the concept of 'leadership' and 'dictatorship' and additionally were very much prone to comparing Hitler with Mussolini, as though they played identical roles in their respective countries. Left wing analysts, however, were already beginning to fit Hitler into their own conceptual framework, based on the notion of the crisis of capitalism; that is to say that Hitler's rise to power had been facilitated by sections of German industry using him as a front man.[4]

The concern to trace the 'roots' of National Socialism which preoccupied historians during the Second World War (see Chapter 2) inevitably meant that somewhat less attention was given to Hitler the man as the Allied Powers struggled to defeat the whole German nation. The drama of Germany's collapse in 1945 and the circumstances surrounding Hitler's own suicide were directly responsible for producing the first important postwar study of the Führer. In Trevor-Roper's classic account of how the Third Reich met its end, published in 1947, Hitler once again assumed the centre of the stage. 'How wrong many of us were', Trevor-Roper commented, 'about that despot too, who has often been represented as a tool, but whose personal power was in fact so undisputed that he rode to the end above the chaos he had created, and concealed its true nature'.[5] Trevor-Roper was certainly aware of the limits to Hitler's rule, but his main concern was with the all-powerful leader, whom he placed firmly in the foreground.

There he remained in Alan Bullock's biography, still often referred to as the standard work. His Hitler seems to be a man who achieved power almost entirely through the exercise of his own demonic will, totally overshadowing his associates among the leaders of the Party. Bullock's Hitler, particularly as delineated in the chapter called 'The dictator', has exerted a powerful spell on a whole generation of historians in Europe and America.[6] Yet to re-read Bullock now is to be struck by the curiously one-dimensional nature of the portrait. There is virtually no glimpse of a real human being behind the facade of a 'consummate actor, with the actor's and orator's facility for absorbing himself in a role and convincing himself of the truth of what he was saying at the time he said it'.[7] The image remains of an enormous source of energy and power, disturbing yet oddly flat at the same time.

Moreover the vision of Hitler in this pioneer study has served as a starting point for lesser writers, not all of them professional historians, who have elaborated on Bullock's views to the point almost of distortion. The so-called 'Hitler wave', which has sometimes simply served financial or political ends, has undoubtedly helped to widen the gap between the popular and the scholarly views of the Führer.[8] In many of these books he appears as a personification of evil itself, no longer recognizable as a human being at all. Quite often it is the very imagery which creates the impression. For Fabry, 'A man emerges from the depths...embarks on an unparalleled rise to the summit of the state, makes this state the mightiest on the continent, in rapid campaigns brings the greater part of Europe under his yoke...and finally commits suicide in the ruins of his palace after the desperate struggles of his army'.[9] Even Golo Mann's normal objectivity seems to desert him when writing about Hitler in the foreword of Calic's *Hitler Ohne Maske*.[10] It is of course possible as historians to see quite clear reasons for the 'demonization' of Hitler. In one respect the undue concentration on Hitler's personality among postwar Anglo-Saxon historians was in some measure due to their unfamiliarity with previous German history. Apart from anything else this led them to exaggerate Hitler's originality as a thinker. For the West Germans a more pressing reason, especially for those who had helped Hitler into office, was the need to distance themselves and contemporary West German society from him, in the course of which Hitler became a general alibi.[11]

In retrospect it is clear that the exaggeration of Hitler's demonic personality in the postwar era has been in part, ironically enough, a testimony, to the durability of National Socialist propaganda, with its incessant presentation of the omniscient, omnipotent Führer.[12] Inherent in the demonization process was the production of the often unfounded assertions by writers on Hitler which in themselves became part of the legend.[13] The question remains open as to whether a biographical approach will ever fully explain Hitler's place in National Socialism, although his personality is bound to be a central problem. Both Hildebrand and Mommsen recognize that National Socialism and Hitler are not identical, but the former goes on to suggest that the NSDAP was in practice tied so closely to Hitler's personality and policies that it would be impossible to imagine the movement as a real historical phenomenon without him.[14] In effect this is a conceptually refined argument which evades tackling the problem head on and does not in any significant way advance our understanding. At the most it must mean that without Hitler National Socialism would not have come to *power,* since the movement did have an almost autonomous existence, dependent both on previous German tradition and on many local leaders other than Hitler (see Chapter 3).

The counterpart to Bullock's portrait is not to be found in the works of Hildebrand and Mommsen, who in this respect stand halfway between him and K. D. Bracher. The latter roundly asserts that Hitler is not in fact one of the great personalities of history but a man with 'little to arouse one's interest', whose personality is 'almost totally submerged in the history of his political movement and the Third Reich.'[15] Of course Bracher understands the historical significance of Hitler's leadership; nonetheless he still finds it difficult to give a convincing analysis of the Führer as a man. On another level, Fest has found it hard to explain why Hitler and National Socialism came to incorporate the most radical form of fascism in practice when arguing that Hitler was a child of his era.[16] In that case why him rather than any other 'child' of that era? At least the accounts which dwell on Hitler's 'dynamic' personality provide some kind of explanation for why he was able to raise himself above the mass of his followers. Equally the suggestion by Kühnl that Hitler was one factor amongst many in the explanation of National Socialism is inadequate as it stands.[17] Any attempt to write the history of National Socialism as the history of Adolf Hitler can only be superficial and has the effect of distorting the entire picture. Above all, a one-sided personification of the complex socio-historical context undoubtedly conceals the interests of different political and interest groups behind National Socialism.[18]

It is precisely on these that East German historians have focused their attention since the war when examining the Hitler phenomenon. Their point of departure is that bourgeois historians are obsessed with Hitler's personality to the point of ignoring, for party political reasons, the traditional power elites of Germany. There was no doubt a great deal of justification for this charge, at least until the late 1960s and the arrival of the 'New Left' in West Germany. In the East German view State Monopoly Capitalism (Stamokap) operated the strings of Hitler, the puppet of capitalism in crisis. In a very real sense this represents a refinement of left wing views already current in the 1930s. It must be emphasized at once that contrary to many western criticisms of Stamokap explanations, not all East German historians hold identical views on Hitler and his relations with big business and landowners (see Chapters 4 and 7). Nonetheless, Stamokap historians cannot escape the charge of oversimplification and in effect producing their own model of 'demonization', although of course they do not actually use this term.[19] In other words, by making Hitler the tool of monopoly capitalism the Eastern bloc historians have stood bourgeois theory on its head. Whilst western explanations of Hitlerism frequently exculpate both big business and the 'duped masses', eastern accounts excuse not merely the latter but, in effect, Hitler as well. After all, how can a puppet be held responsible for its actions?

The debate on Hitler's personal role is not merely academic but has very obvious implications for the understanding of National Socialism as such and its accession to power. For historians such as Bracher, National Socialist Germany would certainly have been different without Hitler, whereas if Bullock's thesis is taken to its logical conclusion, Hitler's absence would preclude the coming into being of the Third Reich at all. This either/or approach to Hitler's personality is in both cases unsatisfactory. Neither Hitler the demon nor Hitler the nonentity/puppet adequately explain his place in the history of the twentieth century. Hitler must be kept in perspective as a human being; this neither diminishes the cataclysmic nature of the events which are inseparable from him nor allows them to dwarf his importance as a personality. It is surely also important to remember that like everyone else Hitler was not wholly evil. If Cromwell asked to be depicted 'warts and all', the image of Hitler painted by most western historians seems to have little room for anything but the warts. However understandable the concentration on the devilish side of Hitler's nature, it utterly fails to make him intelligible as a man. Interestingly, exactly the same criticism can be made of his tendency to disappear as a human being behind the mask of the Stamokap puppet. The concept of the 'banality of evil', as floated long ago by Hannah Arendt in her major study of totalitarian democracy, does not preclude the possibility that Hitler also possessed normal human attributes. Those studies which have sought to present him as a credible human being serve to remind us not simply of Hitler's instability but also of his sense of humour, his almost excessive good manner to visitors, his popularity with his entourage, as well as his feelings of social inferiority in relation to the traditional elites of German society. There are, however, things about Hitler that we do not need to know. Studies of his personality should not degenerate into an exhaustive and exhausting catalogue of the everyday trivia of Hitler's daily life from cradle to grave.[20]

An examination of his intelligence and ability is clearly more to the point than what he may have had for breakfast. A pointer to the more important aspects of Hitler's personality is continued in the question posed by Francois Poncet (French Ambassador to Berlin in the 1930s): namely how a man so gifted in some areas could be so limited in others. Not that the Führer himself recognized such limits. Hitler after all was a man of very strong opinions and confidence in his own ability. Whatever historians may have said, Hitler was wholly convinced not only that great men make history but that he was most certainly one of them. For this reason alone, some brief account of his mental world is in order.

The point of departure here is his primitive Social Darwinism. At least part of Hitler's opposition to Marxism stemmed from his conviction that as a doctrine it sought to deny the natural struggle of existence and the real worth of those gifted individuals who are successful.[21] When, for example, Hitler encouraged private enterprise after 1933 it was not because he was the tool of 'monopoly capitalism'; it was rather that entrepreneurial competition represented for him

Social Darwinism transferred to the sphere of economics. What was true for Hitler in respect of the individual was also valid at the level of international rivalry, which he saw in terms of a battle for daily bread, the most pressing problem for any nation.[22] Hitler was therefore quite logical in his assertion that for a people to survive it was absolutely crucial to preserve what he called its 'racial core'. He said this in 1928 and repeated it in a speech to his generals in 1944. The state's task was to search out the biological elite, to ensure the selection of the most gifted for leadership positions. Such innately gifted leaders would then run the state, an outcome which has led Steinert to describe this programme as a form of racial St Simonianism.[23] Breitling also insists that Hitler believed in his own racial doctrines, which were based on the principle of seeking out a natural aristocracy.[24] If this were taken at face value then for Hitler a 'superior race' would mean any group of gifted individuals, irrespective of ethnic or national origins. Closer investigation however reveals an apparent inconsistency in his views. Apart from his lasting hatred of the Jews (Chapter 2), which historians have indiscriminately lumped together with his views on racial policy in this narrower sense, Hitler never really bothered to formulate a coherent picture of what he meant by 'race'. Admittedly he went as far as describing a racial hierarchy, with the 'Nordic race' at its apex and the other European peoples somewhere around the middle of the pyramid, which at times he appeared to believe categorically. Yet he allegedly told Rauschning that he knew perfectly well, scientifically speaking, there was no such thing as a race.

At first sight this would explain his derogatory asides about the concept of Nordic superiority, despite his refusal to say this publicly.[25] A problem arises, however, because on other occasions, even in private, he did appear to subscribe to the idea. Hitler did not exactly clarify his racial views by his frequent recourse to the classical world of the Mediterranean and to foreign powers in general for his precepts and models, rather than to the Germanic past.[26] And yet when he examined the ancient world on other occasions he became convinced that it had declined because it had failed to maintain the aristocracy of leadership (its racial core) by means of a proper policy of eugenics. Villard's suggestion that Hitler was aware of the practical value of the public cult of Nordic superiority as a romantic ideal which lent some colour to his regime in contrast to the flatness of Weimar is interesting.[27] Yet there was surely a pitfall for him in this line in that

National Socialist literature openly admitted that not all Germans were in fact Nordic. Thus if Hitler had carried the Nordic myth to its logical conclusion it could have had dangerous internal consequences. It was therefore better for him to use the concept vaguely. Its propagation inspired nationalism without committing him to any clear cut policy, a point which Hillgruber has made.[28] Such an explanation is too neat and epitomizes the academic's desire to find significance and motives in all of Hitler's utterances. It has clearly been difficult for historians to accept that Hitler did not think through all of his ideas, in this case in respect of Aryan or Nordic superiority. The loose ends of Hitler's racial conceptions may, however, tell us more about him and the way in which he functioned as a leader than any assumption that he always followed a wholly consistent line of thought. It is indeed a feature of the historiography of Adolf Hitler that he is invariably expected to be consistent in every respect in his ideology, which is asking too much of any human being and is not expected of other major historical figures. Certainly Hitler could show a remarkable tenacity in pursuing fixed aims, as in the case of his ruthless anti-semitism and his determination to eliminate the ideologically unfit in German society (Chapter 2). It is, however, a fallacy to assume that he was equally clear on all of his 'racial' concepts.

In addition to his sometimes contradictory thought patterns, Hitler frequently displayed a primitive view both of history and the world, stemming from a tendency to over-simplify. The use of biological models for human affairs, which Hitler often resorted to, illustrates this tendency as well as anything, as Turner pointed out.[29] Thus the actual growth of population was used by Hitler as the most reliable yardstick for the health and viability of a people.[30] Such crude and inappropriate arguments were in keeping with what Nolte has referred to as the trait of infantilism in Hitler's nature, which he suggests was the most dominating.[31] He instances Hitler's obsession with the cowboy and Indian stories of Karl May, which he devoured so avidly in his childhood and which left such an indelible impression on him that he frequently referred to them later in life. Human as this trait may be, it must be said that it is not an encouraging basis for the conduct of the foreign policy of a major power. Moreover such childish tendencies come out strongly in other facets of Hitler's character, for example his obsession with speed and his demand to pass every other car on the road. As Hanfstaengl has said, Hitler referred to any vehicle incapable of travelling above 80 m.p.h. as an oxcart.

Again, like a child, Hitler appears to have taken most things on a very personal level, especially opposition. As Bullock puts it, 'the hostility Hitler showed towards freedom of thought or discussion represented a personal dislike quite as much as a political expedient.'[32] Equally, every enemy was personalized, not merely the 'Jew' but also the 'November criminals', that is to say the SPD in 1918. Even the Habsburg Monarchy was reduced to this level. Such was Hitler's manicheistic view of the world, divided by definition into the good and the bad, that virtually every problem was conceived of on an either/or basis. Thus he seems to have recognized only two social categories, the master and the slave.[33] Too many biographers of Hitler have been inclined to see in his reduction of problems to a series of absolute categories evidence of an almost inhuman consistency of purpose. In fact it was Hitler's inability to see the world in terms other than black and white which ensured that he would at times adopt contradictory positions, since reality is infinitely complex. This is precisely the point made earlier about his mental confusion in respect of racial policy. Hitler's public commitment to Nordic superiority and German nationalism was in effect an acceptance of two concepts which were not merely hard to reconcile but mutually exclusive. The pursuit of the second would mean producing a state in which large numbers of people were not Nordic whilst excluding many who were. Here inconsistency was produced by simultaneous acceptance of two contradictory absolutes.

Faced with such contradictions and difficulties in arriving at a rational explanation of Hitler's actions and beliefs it is not surprising that historians have been increasingly driven to draw upon the findings of psychology. Of course, psychologists have been involved to some extent in the study of Hitler from the period of the Second World War onwards. The recent book by W. Langer, *The Mind of Adolf Hitler,* was actually written in 1942. In the same year Erikson could suggest that the whole of Hitler's *Mein Kampf* was 'a skilful projection of the image of an adolescent who never gave in, who refused to surrender to the domineering father and insisted on protecting the loving mother; an image designed to appeal to the unconscious fantasies engendered by German family patterns.'[34] Similarly, the chief psychiatrist at Nuremberg, Douglas Kelley, analysed Hitler 'based on the description of his closest associates... (as) an obsessive/compulsive neurotic with an Oedipus complex and perhaps a latent homosexual'.[35] A more recent account by a German professor of neurology identified in Hitler 'paranoid tendencies, incipient psychosis and megalomania': in sum, 'Hitler... was not a paralytic (meaning syphilitic) or schizophrenic, because there was no progression of the disease; he was a psychopathic character.'[36] The validity of such comments is limited by their lack of any real understanding of the socio-economic, political and historical context in which Hitler operated.

Historians do not of course reject outright every possible use of psychology, placing as they do such a central emphasis on Hitler's personality. This interest accounts for the newer application of 'psychohistory' in Third Reich studies, combining the traditional tools of the historian's craft with the insights of modern psychology. Within this framework Hitler's childhood and early origins have now become quite well documented. Here it at once becomes apparent that there is little evidence to support any sign of abnormality in his childhood, in spite of the historian's attempt to discover this.[37] In that respect Bullock's description of Hitler's rise to power as manifested after 1918 is really an admission of failure to provide a genuine character analysis, since he is reduced to saying, 'Although, looking backwards, it is possible to detect anticipations of this monstrous will to power in Hitler's early years, it remained latent until the end of the First World War, and only began to appear noticeable when he reached his thirties.'[38] Here again, as in the case of certain psychiatrists, Hitler seems to have been divorced from his background. Surely the impact of the First World War and its consequences had more to do with Hitler's changed attitudes than this early childhood? As Hildebrand has argued, not only is there no evidence of Hitler ever having been a 'monster child' but in fact an account of his childhood tends to arouse sympathy in the reader.[39] This makes Hitler more puzzling and enables more interesting questions to be raised. It is not of course seriously denied here that Hitler's early years played any part in forming his character, but too many historians have read adult traits back into his childhood, as witness the use of the word 'latent' where no positive evidence is forthcoming from his earliest years (as for example in the case of his 'latent' homosexuality). This is bad history as well as bad psychology.

The fact is that Hitler's childhood is interesting simply because it was that of a major historical figure, but as yet it has failed to lead us to any clearer understanding of Hitler the man. More promising in this respect are those studies of his adolescent years in Vienna, where he at last begins to emerge as a real human being in a specific setting. Although Maser's relentlessly detailed descriptions of Hitler the child have not significantly advanced our comprehension, his investigation into Hitler's youth has helped to destroy the self-created image in *Mein Kampf* of a man struggling with poverty.[40] This in turn raises the sort of intriguing question which has not yet been answered, namely why should Hitler have gone to such lengths to pretend that he had been so poor? It is of course possible that this was a corollary of his other deep conviction about himself, that he was by nature an artist. Poverty presumably has its place in the list of desirable qualities of the 'bohemian' painter. More to the point, there is perhaps a link between Hitler's artistic temperament, his inability to make painting his career and his later conduct as leader of Germany. Thies makes the point that Hitler's own statement in his *Table Talk*, that he became a politician against his better judgement after failing as an artist, is probably true.[41] To assume, however, that he became a politician simply because he did not succeed in another career is to raise more questions than it answers. It emphatically does not tell us why Hitler, once in power as a politician, pursued the goals he did. It has been argued that 'In the final analysis he was a frustrated architect, a failed painter, a petit-bourgeois drop-out, now armed with a panoply of powers who was able to seek a kind of self-fulfilment in the construction of enormous buildings.'[42] The most obvious puzzle here, particularly bearing in mind how many failed artists there were in Germany as elsewhere, is how this particular one came to be leader of his country and thereafter, by the usual criteria applied to statesmen, a major international figure of his era. Again, the study of Hitler's personality divorced from his social, economic and historical context cannot alone provide answers to these questions.

This becomes only too painfully obvious in what may be charitably termed the less successful of the Hitler 'psycho-biographies'. Whereas a historian such as Maser belongs to the empirical school par excellence and collects details without any particular conceptual framework, the 'psychohistorians' at their worst seem determined to go to the other extreme. Consequently their work is marred by a great deal of abstract speculation, divorced from any real study of the overall backgound. Loewenberg, in saying of Maser's 'explanations' that they are 'scarcely worthy of the name' provides a particularly clear example of the sort of conflict possible between the two opposing schools.[43] The counterpart to Maser's painstaking, if admittedly frequently trivial empirical data, is provided by Waite's probing of the issues of 'Hitler's anti-semitism, including his psycho-dynamic defence of projection, displacement, denial and identification.'[44] Waite does not hesitate to use Hitler's fantasies as a means of interpreting his character, for example his anxiety that he was part Jewish.[45] Whilst there may be some truth in this, what is the evidence for wild statements, for example, to the effect that for Hitler his Jewish family doctor, Bloch, became a substitute for his hated father Alois; thus: 'In attempting to destroy the Jews, Hitler was attempting to destroy his father.'?[46] Exaggerated claims like this can only alienate historians, are potentially misleading for the general public and detract from the value of serious psychological insights as part of a fuller explanation. The latter is certainly not provided in the recent biography by Binion.

Bloch also figures prominently in Binion's explanation, where the fact that Hitler's mother died of cancer whilst under the Jewish doctor's treatment was one of two main reasons for Hitler's murderous anti-semitism. Binion links this to Hitler's personal participation in the national German trauma of defeat in 1918: he argues that his 'gassing and temporary blindness in 1918 traumatized Hitler to such an extent that it caused the repressed guilt conflict of 1907 (the year of his mother's death) to surface'.[47] There are serious objections to such a line of argument. Firstly, it is another form of the demonization of Hitler in the sense that the inability to find any explanation for the murder of six million people pushes Binion to seek an irrational one. It is as if, in trying to exaggerate the degree of Hitler's early guilt and hatred, Binion is trying to grapple with the mathematical enormity of the Holocaust. Binion's error here seems to be to confuse views which are both repulsive and mistaken, with irrationality as such. In other words, if Hitler did not have a 'reason' for killing Jews, then we must look for a 'cause'. Yet Hitler's world view did have its own innate logic, as Jäckl has convincingly argued. The fact is that Hitler did consider the Jews as a cancer in the body politic and moreover in his own mind made them responsible for Germany's defeat in the First World War, as a result of which 3 million Germans died in vain. Since such specific events have long been accepted as helping to form Hitler's virulent anti-semitism, it is difficult to see that an examination of his feelings in 1907 adds anything to our understanding. Furthermore, do we have to search through the family records of all Hitler's subordinates who actually participated in the Final Solution to discover whether or not similar incidents took place in their childhood or adolescence? Such a manifestly rhetorical question once more highlights the fact that Hitler has been studied out of his context by the psycho-biographers. This equally applies to Binion's assertions that Hitler was motivated to take revenge on the Jews because he himself had been gassed in the First World War, as well as to his statement that Hitler desired to make Germany great again and restore its old strength as compensation for his mother's death.[48] This is another instance of the abuse of psycho-history, for we hardly need recourse to special disciplines to explain why Hitler, or any other German for that matter, disliked the Treaty of Versailles.

The above criticisms of psycho-history at its worst are not made in support of Bracher's opinion, which we do not accept, that psychological digressions, for example on Hitler's fears of being Jewish, are 'as sensational as they are pointless, for though well-meaning they are rooted in racist superstitions.'[49] On the contrary, we recognize the serious purpose behind psycho-history even if it has resulted at times in inadequate treatment, since it does raise the question as to how someone like Hitler could find such an echo in the German public at large.[50] Wehler is undoubtedly correct in stating that the real problem historians have to solve is not only the 'Hitler file' but the condition of the society which let him come to power and rule until 1945.[51] Fest touches on this with his statement that Hitler was as much a child of his era as that era, with its irrational longing, was prepared for the appearance of the Führer. At the same time this judgement underlines the need to be cautious when resorting to psychological descriptions of Hitler, with an implicit or explicit emphasis on Hitler's or on Germany's irrationalism. What is irrational, in twentieth century terms, in desiring the restoration of the power and prestige of one's own country? It is surely inevitable that in the 1920s, when it appeared that Germany held an inferior place in the world order with no immediate prospect of improvement, that large sections of the German public should have become frustrated. It is worth remembering firstly that there were numerous pre-Hitler radical right wing organizations, many of which joined the NSDAP, but all of which originated without the slightest help from Hitler. In addition, the growth of the Party in areas where he never spoke, but where local NSDAP leaders mobilized support for the movement, illustrates how widespread was the appeal of right-wing radical nationalism in the

1920s. This is the sort of area where studies of group psychology will have value in helping to fill out an explanation as to how such frustration existed and its connection with Hitler's leadership. As Steinert underlined, it was Hitler who set the spark to this potentially explosive mixture of bitterness and resentment.[52] All this has been of considerable help in fixing the background in which Hitler came to power but the failure of other would-be 'Führers' emphasizes that the historian will always have to return to the central personality of Hitler himself.

Other crucial questions concern not so much Hitler's personality as its effect on his capacity for leadership. (The related issue of the function of Hitler's role in the machinery of government in the Third Reich and as an integrating factor in his own Party will be mainly dealt with in Chapter 3.) Earlier studies of Hitler inevitably stressed his determination from the outset to assume leadership of his Party, which was very much in keeping with his own statements in *Mein Kampf*. Bullock and Trevor Roper certainly did not change this image and most of the subsequent writers have preserved the impression more or less intact, even in comparative studies of fascism. Nolte suggests that Hitler's drive to acquire dictatorial powers over the Party begins with the leadership crisis in July 1921.[53] Others, like Horn, point out in conjunction with the failed putsch of November 1923, that Hitler's own ambitions did not stop at being leader of his own Party but that he was already consciously trying to dominate the entire *völkisch* movement.[54] Hitler was not content to be a mere 'drummer up' of support for military circles at that time. In fact the one-sided emphasis on his early claim to total leadership was a corollary of the concentration on Hitler the sole dictator.[55] Conversely, the climate created by the more recent tendency to undermine the idea of monolithic government in the Third Reich (see Chapter 3) has made it possible to question Hitler's earlier intentions and the extent of his dominance over the Party. Even so, Tyrell in his study of the transition from drummer to leader is virtually alone in throwing doubt on Hitler's readiness to assume leadership in its fullest sense in the early 1920s. In Tyrell's view, Hitler only developed his ambition to dominate the movement during his term of imprisonment in Landsberg in 1924, having been until then content to be the drummer.[56] Tyrell may well be on to something in suggesting that Hitler was above all excited by the novel experience of success as a public speaker, but the future Führer can hardly have been unaware of the extent to which the infant Party was already becoming dependent on him. It is difficult to accept Tyrell's view that Hitler was hesitant about assuming the role in which the movement seemed to be casting him, in view of the fact that at the 46 meetings held between Nov. 1919 and Nov. 1920 he was the main platform speaker on 31 occasions.[57] It is more likely that his superiority as an orator reflected his already established position as a leader and at the same time reinforced it.

Moreover his major speaking role confirms at the very least the part which Hitler played in integrating the movement, whether he was reluctant to assume its leadership or not. Historians have long resorted to the concept of 'charisma' to explain Hitler's dominance, in that it placed him above factional conflicts: Hitler was 'the primary source of group cohesion, the focus of loyalty and the personification of the utopian ideal...in short, a charismatic leader.'[58] A forerunner of such an explicatory model for Hitler's leadership can be found as early as 1935, where he was compared with a film star who was 'romanticized' by National Socialist propaganda organs.[59]

The now familiar emphasis on Hitler's charisma and on the way in which he saw himself as being indispensable to Germany and to the movement did not preclude self-doubt in some respects. In particular his normal preoccupation with his health became intensified after 1933, when he was haunted by the fear of dying before his work was completed. The question which historians have often considered is: Would Hitler's premature death have meant a total revision of the system? Buchheim is firmly of the opinion that it would: '...Hitler's premature death would have brought a fundamental change in the regime; all the more so because all his probable successors were so dependent on his personal influence and so divided among themselves that not one of them would have won through his own efforts.'[60] This was a problem to which Hitler gave considerable thought, since he floated the idea of a senate to choose his successor. His concern with his health obviously has implications far beyond the government of Germany, in that it was bound to affect his foreign policy as well. Carr's short but concise study of Hitler puts it as follows: 'All the same, Hitler's preoccupation with his health was a factor in the situation which should not be ignored just because it cannot be precisely quantified. At the very least, times of illness probably confirmed him in the belief that he must act in the near future and contributed their share to events which have changed the face of our world.'[61] It is also possible that Hitler's hypochondria made him less effective in actually taking decisions but this is an area of considerable speculation. Indeed, for Hildebrand, the point that Hitler may have suffered from Parkinson's disease is only of marginal importance.[62]

Although the study of Hitler's health is interesting, it can never in itself wholly explain his decision-making process; his obsession with not missing chances was also shared by other National Socialist leaders, according to Heiber. In the florid oratory of Goebbels in 1943: 'Only seldom does the Goddess of History bestow her favours on the people of our globe, when the hem of her mantle touches this earth.'[63] In other words, every opportunity has to be exploited as it presents itself or the chance will be missed, possibly for ever. Heiber suggests that this preoccupation which Hitler shared with his followers led to hasty measures and thereby contributed to the downfall of the regime. An additional factor and perhaps more to the point in questions concerning Hitler's decision-making, was the logic of the European situation in the late 1930s. This obliged Germany to go to war far too soon in the Führer's view, because of the moral unpreparedness of the movement: 'My disciples have not yet had time to attain their full manhood. I should really have had another twenty years in which to bring this new elite to maturity.'[64] As Hitler saw it, 'The tragedy for us Germans is that we never have enough time. Circumstances always conspire to force us to hurry.' Here is another interesting facet of Hitler's personality, namely his capacity to blame his own or Germany's failure on ill luck. In reality his own hasty decisions frequently caused the bad luck for him. Although Hitler prided himself on being an ice-cold planner, who reached decisions by reason and not by emotion, his practice did not always accord with this. It is, then, almost certainly so that the central obsession of the National Socialists with seizing opportunities whenever they seemed to occur, combined with the simple logic of the situation in which Germany found herself, provide a far more convincing explanation for Hitler's often hasty actions than worries about the state of his health.

Bullock on the other hand has a more positive judgement of Hitler's grasp of political tactics and ability to exploit the occasion when it presented itself: 'A German word, *Fingerspitzengefühl*—which was often applied to Hitler, well describes his sense of opportunity and timing.'[65] Freymond agreed, particularly in regard to foreign policy, which is very often the arena in which this particular aspect of the debate occurs. 'In this respect he adopted a pragmatic attitude and was prepared to wait for the opportune moment to take every decision.'[66] It must be said that this is in many respects a somewhat flattering portrait of Hitler's ability. For example, on the timing of the war, he asserted: 'I ought to have seized the initiative in 1938 instead of allowing myself to be forced into war in 1939,'[67] whereas as we have just seen he was later to blame Germany's ultimate defeat on having had to fight too soon. At the heart of this debate lies real confusion about the concept 'opportunism'. What precisely does it imply? On Bullock's model the term is used to indicate a skilful, tactical wait until the time is absolutely right for the move (see Chapter 5). On the Goebbels model, a chance has to be taken whenever it presents itself, whether objective circumstances are generally propitious or not. Hitler did in fact act in both senses of the meaning of 'opportunism', but his own personality traits, linked with the dynamism of the regime and the exigencies of the external situation, tipped the scales more in the direction of the second sense. The progress of historical research suggests that the whole controversy concerning Hitler's opportunism and its relation to the decision-making process, reflected an early preoccupation among historians with foreign policy, where the Führer assumed a larger role than he did in the conduct of internal affairs. Hildebrand is no doubt correct therefore in his asssumption that Bullock's original picture of Hitler the opportunist needs retouching.[68] Bullock's subsequent suggestion that opportunism and long-term planning are by no means mutually exclusive was an obvious but not wholly convincing one and does little to clear up the confusion caused by his initial use of the term.[69]

A related question is that concerning Hitler's alleged pragmatism. Turner is insistent that Hitler could act so when it suited him, for instance in the case of the economic sections of the original Party programme. In 1927 Hitler told Keppler, his economic adviser, at their first meeting, that the economic goals of the Party as outlined in 1920 were 'unusable'. The Führer meant that the beliefs to which he had originally been committed in this instance were those of a young man, and that he had since changed his mind.[70] Hitler's willingness to depart from previously enunciated doctrine, at least in some areas, does not of course imply that he was completely devoid of fixed principles and was animated solely by a lust for power as asserted by Bullock: 'The Strasser brothers did not share Hitler's cynical disregard of any programme except as a means to power.'[71] Fest appears to support this view of Bullock's by stating that not only was Hitler prepared to accept any factor bringing power but also to give up any principle to get it: 'If

National Socialism, apart from certain racialist and expansionist fixations, ever did have a binding ideological or day to day political programme, this was finally abandoned in the course of seizing power and preserved only by a few eccentrics who were ridiculed or eliminated.'[72] It is too generous to say that such a line of argument takes the idea of pragmatism to extremes: it simply overlooks the extent to which fixed principles from the day to day approach of a political movement once it attains power in the state. Policy for Hitler was not characterized by any absence of long-term goals, but by his flexibility in pursuit of them. What Hitler had above all was an ability to order priorities, as for example when he decided to give more weight to the alliance with Italy than to the claims of the German speaking minority in the Tyrol, despite the Party programme's commitment to the support of Germans outside the Reich: 'The babble about South Tyrol, the futile protests against the fascists, only damage us, because they alienate us from Italy. In politics there is no sentiment.'[73] By contrast, where no foreign alliance was at stake, Hitler adopted a totally different attitude towards the Sudeten Germans in 1938. This is not to say that he abandoned the Tyrolese but rather that he had a reason for subordinating their interests to what he conceived of as the higher goal. It is therefore an error to seize on such examples as illustrating Hitler's cynical disregard of principles.

Hitler's pragmatism was in fact compatible with a well-known dislike of routine work, as witness his instruction to Lammers, head of the Reich Chancellery in 1933, that he was not to be bothered by details. For Hitler this was indeed an apparently integral part of the leadership process. Goering's statement in 1938, that: 'The Führer wants to take as few decisions as possible', was used by Winkler to prove that Hitler wished to use a policy of divide and rule to increase his personal power to arbitrate in Party and state disputes.[74]

In fact he was primarily concerned to concentrate his energies and attentions on certain areas, especially relating to the Reichswehr and heavy industry.[75] A clearer statement of Hitler's philosophy of government, as it were, is provided by his attitude towards the autobahn programme under Fritz Todt, whom he wished to be able to work free of all restrictions: '(Todt's) proposed authority only needs to be ministerial in character...' but it should 'be freed of any routine work to preserve the vitality essential to carrying out the allotted task.' The authority had above all 'to provide inspiration' and should 'have nothing to do with administration as such.'[76] In this context any attempt to present Hitler's lack of interest in routine as evidence of a lack of interest in the subject matter as such, is entirely ill-founded. For Hitler the task of the leader above all was to take the great decisions; a priority surely of most leaders of large nations.

In Hitler's case there was the additional fact that: 'He had a particular and inveterate distrust of experts. He refused to be impressed by the complexity of problems, insisting until it became monotonous that if only the will was there any problem could be solved.'[77] Schacht, like Hitler himself, considered this to be the Führer's greatest strength, namely the ability to find direct, if often brutal solutions to problems which had perplexed others. Even prior to 1933 Goebbels was already lauding this as Hitler's greatest gift, in his description of him as the 'greatest simplifier', a point which Schramm confirmed from his own observations of the Führer: 'Hitler saw his particular strength in an ability to simplify complex problems and to think consistently.'[78] Even his choice of personal entourage and advisers seems to have been dictated more by his familiarity and friendship with the people in question than by any appreciation of their intellectual abilities. Here a real problem arises because of the relationship between Hitler and his entourage on the one hand, and his function as a leader on the other. Hitler was capable of putting up with associates because of their loyalty to him even if they were not in fact competent. Overy has provided an important example of this in his analysis of the part played by Göring and by Hitler in German aircraft production, and in the management of the Luftwaffe in general. When the Führer's circle asked him quite simply why he continued to tolerate Göring's apparent incompetence, Hitler justified retaining him on the grounds of his personal devotion and by the way in which he kept his nerve in a political crisis.[79]

It is both significant and surprising that although this capacity for personal loyalty on the part of Hitler was described as early as 1949 in Zoller's *Hitler Privat,* it was largely overlooked, together with his other human qualities, because of the dominance of what we have called the 'demonization' trend in biographies of the Führer. Hitler was human and it ought not to surprise us that he had a keen sense of humour.[80] The 'humanization' of Hitler, that is to say the presentation of him as a recognizeable member of the human race, is a welcome trend in recent historiography. Historians such as Fest and Schramm are not of course attempting to exculpate Hitler in this way or to make him more attractive, let alone to excuse his atrocities. Their object is simply to make it plain to the reader that no assessment either of Hitler or the way in which he ran his country can possibly be made without a basic understanding of his whole personality. In this connection the longstanding tendency in many books and even films to portray Hitler as a frenzied hysteric devoid of any form of self-control simply feeds the demonization legend. In no other respect does the public image of Hitler differ so widely from that presented by those who actually met him. Backe insists that the picture of Hitler as a man who habitually ranted and raved at his subordinates belongs to the world of fable.[81] This is not to deny that Hitler lost his temper on many occasions both before and during the war, as any statesman faced with his responsibilities would be likely to do. But those contemporaries whc expected, before meeting Hitler, to be confronted with a raving madman, were often struck by his relative degree of self-control.[82] What bothered them was his unpredictability, and the difficulty for the observer to determine in advance how he would next react. The question here is how far this was an actual weapon in Hitler's own armoury. Domarus mentions several occasions when after an apparently uncontrolled outburst of hysterical rage, Hitler's demeanour changed in such a way as to make it obvious that the entire scene had been a calculated ploy.[83] This was not exactly a pleasant trait, but it is hardly unique amongst politicians. The real issue is that it is impossible to show that Hitler was a mere hysteric, unable to control his temper.

An interesting case study of how all these different aspects of Hitler's whole personality could come together and influence his capacity as a leader can be found in the military sphere. In the first place, it is difficult to find another area in German life (with the possible exception of the law) where Hitler's indifference to experts was so visible. How else is one to account for the fact that in five years of service under Hitler, Beck, the Chief of the General Staff, claimed that he never had a chance to brief Hitler on his views regarding defence? In fact the only chance he had for a proper conversation at all lasted five minutes.[84] Keitel, the Chief of the *Wehrmacht Amt,* which was the office preparing the Defence Ministry Directives for the armed forces, 'only met Hitler face to face three times between 1935 and the beginning of 1938'.[85] What better illustration could there be for the way in which Hitler's personality affected the whole process of government in Germany, since he manifestly *was* extremely interested in both defence and foreign policy? As Göring testified at Nuremberg, he regarded them both as his own special province. For Hitler the more narrowly professional concerns of the military mind could never alone provide the basis for a proper defence strategy, with which his foreign policy was so closely linked. This provides yet another instance of Hitler's extraordinary belief in his own ability in certain areas, a belief which often prevented him taking the advice of those he dismissed as 'mere experts'. Alongside this went a strong gambler's streak in Hitler's personality, together with his feeling that Germany was short of time in any case. All these factors conspired to reinforce Hitler's conviction that he should pursue a policy of Blitzkrieg at the strategic level as well as at the tactical. According to Thomas, it was precisely this which prevented proper preparations being made for the sort of war which Germany would almost certainly have to wage.[86] (see Chapters 5 and 6.) Historiographically, the debate about Hitler's capacity as a wartime leader, which by definition could only begin seriously after 1945, brought general agreement that the Führer was responsible for many of the failures of the German Army in the Second World War.[87] It was only somewhat later that Hitler began to get credit for the successes as well,[88] for example: 'In addition Hitler personally supervised the planning and preparation of some of the most daring coups of the War, such as the capture of Dirschau bridge in Poland, that of the Eben Emael fort in Belgium and the conquest of Crete.'[89]

Such audacious strokes could not, however, disguise Germany's basic weaknesses and these became an insuperable obstacle to such a method of waging a world war. In that respect limits were set to Hitler's capacity as a war leader by the circumstances in which Germany found itself; but there is no doubt that his own inability systematically contributed to Germany's defeat. Hitler could not endlessly pull off a series of bold actions in the face of mounting Allied material and technical superiority. As these factors began to make themselves more and more evident, Hitler's luck ran out. It must be emphasized, however, that it was ultimately Hitler's errors in the political field which had contributed to uniting such extensive foreign resistance against Germany and which in so doing had made virtually impossible the task of any German military leader. A list of Hitler's successes and failures during the War has led Carr to suggest that as a military leader: 'He was a veritable jack-in-the-box, who interpreted every situation to suit himself regardless of inconsistency. This habit points to the profound struggle taking place in Hitler between...his acute intelligence, which left him in no doubt about the likely outcome of the War and...his deeply held conviction that he was a man with a mission to accomplish, whom "providence" would protect.'[90] The willpower which had been so important in bringing Hitler to office and in running Germany prior to 1939 increasingly became a liability the longer the War continued. He was not able emotionally to accept the objective facts of the military situation. As Roper said: 'To him, the reality...was not a fact but an artefact: it was made by the human mind, the human will.'[91] This is a dangerous trait at any time in a leader but especially in time of war.

Hitler's distrust of experts almost inevitably distanced him from his generals in regard to the conduct of the campaigns. Despite his undoubted technical expertise there were considerable gaps in his knowledge, though these were greatly exaggerated by F. Halder, the Chief of General Staff from 1938 to 1942. Hitler tended to judge Germany's military situation by how many troops there were in the front line at any given moment, especially the number of divisions. According to Göring this had a serious effect on the Russian campaign, since Hitler neglected reinforcement back-up and logistics.[92] Another example is provided by the German Army request that Germany should not declare war unless it had four months' reserves of ammunition: in fact, when hostilities commenced there were only six weeks' supply.[93] (see Chapter 6.) Equally, Hitler was less technically gifted than he supposed himself to be, in respect above all of modern weapons, many of which he failed to understand. Both Overy and Carr agree that Hitler was basically an infantryman from the First World War who did not understand either sea or air warfare or the armaments associated with them.[94] More dramatically, the contempt with which Hitler dismissed atomic research as 'Jewish physics' had obvious implications for any German attempt to produce a nuclear weapon.

Taken together such examples confirm the way in which war highlighted Hitler's personality defects. The most serious of these turned out to be his indecisiveness under pressure, which manifested itself in two particularly important areas, namely the actual conduct of operations and the forward planning of the German rearmament programme. An instance of the former would be the way in which Hitler in panic very nearly ordered the surrender of Narvik just when the German troops were about to achieve victory. For the latter aspect of Hitler's leadership Thomas provides several instances of his changing his mind under pressure in 1940 and 1942.[95] Such indecisiveness was not proof of physical cowardice, as his conduct in the trenches in World War One had proved. Yet he does seem to have lacked moral fibre on occasions, in his reluctance to face up to the consequences of the Second World War for the German people. As Heiber points out, unlike Goebbels Hitler seems to have been afraid of visiting any bombed cities. Indeed the longer the war continued the more reluctant Hitler became to appear in public at all, again in contrast to the Minister of Propaganda.[96] In this respect the incident in Speer's memoirs is informative; when Hitler, sitting in his private train, saw some wounded soldiers outside, he immediately pulled down the blind to avoid the sight of the suffering which his own policies had caused.

Yet although Hitler was inadequate as a war leader, there was, according to Keitel, nobody to replace him in the overall direction of the war and in particular in the conduct of the campaigns against the Soviet Union. In the last resort Hitler's character defects have to be set alongside what he actually achieved in his own lifetime. 'He may have been a hideous historical phenomenon, but at least he was an important historical phenomenon, and we cannot afford to pass him by.'[97] By comparison with other major historical figures of this century his achievements were considerable even if ultimately overshadowed by the repulsion which we feel towards the policies which he followed. Hitler rose from nothing to become leader of a

country of which he had only recently become a citizen; he found it in a state of decline, both economically and militarily, and yet eight years after his assumption of power Germany was mistress of Europe. Ultimately, he failed chiefly because of the overwhelming superiority of his enemies, but it must be borne in mind that this hostile coalition was one which his own mistakes had conjured up.

Nothing has so imprinted itself on the history of the twentieth centruy as this powerful if flawed personality. In one respect at least he was truly a child of his era in that his relatively modest social origins were similar to those of other twentieth century dictators. As to his personality, it must always be given full weight in the assessment of that era as a whole. Yet we do not have to go as far as Speer in arguing that 'The whole demonic figure of the man can never be explained simply as the product of events...They could just as easily have found expression in a national leader of mediocre stature. For Hitler was one of those inexplicable historical phenomena which emerge at rare intervals among mankind. His person determined the fate of the nation. He alone placed, and kept it, upon the path which has led to this dreadful ending.'[98] The attraction of this sort of approach at first glance, and it is characteristic also of most Hitler biographies, is that it appears to do justice to Hitler's own great ability. As we have argued, however, this would be to take Hitler's own assessment of himself too much at face value and it does not give sufficient weight to the background and circumstances in which he actually came to power.

Conversely, although providing a valuable corrective to some Hitler biographies, such objective realities figure somewhat too largely in what is described as structural history, of which Stamokap theories are one variant and indeed the oldest. Here the central emphasis is not so much on Hitler as on the socio-economic and political circumstances in which he came to power and governed. Additionally such studies analyse the actual structures of the state and society which he ruled. However, all variations on this approach are in the final analysis unable to do justice to his personality and policies. Hitler was not directly interchangeable with any other German of his era who grew up in the same circumstances.[99] The problem of achieving a real balance between 'structural history' on the one hand and biographies on the other has not been satisfactorily resolved. In the latter there is too much attention to Hitler's demonic will, even in the best books. At their worst some biographies seem over concerned to tell us what Hitler had for breakfast, or to draw questionable conclusions from his alleged sexual deviance or from incidents in his childhood. The 'Hitler wave' has been a mixed blessing, confirming that the discovery of more and more detail about Hitler's private life does not necessarily lead to a better understanding of him as a man or as a leader. It must be complemented by continuing research into the socio-political, economic context in which Hitler operated, which alone can make his world view and his subsequent actions intelligible. The longstanding concentration on Hitler's personality *per se* produced too much talk about the irrationality both of Hitler and of National Socialism. That arose from an understandable preoccupation with the Final Solution. The sheer extent of Hitler's murderous anti-semitism continues to defy rational explanation, based as it is on the notion of a Jewish world conspiracy. But anti-semitism alone would never have brought Hitler to power, let alone kept him there, and this is a perception which structural history can provide.

That we are in many respects still too close to the events was confirmed by the many criticisms of Fest, Hitler's current major biographer, to the effect that by writing and talking about Hitler in human terms he was somehow sanctioning his actions. As Fest answered, however, there would never be a proper understanding of how and why Hitler came to power if people simply threw up their hands in horror and refused to examine the Hitler phenomenon objectively.[100] On the contrary the slow, painstaking accumulation of detail about Hitler and his rise to power will serve to remind us that he was not some kind of demon appearing from nowhere, but that far more dangerously a repetition of similar developments could produce a similar outcome in the future. This certainly does not apply to Germany alone. By the same token the humanization of Hitler, that is to say the recognition that he did actually possess some likeable characteristics as well as unpleasant ones, is not to exculpate Hitler but rather to flesh out Hannah Arendt's idea about the 'banality of evil'. In fact the more balanced picture of Hitler the man which is now slowly emerging provides us with a striking contrast between the wickedness of his character on the one hand and its sheer ordinariness on the other. It is the latter aspect which many earlier studies omitted. Much more is now demanded of the modern biographer of Hitler, who is expected not only to have a fuller knowledge of the context in which Hitler came to power but a grasp of the theoretical insights of related disciplines.[101] It is all the more regrettable that the most recent biography in English, by Stone, contained not only factual errors but claimed a novelty for its findings and insights which they do not possess: it will do nothing to close the gap between scholarly studies of the Third Reich and popular but ill-informed perceptions of it.[102]

It may be that the least disputable statement that has ever been made about Hitler related to his self-confidence. 'His own firm belief in his messianic mission was perhaps the most important element in the extraordinary power of his personality'.[103] It could easily be said that this was also the reason for his ultimate failure, in that he became intoxicated with his vision of himself and eventually its prisoner. He wholeheartedly played the part in which he had cast himself and in so doing forgot his limitations as a human being. Thus Hitler was to take his final bow as vanquished and not as victor. Yet right to the very end he could find little wrong with his basic ideas as such; he blamed the catastrophe and imminent defeat on almost everyone but himself and remained convinced of the correctness of National Socialist ideals. To these we can now turn.

# 2 Ideology and the nationalization of the masses

> 'The ideology is intolerant and cannot be content with the role of a "party among other parties". It imperiously demands its own, exclusive and unqualified recognition as well as the complete transformation of the whole public life according to its views.'[1]

Despite this very clear expression by Hitler himself of the significance which he attributed to the ideology of the National Socialist movement, historians have only comparatively recently come to a fuller appreciation of the part played by ideas in the formation of policies in the Third Reich. The attitude of many early accounts is best exemplified by Trevor-Roper's undifferentiated description of 'that dispiriting subject' as a 'vast system of bestial, Nordic nonsense'.[2] Nonetheless, it was Trevor-Roper himself who was among the first postwar scholars to recognize the crucial importance of certain key concepts in National Socialist thinking, in particular regarding foreign policy. Since then there has been general agreement amongst historians at least on what constituted the four main pillars of the Party's racial ideology, with which we are chiefly concerned in this chapter : namely, Social Darwinism, *Rassenpolitik* (i.e. elimination of the 'unfit', etc.) anti-semitism and, of far less importance in practice, Nordic superiority.

However apparent this consensus may be there are more serious problems about the way in which scholars have treated ideology. Political scientists for example, when analysing 'fascism' and 'totalitarianism' have often fallen into the trap of regarding National Socialist ideas as a fixed and constant system, as though they existed in some curious socio-economic vacuum, unrelated to everyday life.[3] This is not the way to arrive at a proper understanding of the part which ideology played in German society between 1933 and 1945. Additionally, such an approach insists too much on Hitler's role in ideology, due to the emphasis on the leader and personality cult in so-called 'totalitarian' systems. Obviously the whole subject of Hitler's contribution to this area has occasioned lively debate, but before this issue is tackled it is logically necessary to consider the wider question of the origins of National Socialist ideas.

It is understandable that historians should wish to delve back into the past to discover the sources of National Socialist thought, in the hope of establishing a clear line between Hitler and whatever predecessors he may have had. There is little doubt, however, that in many cases this process has degenerated into what at times amounts to an almost frantic ransacking of Germany's past to find anyone who sounds as though he might have had some connection, however remote, with National Socialism. The outbreak of hostilities in 1939 was itself a spur to writers of this school, whose attitude can clearly be seen in titles like *The roots of National Socialism 1783-1933*.[4] For all the seriousness of purpose and scholarly approach of this work the basic premise is flawed, in that the timespan under consideration is too long to permit any meaningful comparisons to be made. Even worse are attempts to go back into history in order to link Hitler with some mythical German national character, as though Germans were as a nation always particularly prone to fall victim to National Socialist ideas. A typical example of this line of argument is Shirer's description of the behaviour of members of the Reichstag in 1936, when Hitler announced the re-entry of German troops into the Rhineland: 'All the militarism in their German blood surges to their heads.'[5] This sort of judgement descends to the level of National Socialist propaganda itself, which the book is dedicated to attacking; one over-simplification answers another. Equally, to the latter day scholar such concepts as the 'mind of Germany' have a somewhat curious ring, in that they seem to place the Germans perpetually apart from other people in their development.[6] To take another example: 'With the older Fichte began the community idolatry that can be traced from the romantics to the Pan-Germans and the racialists, and on to the crude doctrines of the National Socialists in the twentieth century.'[7]

There is of course no shortage of able historians who, unlike Shirer, do not attribute National Socialism directly to some long-standing flaw in the German psyche but who have nonetheless been unable to break away from a certain fixation with the course of nineteenth century German history as a whole, and particularly with its intellectual history, when trying to explain National Socialism. The 1960s saw a spate of works dealing with German intellectual history in global terms, in which expressions such as 'cultural despair' played a key role. The presumption was that some kind of crisis occurred in the development of ideas in Germany in the last century, from which a clear line leading to Adolf Hitler and his works may be traced. Such writers have correctly stressed the influence exerted by earlier *völkisch* thinkers on many members of the National Socialist movement. From the information which we now possess on Himmler's formative years we know how fascinated he was by the Felix Dahn novel, *Ein Kampf um Rom*, as well as by other fiction dealing with the ancient Germans, particularly that written by Werner Jansen and Gustav Freytag. As he noted in his diary in February 1926: 'If only we were still like the ancient Germans *(Germanen)* with their morals and their sound precepts.' Carsten is therefore quite justified when, after rejecting the notion that Hitler was the inevitable outcome of a long historical process, he states: 'The National Socialist dictatorship was not alien to the German people, nor was Germany an "occupied country"... Professor Bracher is entirely right when he calls his [then] last book: "The German Dictatorship."'[8]

This perception has been precisely the point of departure for much new research into the ideological background of National Socialism as an attempt to understand how the Third Reich could have come about. Significantly much of the attention has been focused on the period since the foundation of Bismarck's Germany in 1871, right up to the final phase of the Weimar Republic. There are broadly two groups of thinkers who have been the subject of research, the *völkisch* and the authoritarian/conservative. Bracher's book, for example, has extensive sections on 19th century *völkisch* precursors of National Socialism and it has to be said that our greater knowledge of such figures as Schoenerer and Rudolf Jung has helped historians to a better understanding of the true 'roots' of National Socialism.[9] Yet of far more immediate interest are the second group, those thinkers who attempted to find a viable constitutional and ideological alternative to the Weimar Republic. Such critics did not by any means confine themselves to sterile opposition to the Republic as such, but conceived of a new order orientated above all to the restoration of 'natural' principles and authoritarianism.[10] Foremost in the field of constitutional theory were Johannes Popitz and Carl Schmitt, with their shared dislike of party-politics and the 'party state'. This is not of course to say that they agreed in every respect over the possible alternatives, since Schmitt was later to stand far closer to the NSDAP than was Popitz.[11]

A very different school of anti-democratic thought found its expression in the so-called Spann Circle, based on the ideas of the Viennese Professor Othmar Spann. From his relationship to the Dollfuss regime in Austria Spann's ideas have often been summarised as a kind of clerical fascism, particularly as represented in his *Der wahre Staat* (The true state) published in 1923. Despite the fact that the National Socialists removed Spann from his teaching post when they occupied Vienna in 1938, recent historical research has underlined that his somewhat nebulous ideas on universalism and the 'corporative state' found an echo in the Third Reich, through the agency of the Düsseldorf Institute for Corporative Organisation *(Ständewesen)*. Siegfried has pointed out that the courses and lectures run by this Institute reached about 7000 entrepreneurs and German Labour Front officials in less than two years.[12] This kind of evidence demands a cautious approach in assessing the exact nature of the role played by conservative thinking in the NSDAP. In fact it is unwise to assume, merely because Spann did not see eye to eye with National Socialist racial doctrines (which ultimately caused his downfall), that his ideas were wholly at variance with NSDAP thinking. Additionally it has been argued that one of the most prominent points of contact between Spann and fascism in general was exactly his advocacy of the 'Leader principle'.[14]

Newer studies of other conservative thinkers such as Edgar Jung and the Tat-Circle have allowed further light to penetrate the tangled undergrowth of anti-democratic ideology which existed prior to Hitler.[15] One important aspect of Jung's ideas is precisely the way in which they illustrate to what extent he was the intellectual heir to such nineteenth century thinkers as Nietzsche, Bergson, Sorel and Pareto, as well as his considerable affinity to both Othmar Spann and Oswald Spengler. Despite the fact that Jung's radical-elitist ideas were less racial, they were remarkably similar to National Socialist propaganda, in that Jung was fundamentally against western democracy: 'therefore for Jung National Socialism was a natural ally in the battle against Weimar'.[16] What he feared above all in pluralistic democracy was, in his own words, 'rule by the inferior', on the basis of one man, one vote. As in the case of Spann, however, no affinity of thought with National Socialism could ultimately save Jung from the consequences of what remained important differences. Unlike Spann this actually cost him his life, during the Röhm putsch, by which time he had already become classified as a dangerous opponent of the regime. This in spite of the fact that he could still, in the famous Marburg speech which he wrote for Vice Chancellor von Papen, demonstrate his clear commitment to fascism in principle. The two great stumbling blocks for Jung were the excesses of the regime and the Hitlerian concept of plebiscitary legitimation of his measures. In this new and more powerful form of popular acclamation Jung seems to have seen another form of rule by the inferior, which he had already found in Weimar democracy.[17]

It was not that such neo-conservative thinkers desired merely a restoration of the old pre-1914 state with its traditional ruling class. For example Moeller van den Bruck explicitly formulated Germany's needs for 'popular leaders whose only party is Germany—it matters little whether they spring from the old leader class or themselves create a new one.'[18] As Bruck saw it, the task of the new conservative leader lay essentially in creating what he called a 'Third Party which cuts across all party political lines, repudiates the (western) political thought that brought Germany and Europe to ruin, and appeals to the man in every German and to the German in every man.'[19] Small wonder that the East German historian Petzold could analyse Bruck's concept of the 'Third Party' as one attempting to conceal the conflict between Left and Right, which would simultaneously be both 'national' and 'social' and would have as its bedrock the principle of the 'conservative revolution'.[20] The task of the 'Third Party' was to introduce the 'Third Empire' *(Reich)*, a future German state free of factional conflicts. It seems to have been the case in the 1930s that the phrase 'The Third Reich' was understood in English speaking countries as a literal description of Hitler's Germany. Indeed when van den Bruck's book was first translated into English in 1934 it was actually described by the publishers as the 'Bible of Nazi Germany'. It was also roundly asserted that 'It is impossible fully to understand Hitler's Germany without reading this remarkable book, which occupies so central a position in Nazi ideology'. This grotesque error serves only to highlight how necessary it is to distinguish between the affinity which many conservative thinkers had with Hitler's ideas on the one hand, and absolute identity with them on the other. Here the case for the first is being presented, but not for the second. This distinction is also valid for that group of thinkers normally called the Tat-Circle, with which Carl Schmitt was so closely associated as the advocate of the 'total state'.[21]

As in the case of Moeller van den Bruck, these figures cannot fairly be described as National Socialists themselves. Moeller van den Bruck died before Hitler came to power, but there is little doubt that the divergence of his views from the Party's would have precluded him from active participation in the ideology of Hitler's Third Reich, which ultimately differed in important respects from his own vision of a new Germany. This places Moeller and the Tat-Circle firmly in the same category as the other thinkers discussed here. What all these people had in common was an abhorrence of the idea of one man, one vote and its concomitant, the 'party state'. What they all desired was an authoritarian successor based on the leadership principle, concepts in other words which are invariably characterised by the term 'conservative revolution'. They shared with the National Socialists the belief that November 1918 had been a genuine watershed in German history, whilst at the same time holding firmly to the notion that its outcome was not irreversible. Again like Hitler, these conservative ideologists had no wish merely to restore the old pre-1918 order, because events had compelled them to recognize the bankruptcy of the old ruling classes. In Bruck's words: 'The history of every revolution, whether Roman, English or French, shows that it ultimately meant a recruiting of new men and human forces for the strengthening of the nation. So it will prove with the (coming) German Revolution—unless German history ends with the Revolution of 1918.'[22]

In this sense Moeller and the other neo-conservatives represented the first intellectual assault on the citadel of Weimar Republican democracy. This is why any book on National Socialism needs to devote some space to the examination of their ideas, even though it has to be recognized that they failed themselves to mobilise any degree of popular support, not least because of their social and intellectual isolation from the masses, without whose help the Weimar system could not have been overthrown. Their lack of popular appeal was not of course their only difference from the National Socialist Party, the real point of divergence between them and National Socialism being precisely the far greater emphasis placed by Hitler and his movement on racial ideology.

Further research on those who actually were National Socialists has undermined the tendency in earlier works to focus the study of NSDAP racial concepts solely on the mind of Adolf Hitler. This tendency comes out strongly, for example, in an article by Holborn in 1964, where he commits himself to the assertion that 'Hitler's *Mein*

*Kampf* is by far the most important source for Nazi ideology'.[23] The article makes clear that this is part and parcel of Holborn's general belief that prior to 1933 National Socialism possessed few canonical writings, a view shared by many British historians in their earliest contacts with Hitlerism, when they assumed *Mein Kampf* to have been the sole fount of National Socialist ideas.[24] The preoccupation with *Mein Kampf* almost certainly derived from the excessive concentration on Hitler's foreign policy. This is also very apparent in Jäckl's major work on Hitler's *Weltanschauung* which, when it appeared in 1969, was hailed by historians as the first comprehensive re-examination of the Führer's ideas. Impressive as the work was, it can now be seen as a culmination of a long-standing trend in historiography rather than the initiation of a new one, in that it was primarily concerned with Hitler alone.[25] There is then some truth in the assertion by the American historian Barbara Miller Lane in 1974, that no really sound overall analysis of National Socialist ideology had yet appeared, although as she pointed out, 'The Party publishing houses...issued dozens of books and pamphlets (before 1933) some by Hitler, but most by other Party leaders. Of those other leaders, the most prolific were Dietrich Eckart, Gottfried Feder, Alfred Rosenberg, Gregor and Otto Strasser and Richard Walther Darré.'[26]

In fact this assertion needs qualifying, in that such figures as well as Himmler have long been familiar in the annals of the Third Reich.[27] Additionally the growing awareness of the way in which the Third Reich was actually run, and of its ceaseless internal conflicts, has forced historians to keep on moving the spotlight away from the centre of the stage towards the wings. As Hitler's chief lieutenants became increasingly illuminated, the origin of their ideas in turn became the subject of historical research. The trouble is that they tend on the whole to have been treated individually, and there has been less of an attempt at an overall assessment of National Socialist ideology as that set of principles which actually held the entire movement together. This is in effect what Lane means by 'unfinished business'. It is important to see Hitler in relation both to contemporary National Socialists and to modern German history and society.

Justice also needs to be done to the ideological ferment at grassroots level. Again, the evidence for this has often been published but has not been sufficiently related to the larger problem of National

Socialist ideology as a whole. Some indication of early activity at local level is afforded by the National Socialist circle in Göttingen in 1924, which included Herbert Backe, Hitler's later Minister of Agriculture, and Ludolf Haase. Backe's own report makes clear that he had never heard Hitler speak until 1926, but his views on *Lebensraum* and the need for self-sufficiency were evolving independently of Hitler and the Party leadership in Munich; for example: 'Our living space is too confined', therefore, '(we need) colonies or breathing space *(Luft)* in Europe'[28] Another instance is the Göttingen group's view of the unalterable influence on the human race of hereditary factors in determining the ineluctable division into leaders and led. Clearly then, such views were not confined merely to the National Socialist leadership. The investigation of the beliefs of those once held to be relatively minor figures in the history of the Third Reich will continue to yield fruitful results.[29] It will also underline the autonomy of National Socialist ideology. In so doing, it must necessarily cast serious doubt on East German historians' views of Adolf Hitler, based on the assumption that he was nothing more than a tool of German capitalism. That surely reduces ideology to the role of the purely instrumental, depicting it as a deliberate ploy by 'monopoly capitalism' aimed at the integration of the 'non-monopolistic sectors of German society', that is, covering up the class struggle.[30]

Autonomy of course is not the same thing as unanimity; there was never any exact agreement between Party members on every detail of the various aspects of the movement's ideology, a situation which reflects the heterogeneous nature of the actual membership.[31] This is not to take the negative view that 'political thought played a relatively unimportant part in the rise (and fall) of the Third Reich.'[32] Hitler and Himmler may well have had different views about the role which Charlemagne had played in the formation of the German people[33]; similarly, the Führer sneered at what he called Himmler's 'biological fishing expeditions' during the war, when the Reichsführer SS was scouring the occupied territories for valuable foreign blood to ensure the future of the German race. Such differences of opinion, which ran throughout the movement, must never be allowed to obscure the fact that notwithstanding inevitable ideological variations, there was general agreement, particularly among the 'old warriors', as to what constituted the key principles. That Hitler and Himmler should have diverged in their views about the past is clearly of far less importance than their shared belief that Germany's future lay in the exploitation above all of Poles and Russians. And this is obviously true of their attitudes on anti-semitism and *Rassenpolitik*. These are ideas which all the National Socialist leaders had in common, the existence and significance of which cannot be explained by any Marxist reduction of Hitlerism to a mere function, that is to say as the agent of capitalism in crisis. Such shared ideals were the very stuff of National Socialism and cannot be treated as merely an epiphenomenon. Whatever historians may feel personally about these beliefs they must, as Jäckl argued, overcome their revulsion and subject them to serious analysis.[34]

Any reader looking through the literature on National Socialist racial ideology will become aware that although its fundamentals have been separately identified (see p. 33) they have not all been subjected to an equally rigorous analysis. Understandably, because of the Holocaust, the anti-semitism inherent to Hitlerism has received most attention, which has had the consequence not only of hindering a fuller treatment of racial policy as such, but has also overshadowed the discussion of ideology as a whole. This is not to deny that National Socialists frequently thought of anti-semitism in the context of racial purification in general, but historians lost sight of the more restricted application of the term, in determining the biological fitness of non-Jewish Germans. Naturally the close secrecy surrounding the elimination of the 'unfit' prevented any examination of these events prior to 1945. Nevertheless, it still seems strange that what detailed studies we do possess are of quite recent vintage.[35] Another reason for this was that, in addition to the Holocaust, historians were preoccupied with the myth of 'Nordic superiority', which again is surely a separate issue. It had no necessary connection with the other strands of National Socialist philosophy already identified.[36] The absence until comparatively recently of a more sophisticated analysis of what National Socialism meant by *Rassenpolitik* has been a serious omission in historical research. To take one example, there appears to have been no detailed study of the consequences of one of the earliest National Socialist measures in the area of *Rassenpolitik*, namely the Law for the Prevention of Hereditarily-Diseased Offspring. How was this law applied in practice and to how many? One of the newer 'growth areas' in Third Reich studies, that concerning the development and practice of the legal system, is only just beginning to yield answers to such questions and indeed promises to give a more concrete dimension to the discussion of ideology as a whole.

The way in which National Socialist legislation was actually interpreted by the courts illustrates the impact on the life of the German people of these central concepts. Contemporary observers were quick to recognize the racial basis of agrarian laws and to draw attention to the fact that 'those who are held to be incurably weak in body, mind or character should be debarred altogether from contracting a German marriage.'[38] This serves as a reminder that the point of departure for lawyers in the Third Reich was the need to give concrete legal expression to what were after all originally a set of fairly nebulous general maxims. Anderbrügge points up the efforts of jurists to transform the law 'in the spirit of National Socialism.'[39] Guidelines for the whole country issued in 1936 specifically stated that the foundation of law should be the National Socialist *Weltanschauung*, 'especially as it finds expression in the Party programme and in the utterances of the Führer.'[40] In practice that meant that the community was to take precedence over the individual; the German citizen enjoyed rights only insofar as he fulfilled his duties towards the ethnic community.[42] This concretization of the racial ideology led in 1934 to the replacement of the old rational legal maxim, 'no punishment without a law' by the assertion of 'no crime without punishment', according to one National Socialist jurist.[43] Anderbrügge insists that what underlay the practice of law in the Third Reich was the affirmation of National Socialist ideas and he further demonstrates the existence of a broad consensus amongst their theorists which had already been formed prior to the *Machtergreifung*.[44]

Such studies confirm that National Socialist ideology was neither a hotchpotch of racial nonsense nor merely a means for electoral mobilization prior to 1933, nor simply a way of inspiring enthusiasm for the regime after that date. On the contrary, it had a radical aim, the object of which was nothing less than the transformation of the whole German people and its way of thought. Of course Marxist historians are correct in arguing that it did have the additional advantage of helping to defeat socialism as a mass movement in Germany.[45] Ironically enough this was to be achieved through the agency of those very people the National Socialists despised most, the legal profession.[46] At the same time we should not forget that prolonged study of the application of racially based law does not exhaust the theme of *Rassenpolitik* in the Third Reich since so many measures were in any case illegally executed.

This was true, certainly in the later stages, of the other main area of racial policy, namely anti-semitism. As previously stated, this is often wrongly taken to be not merely the main plank of National Socialist racial ideology but its only component.[47] Of course, historiographically, there is no debate over the fact that National Socialist leaders were thoroughly imbued with the crudest kind of prejudice against Jews. At the same time it is necessary to avoid the trap of lumping them all together in this respect, as though their views always completely coincided. This is to offer a mirror image of Streicher's stereotype Jew and is equally simplistic. For example, Gregor Strasser, in correspondence with Oswald Spengler in the 1920s, actually referred to anti-semitism as 'a primitive solution'.[48] Again, Dietrich Eckart's view was different to that of both Rosenberg and Streicher, since he regarded 'Jewishness' as a religious concept, whereas for Rosenberg it was biological.[49] Such variations cannot simply be taken as trivial, since one type of anti-semitism may have led to the Final Solution whereas a less racial form would not have, however deeply held. This is precisely why it is so important to recognize the crucial role played by Hitler, Himmler and Goebbels in bringing about the Holocaust. The fact that few Party members actually subscribed to extermination as a solution to the Jewish problem again throws into relief the fact that Hitler's ideas and National Socialism cannot automatically be equated.

On this subject Nolte has pointed to Hitler's obsession with 'purification', as reflected in the vocabulary of *Mein Kampf*, where words such as 'pests', 'parasites', 'bacilli' are brought into the same context as concepts such as 'elimination', 'rooting out' and 'annihilation'. In his *Table Talk* during the war, Hitler actually compared his discovery of what he called the 'Jewish virus' in society to Pasteur's work on germs in the nineteenth century. The use of this imagery shows how Hitler could arrive at a manicheistic division of the world into the good and the bad. From there it was but a short step to the belief in a struggle to the death between them. Thus in September 1923, in referring to the Jews, he said: 'There are only two possibilities; we shall be either victor or sacrificial lamb.'[50] This black and white view of the world was fully shared by Himmler, who began by believing in Freemasonry as the source of all evil before transferring his hatred to world Jewry.[51] There has been no real disagreement that the 'Jew' was psychologically necessary as an enemy to both Himmler and Hitler, but it has been less easy to agree on how important anti-semitism was as a factor in holding the Party together and in mobilising electoral support. Kershaw confirmed in his recent study that it had a vital function to play in education and mobilising the *Party*, where the idea of moving towards a distant utopia was promoted by the exclusion of the Jew.[52] It has also been suggested that the simple personification of the Jew as enemy enormously added to the effectiveness of National Socialist propaganda prior to the takeover, since it also hit at individual political foes.[53] Moreover, like communists, Jews were easy to isolate as targets in the sense that both normally lacked really widespread popular support.[54] Debate has become much more intense, however, over the question of to what extent the general public embraced the anti-semitic views disseminated by the Party, chiefly perhaps because this is so intimately linked with the painful issue of the extermination of the Jews.

Steinert is firmly of the opinion that what she calls the 'wooden mallet' method of repetition was counterproductive, and that both euthanasia and anti-semitism set clear limits to National Socialist manipulation of the masses; the great majority of Germans were allegedly apathetic over the persecution of the Jews.[55] Kershaw recognizes this point when observing what astonishingly little resonance anti-semitism found amongst the German people after 1933, when compared with the regime's anti-Bolshevism. Such a comparison may overlook the way in which the propaganda of the regime deliberately linked the two, but for Kershaw the absence of any popular reaction was not the whole story. The systematic encouragement of latent anti-semitism by the Party had conditioned the population for the Final Solution, in the sense that 'It permitted the execution of radical National Socialist anti-semitism, but did not cause it.'[56] In other words, however revolted Germans were by the intensification of the struggle against the Jews, the atmosphere had been created in which the 'Final Solution' could take place.

Irving has confused the debate by suggesting not merely that the killing was unplanned, but that Hitler was not even privy to it; rather that it was the SS which exploited Hitler's anti-semitic decrees, thus demonstrating the Führer's lack of control over his own subordinates, which became more marked as the war continued.[57] At first sight Irving's arguments can be made to seem more credible by the fact that when Hitler spoke of 'rooting out' the Jews in *Mein Kampf*, he may not necessarily have meant extermination; after all, he had used exactly the same term in connection with Germans under the Habsburg monarchy, where the implication was not that they were physically destroyed but rather that they were 'de-germanized' in the sense of losing their separate identity as the ruling class.[58] Superficially this argument appears to receive further support from historians who have insisted on the improvised nature of the mass murders. Adam argued that the decision to kill all European Jews was taken between September and November 1941, due to the stalemate on the Eastern front. This thwarted plans to re-settle Jews in Siberia, which until then had been a distinct possibility.[59] Adam's firm conclusion, however, that the order for a mass execution was certainly a personal decision by Hitler deprives Irving's thesis of any real support from this quarter. Broszat's magisterial reply to Irving has rightly been seen as the most convincing refutation yet of the argument that Hitler was unaware of and did not agree to the fate suffered by European Jewry at the hands of his subordinates.[60] The crux of Irving's argument lies in his assumption that the absence of a written order from Hitler to exterminate the Jews is in some way significant. Broszat accepts it as improbable that any single specific order was given but, unlike Irving, gives full weight to the whole ideological background of the Third Reich and to the implications of Hitler's own pressure for a radical solution, contained in private correspondence as early as September 1919.[61] The continuity of Hitler's views on the Jewish problem can be seen from his conversation with the Croat Defence Minister, Kvaternik, on the 21 July 1941, where the total removal of the European Jews was already foreseen exactly at the time when he appeared to be on the threshold of victory in the East. This makes it hard to accept Adam's dating of the decision to eliminate the Jews to September/October 1941. Browning confirms an earlier decision from a reference on 28 August 1941 in a letter from Eichmann to the Foreign Office in Berlin. Ominously this document spoke already of the 'coming Final Solution', which accords with Eichmann's own later testimony that he had first heard of the annihilation order in late summer 1941.[63]

It must be stressed that however academically interesting the debate over the timing of the Final Solution may be, it is far from being the heart of the matter. In the final analysis the extermination of the Jews was caused by Hitler's fixed obsession: 'The belief in the Satanic Jew was the central core of the new *Weltanschauung*'.[64] It is instructive to remember the prophecy of doom in *Mein Kampf*, that should the Jew ever triumph over the peoples of this world, his crowning success would be the death of mankind; this planet would then again ride empty through space as it once did thousands of years ago[65]—a conviction which makes it quite clear that the military stalemate on the Eastern Front was at most the occasion for the timing of the Final Solution, but hardly its cause. It also convincingly rebuts Irving's curious attempt to present Hitler's subordinates as an alibi for the Führer's action, thus reversing the trend normally noticeable in West Germany of using Hitler as a general alibi. Although the latter process has been carried too far, Mommsen is surely nonetheless correct in underlining Hitler's basic guilt when he argues that he was dominated throughout his life rather more by fixed ideas than by pragmatic political calculations; historians should give due regard to this when analysing his actions.[66]

This raises the issue of the wider debate on what T. W. Mason has described as the division of historians of Hitler's Germany into two groups, the functionalists and the intentionalists.[67] The former essentially analyse political developments in the Third Reich as a kind of frantic but completely uncoordinated activity by competing power groups, producing a progressive radicalisation of measures. The intentionalists, however, consider the consistency in Hitler's leadership and his proven power as the true characteristic of National Socialist dominance, which leads them to the supposition that the best way of making sense of the Third Reich is by understanding Hitler and his ideology together with what they see as its resulting programme. Mason identifies Mommsen as the leader of the functionalists and K. D. Bracher and K. Hildebrand as the most important representatives of the second school of thought. What has to be decided here is how far the thesis has validity in the case of the Holocaust. The very fact that Hitler's key henchmen, notably Himmler, were so much at one with the Führer in his view of the 'Jewish threat' demonstrates that they shared his 'intentions' in any event.[68] Such an affinity made it almost certain that any system for which Hitler bore the ultimate responsibility would automatically 'function' in accordance with his 'intentions', irrespective of whether a written order was issued or not, at least in the case of such a central idea as anti-semitism. Whether Hitler himself was actually aware of how many Jews were being killed by what was after all his form of government, is in the final analysis immaterial. In the first place, he was tied to the consequences of the system, whether he deliberately fostered 'divide and rule' or not. Secondly, if the fearful consistency between Hitler's stated views and the Holocaust is borne in mind, it then becomes impossible to conceive of Hitler putting an end to the extermination programme even if he had not directly ordered it in the first place. It may well be that the functionalists are correct in assuming that in the case of the Final Solution, as in other aspects of the Third Reich, the very way in which the system operated modified the speed or dynamic of the intentionalist programme, but that it did any more than that remains unproven.

However tragic the dimension of the Holocaust was, it has to be remembered that it was only part of a deliberate attempt by the National Socialists to transform the entire values system of the German people, in which the first stage was the rooting out of the vestiges of Marxism and liberalism in German society. This clearly has relevance for the whole discussion of the role of ideology in moulding public opinion in the Third Reich, in which propaganda is seen as playing a key part. Here the concepts of 'manipulation' and 'mobilization' must be examined more closely. The first of these terms indicates the initial stage in the preparation of public opinion for the full acceptance of the Party's aims.

National Socialists were unable to move directly towards an open declaration of their goals at least partly because of the survival of Marxism and liberalism, not to mention Christianity, among wide sections of the German population. Prior to the *Machtergreifung*, as has frequently been pointed out, racialism and anti-semitism were much less obvious in Hitler's speeches. The same is true of attacks on the Christian religion, which were replaced by a more overt onslaught on Marxism.[69] Concealment of some of the National Socialist aims was essential in order to rally electoral support. That in itself made it more difficult to declare openly the true purpose of the movement even after coming to power. Hitler often recognized in the relative privacy of the cabinet discussions after 1933 that there was bound to be an interim phase between the arrival of National Socialism and the total transformation of German society to National Socialist ideas, i.e., 'mobilization'. The 'nationalisation of the masses', that is to say the conversion of the German people to the belief that *the* most important thing in their lives was their common ethnic relationship, was bound to be a long-term process. Those Germans who could not by now be fully converted to the pure ideals of the movement, because they had been raised under a different political system, could at least be persuaded that the survival of the German nation was of paramount importance. For this reason too, the dominant theme of the National Socialists prior to 1933 was an appeal to nationalism. When Goebbels in a speech in 1932, for example, described the Germans as a 'slave people' having fewer rights than the subjects of a European colony in the Congo, it was clearly to the German sense of national humiliation which he was appealing.[70] The Party's presentation of itself as the spokesman for traditional German patriotism was of course facilitated by its emphasis on the Old Prussian virtues, which by implication they would restore in order to heal the 'sick society'. The dazzling brushwork with which the National Socialists painted this image made it difficult for Germans always to detect the real ideological framework which lay underneath.[71]

Many historians have laboured the point that the ceremony at the Potsdam Garrison Church in early March 1933 was a deliberate attempt to suggest that nothing had permanently changed in German history, in the sense that the temporary 'nightmare' of the Weimar Republic was now at an end, an illusion skilfully fostered by Hitler's appearance at the side of the aged Hindenburg. Indeed the two congratulatory telegrams sent in the President's name to Hitler on 2 July 1934, expressing his deeply felt thanks for the 'Night of the Long Knives', were actually both composed in Goebbels's Propaganda Ministry.[72] That they were, however, signed by Hindenburg was bound to reinforce the impression that the military hero of World War One now stood firmly behind the new regime and his signature was doubtless perceived as a guarantee in itself against further violent upheaval. Yet the appeal to German nationalism has to be seen in a much wider context than this. It was to begin with an essential basic element of the Party's own creed, and must never be seen as merely a means to achieve power. Here it is necessary to emphasize the crucial importance of the trauma of 1918 for National Socialist thinking, since it was the Revolution of that year which in Hitler's view had delivered Germany into the predatory hands of Marxists and liberals. This accounts for the persistent National Socialist attacks on the Revolution and its offspring, the Weimar Republic, prior to 1933, as 'un-German'.

Such is the probable meaning of Hitler's remarks, when he suggested in an interview in 1933 with Colonel Etherton of *The Daily Mail* that Germany now needed a Cromwell to pull it out of the curses it was enduring.[74] This explicatory model makes a parallel with Cromwell's restoration of stability in England after the collapse of the old order following the Civil War, and Hitler's own assumption of power. He saw the German Revolution as an event comparable to the English Civil War, in as much as the old order had been destroyed and this was followed by a period of upheaval and uncertainty like that in Germany after 1918. Mason has repeatedly argued that Hitler's need to win the people to a new *Weltanschauung* was based on his assumption that only in this way could the hold of Marxism on the German working class be broken.[76] A further point of vital importance for the National Socialists was their fear that any future war might be lost by a repetition of the collapse of civilian morale in 1918.[77] Hitler did not of course make the mistake of assuming that he could win the masses over merely by offering them an idea and nothing more. As he said in *Mein Kampf*: 'the national conversion of the mass of the people...requires an indirect approach through social advance'.[78] According to Mason this conviction had grown even stronger in the Führer's mind by the end of the 1920s.[79]

It manifested itself after 1933 in a determination to demand as few sacrifices as possible in order to keep the home front stable and thereby avoid a re-run of the events of 1918 should war occur. It must also be kept in mind, therefore, that the National Socialists did manage to achieve a return to full employment. When contrasted with the recent grim reality of the world economic crisis, such a relative material improvement helped to consolidate the regime and thereby to facilitate the transmission of its ideals to the German people. In that process myth, ritual and ceremony all had an important part to play, an aspect of National Socialism which did not fail to impress contemporary observers. Indeed they became almost obsessed with it. In a way they saw the whole of National Socialism as a gigantic charade, a hollow sham the sole purpose of which was to paper over the cracks in German society. Thus: 'National Socialism has no political or social theory. It has no philosophy and no concern for the truth.'[80] In such accounts myth and ceremony are mono-functional, a vast exercise in propaganda and nothing more. This scarcely does justice to the possibility that National Socialists actually believed in their own ideals as they attempted to convert the

German masses. The obstacle to giving full recognition to this point has been above all the tendency of historians to stress the Hitler movement's obsession with power for its own sake, and to reduce the function of ideology to the overthrow of Marxism.[81]

Yet 'myth' and 'ceremony' are in fact an integral part of all religions and to use such concepts is to accept that National Socialism also has this status. As Broszat pointed out: 'There is evidence even from the beginnings of the NSDAP, that speeches by Hitler were "enjoyed" as a sort of popular entertainment...but demagogic aggression alone could not have achieved this unique effect if Hitler had not at the same time had a masterly understanding of how to convey the impression of "holy seriousness".'[82] Hitler himself, in a circular to the Party in December 1932, referred to it as a 'movement of apostles'. It is not therefore surprising that the Party should have attached so much importance to its festivals. A typical example was the enormous demonstration of no fewer than half a million peasants at the Bückeberg on 1 October 1933, the first of the annual harvest festivals. This event, which the London *Times* found to be a 'magnificent spectacle', was, significantly, organized by the Ministry of Propaganda and not by the Ministry of Food and Agriculture. Apart from their sheer impressiveness it has to be remembered that such festivals encouraged the devotees' readiness to lose their personal identity in the drive towards the common goal, especially when the charismatic leader Adolf Hitler was personally present.[84] In that connection the 'marching column', to refer to Rosenberg's much cited remark, could be seen as the essential style of the new Germany, with its emphasis on uniformity and togetherness. Since orchestrated public demonstrations were so essential in the process of 'nationalizing the masses', the oratorical skills of Hitler, Goebbels and others were as necessary after the seizure of power as they had been before. In this style of politics the spoken word remained all-important. It provided a liturgy which 'transformed political action into a drama supposedly shared by the people themselves.'[85]

More recently a greater importance has been attached to the place of architecture in the Third Reich. Speer confirmed Hitler's obsessive interest with architecture in his memoirs, but modern historians have emphasized that this was something much more than a mere hobby, in the sense that it provided settings for the quasi-religious ceremonies and was an expression in itself of the ideology. Dülffer insists that to consider Hitler's building programmes as mere megalomania is misleading. The *'Kolossal'* was certainly intended to convey to the public a definite impression of German greatness and the buildings were to be seen as symbolizing the power of the new master race.[86] Additionally attention has been drawn to Hitler's revealing remarks at the Party Congress in 1937, which in themselves define yet another function of his building plans: 'The greater the demands the state makes upon its people, the more imposing it must appear to them...opponents may suspect this power but above all supporters must be sure of it: our buildings arise to strengthen this authority.'[87] Modern historiography demonstrates therefore that ridicule of the architecture of the Third Reich merely on the grounds of its grandiose style has been misplaced. Nor can even its art be demeaned as mere bourgeois philistinism on the part of the movement. Large sections of the German public shared its aversion to 'modernism'. Mosse is therefore probably correct in his assumption that there was an element of genuine popularity in National Socialist art and literature.[88] In this respect at least, both people and leader were at one in the new secular movement, which like all religions provided a degree of social control: 'Totalitarianism was never a system of government in which the charismatic leader beguiled his followers like the Pied Piper of Hamelin.'[89] This is not to say, however, that the Germans as a people are necessarily particularly susceptible to the use of myth and ritual. They did not flock to Hitler merely because of a certain irrational desire for a pre-capitalist order or because they were totally dazzled by the drama and liturgy of the movement. Significant as these aspects of the regime were, it is important to emphasize yet again that they have to be seen against a background of continued material improvement which National Socialism brought to Germany after 1933, as well as against Hitler's initial coups in foreign policy.

It is now quite impossible to conceive of Hitler as having total power to manipulate events and people in the manner of some grotesque puppet master, as on the Erdmann model, whereby Hitler was able 'to overcome the self-control of the masses by stifling reason and conscience in quite deliberately manipulated outbreaks of national hysteria.'[91] The German public, however intoxicated by ceremony, was certainly not prepared to accept the mass murder which National Socialist ideology ultimately involved, so the regime therefore frequently had to cloak its real designs and to take account of public opinion. The point has to be made at once that in the Third

Reich there was officially no ‘public opinion’ as such, only talk of conviction and belief.[92] Ribbentrop, for example, averred to Soviet representatives in August 1939 that public opinion was a ‘quantité négligeable’.[93] Steinert qualifies this by pointing out that it by no means does justice to the zeal with which the ruling circles collected information on the state both of opinion and morale among the German people. Both Hitler and Goebbels showed familiarity with SD reports, the latter frequently quoting them in his own diary. Hitler’s well-known determination to avoid price rises, for example in food, where these could entail loss of popularity for the regime, attests to his sensitivity to prevailing moods among the public. This is not to say that matters as important as high strategy were influenced by public opinion, but nonetheless his perception of it may well have affected the timing of some of his manoeuvres.[94] It would therefore be a huge oversimplification to think of the German public as a tabula rasa, upon which the regime drew whatever picture it wished. Public opinion and propaganda were intimately connected in the Third Reich, as in any political system. What Hitler told the masses was in itself partly conditioned by his awareness of how they already felt.

During the debate on ‘manipulation’ versus ‘mobilization’ in the Third Reich it has to be kept in mind that some elements of German society were amenable to neither. What Mason said of the Labour movement was profoundly true: ‘the SA had rawhide whips and rubber truncheons for the enlightenment of “Marxists” who failed to recognize that 30 January had brought a new spirit of national and social unity.’[95] Moreover the frequent capriciousness and unpredictability of this brutality in itself added to its effectiveness. Such an emphasis on terror conflicts with an earlier Marxist view that ‘propaganda is not a substitute for violence, but one of its aspects.’ Mason at least would recognize that Neumann’s definition of propaganda as ‘violence committed against the soul’ scarcely does justice to National Socialist terror.[97] Neither does Kühnl’s remarkable assertion that since class society began all ruling systems have been based on a ‘combination of physical oppression and ideological manipulation.’[98] This is surely to minimise the difference in degree between governmental systems. Of course justice has been done to the full extent and nature of National Socialist terror as such, in the many documented studies we have of the SS, the Gestapo and the concentration camps.[99] Yet that terror and propaganda were not merely the same thing was acknowledged at least as early as 1939 by such an acute contemporary observer as Emil Lederer, like Neumann a Marxist. He argued that winning over the masses was not merely more important than brutality as a means of control but was the necessary prerequisite for the use of terror.[100] Another student of the fascist movements wrote in the same year that 'National Socialism triumphed because it promised a policy of reform instead of a policy of liquidation.'[101] It hardly needs to be said that this was a retrospective comment on the 1930s and applied to the non-Jewish German population.

The passage of time has inevitably clarified the debate over the use of terror, and in particular its relationship to persuasion, without which the terror would have been impossible. Indeed, it has been argued that Hitler actually preferred conversion to force, his ideal being the individual citizen who acted always from purely idealistic motives rather than from intimidation; this preference may well have emanated from the comradeship of the trenches in World War One.[102] Whatever the scale of terror and however systematically it was used, it necessarily had to have limits. Some National Socialists were certainly aware of the counter-productive effects of too much brutality; the material success of the regime depended in the final analysis on the goodwill of large sections of the German community, whose technical expertise was indispensable. As Darré put it, no gendarme could teach a peasant how to manage his manure heap.

Admittedly, terror was applied on a far greater scale once war broke out, especially when losing the war became a distinct possibility. Defeatism had to be overcome by all possible means. This is part of the explanation for the dramatic increase in the application of the death penalty from three categories of crime in 1933 to 46 by 1944. Conversely, the limitations imposed upon the use of terror prior to the outbreak of hostilities are revealed in the statistic that in 1938 the total number of death sentences confirmed was 23 for the whole Reich (compare this with the figure of 4438 for 1943).[103] Such figures offer support to Mason's argument that by 1939 the attempt to 'nationalize the masses' had simply failed, which in turn implies that the terror must not be seen simply as a kind of function of the war itself, but rather as a confession of failure. Broszat was correct when he argued that 'such a robust toughening up of criminal law went far beyond what could be regarded as a legitimate increase in precautions against crime during the war.' No doubt this was due to the fact that Hitler and his entourage were increasingly haunted by the spectre of another 1918 as the war progressed.[104]

Without doubt this failure lay in the logic of the situation, in that when Hitler assumed power so many Germans had already grown up under a different set of values to those preached by the National Socialists. These formed for Hitler a lost generation. As he himself always recognized in cabinet debates at the outset of his government, the conversion of the German people would necessarily take 30 to 40 years. For children, however, the case was different, in that a sustained attempt could at once be made to indoctrinate them with National Socialist thought. Like the Jesuits, National Socialists clearly believed that what are normally referred to as the formative years of a child's life are the most important. Here, however, National Socialism cannot be seen as a complete watershed in German history; as Flessau has shown, the Party tended to build on certain existing tendencies in the German educational system. Prominent among these was a certain chauvinism already evident in the teaching of the German language, which the National Socialists simply took up and exploited.[105] Indeed between 1933 and 1937 in many cases the National Socialists availed themselves of the educational guidelines drawn up during the Weimar Republic. Nonetheless the appointment of a national Minister for Education, Bernard Rust, emphasized the immediate move from the federal democracy of Weimar towards the policy of centralization. Moreover, outside the school gates the Hitler Youth had already begun the work of converting the young.[106] What prevented more rapid progress in the implementation of a National Socialist programme for education was in the first instance the administrative conflict between Rust's new office and the Party Headquarters at Munich, in the shape of Hess and Bormann. Between them they managed to hold up the publication of guidelines for elementary schools until 1939, although Rust had been working on these for four years.[107] Additionally various other bodies in the Third Reich, such as the Hitler Youth, the SS, and even the Wehrmacht, tried to attain influence over the schools policy for their own ends.[108] By 1938, however, sufficient progress had been made in overcoming these characteristic power struggles for the Party at least to commence using its own unified teaching plans for secondary schools, a process which was to continue until 1942. The ultimate aim of the National Socialist education system was made abundantly plain in the section on science in the 1939 directives, where it stated: 'It is not the task of the elementary school to convey all sorts of knowledge to the individual merely for his own use. It has rather to develop all the abilities of youth so that they may be utilized in the service of people and state.' National Socialist educational principles were obviously aimed at arousing the feeling in children of being above all a member of a group, which shared history, beliefs, goals and faith in common.[109]

Such general aims found practical expression particularly in three areas, namely, history, natural sciences and German language and literature. In the first discipline military history was brought in as a new theme, together with the study of the 'National Revolution' and Nordic history. The sciences were chiefly affected by the introduction of the 'theory of race' into biology. German language and literature was augmented by *völkisch* poetry and 'blood and soil' literature.[110] All these studies helped to forge the awareness of belonging to a common race with a common fate. Even the study of English was recommended partly on racial grounds. The higher school guidelines for 1938 urged, for example, that English should be learnt: 'Since it is the language of a people racially related to us.' That it was also the language of the world economy was advanced only as a secondary reason for its study.[111] The same document reminded teachers that the children must be made aware of the relationship between the Latins and the Greeks of antiquity, and the Nordic Germanic peoples. Even subjects apparently immune to ideology, like mathematics, could be exploited in elementary school textbooks. Part one of the official mathematic textbook has some ideological content on no fewer than 22 pages out of 76, including implied references to racial policy. For example, one sum asked children to calculate, if a lunatic asylum cost six million Reichsmarks to build, and a worker's apartment on average six thousand marks, how many families could have been housed for the money devoted to the mentally unfit. Other sums were based on the assumption that hereditarily unfit families had more children than healthy ones, and asked pupils to work out what proportion of the whole people would be unfit in a hundred or two hundred years' time.

As to other aspects of the curriculum sport took a far greater share of the timetable than had formerly been the case. This doubtless reflected Hitler's own view in *Mein Kampf*, where he suggested that the true object of education was not to pump in factual knowledge but rather to produce thoroughly fit children through intensive physical training. His order of priorities seems to have been: firstly, physical education, then ideological *(seelisch)* schooling with intellectual *(geistig)* training coming last. This was echoed in the directives for 1938 which stated roundly: 'The traditional attitude of merely critical intellectual and aesthetic reflection must be replaced by a vigorous, purposeful and combative approach.'[113]

National Socialist attempts to use the schools to produce 'doers' rather than 'thinkers' would hardly impress educationalists but there is no doubting the deadly seriousness of purpose behind such efforts. As this chapter has argued, the role of ideology was absolutely crucial in the Third Reich, permeating almost every activity. There is a growing tendency amongst historians to accept this point. No-one would now describe the National Socialist beliefs in the way in which Trevor-Roper once did, at least as they applied to domestic politics. Undoubtedly most historians continue to share his aversion to National Socialist ideology, but they have increasingly been forced to recognise the impact which it had on daily life in the Third Reich. Our greater awareness of the importance of the movement's ideology has in itself been partly responsible for research into the origins and evolution of National Socialist ideas. The *völkisch* and conservative predecessors or contemporaries of National Socialism have been more sharply delineated, so that Hitler can now be seen in his proper historical perspective.

Such research has eliminated two persistent misinterpretations. The first is to assume that National Socialism was the inevitable outcome of a long drawn out historical process which began centuries before Hitler's birth. As Carsten has implied, Martin Luther had very little to do with Hitler![114] Explanations of this type have very often been linked with vague talk about a 'German national character', which has supposedly existed through the ages. The second error is to divorce Hitler completely from previous German history, so that he suddenly appears in the centre of the stage, complete with his ideology, like some *deus ex machina*. The banal truth is to be found somewhere in between. In short, the National Socialist ideology can be seen to have represented an extreme variant of the struggle on the part of Germany's ruling classes to solve the problems posed for them by the late and rapid industrialization of Germany, and the social and political difficulties inherent in this process. As early as the 1890s Friedrich Naumann had suggested that the most effective way to combat Marxism was through a method of secondary integration, that is to say workers would become reconciled to the bourgeois state both by an appeal to their nationalism and simultaneously through a programme of social welfare. National Socialists were later to pervert this 'nationalization of the masses' to their own racial ends, which needless to say were very different from Naumann's aims.

National Socialist propaganda, it is now clear, served a dual function. Whilst preparing the ground for the long-term conversion of the German people to an acceptance of the National Socialist ethos, with all its implications, it also served to conceal the immediate reality of the class struggle inside Germany during the 1930s. In that sense it enjoyed the distinct advantage that material conditions had improved relative to the period prior to 1933, but not to the extent that the National Socialists could exercise the control they required through persuasion alone. Nonetheless, historians have now been able to attain a better insight into the relationship between terror and persuasion in Hitler's Germany, and to understand the fluctuating nature of the balance between them. Prior to 1939, the limits of terror were determined by the acceptance of the regime on the part of the masses, and by the Party's own apprehension about the consequences of inflicting unpopular measures. The war, by imposing greater demands on the German people, almost inevitably began to tip the scales in favour of terror as a means of social control, particularly once the possibility of defeat became apparent. On this level then, ideological persuasion had proved ineffective in the short term. This judgement needs to be qualified, however, by reference to the stoic endurance of the German people during six years of war and the way in which their belief in Hitler apparently remained unshaken to the very end. There were of course other reasons for such tenacity, but it is difficult not to be impressed by the fact that the will of the German people did not break in the face of overwhelming Allied superiority. Faced with this evidence, the possibility has to be admitted that National Socialist indoctrination also played its part. Its impact on the younger generation in particular has been well attested by Allied observers in postwar occupied Germany.

This is the point at which the connection between myth and reality in National Socialist propaganda becomes crucial. If a belief is deliberately fostered it can indeed become a kind of self-fulfilling prophecy. If Germans were prepared to act as though they were a master race, it would then be pointless to speculate on whether Hitler believed in his own ideology or not. The discussion is further complicated by Hitler's own attitude towards the criteria adopted in respect of the ideals set by the charismatic leader. As Baynes argued, the Führer perceived that the usefulness of a political ideal does not necessarily depend on its being ultimately fully realizable in practice. As long as people became 'better' in attempting to attain the ideal, this in itself would justify its existence.[115] Moreover, were the process to be continued, it would offer the leadership the distinct possibility that the point could be reached where the ultimate consequences of National Socialist ideology, even the Final Solution, could be spelled out directly to the German public. The fact that right up to 1945 they had not been able to do this, demonstrates the gap in the Third Reich between overt propaganda and the real goals of the National Socialist leaders. To those aims their commitment, however secret, remained firm until the very end. The determination and above all precision with which those aims were realized is precisely why, during the course of the recent *Historikerstreist* in West Germany, so many historians wished to stress the unique nature of the Holocaust.[116]

# 3 Centralized or polycentric dictatorship?

> 'The men about me are four-square and upstanding men, each of them a powerful personality, each of them a man of will and ambition. If they had not ambition they would not be where they are today. I welcome ambition. When you have a group of powerful personalities, it is inevitable that occasionally friction is produced.'[1]

Despite the implications of the above remark the persistent popular image of the Third Reich as a monolithic society subject to the personal rule and will of one man has scarcely changed. In this view Hitler operated at the pinnacle of a tightly organized society which he manipulated in all respects. His regime was seen as centralized and highly. efficient, and has often been contrasted with the more protracted decision-making process characteristic of parliamentary democracy. Probably the most widespread and popular manifestation of this belief was the facile acceptance by so many in the West that under dictatorship the trains *did* always run on time. The point is raised here precisely because the idea of a super-efficient and above all centralized system derived from the obsessive concentration on Hitler himself, and therefore on his personal rule. The study of the Third Reich has been dogged by this approach from the earliest days and partly stems from the National Socialist propaganda on Hitler as the unchallenged leader of his party; quite apart from other considerations this was felt necessary in order to win votes. The very activity of battling for electoral success after 1925 under the conditions of Weimar required that a facade of unity be presented to the public. Contemporary observers were already stressing that Adolf Hitler was 'its (NSDAP's) leader in the strictest sense of the word', and then proceeded to offer a 'few examples of the absolute power which he seems to exercise within his party'.[2] After January 1933 there was an even greater need to accentuate the idea of Hitler as the omnipotent leader, almost single-handedly steering the ship of state. And of course this approach had been essential to help free Hitler from the constraints of his Nationalist coalition partners. A further factor was Hitler's attempt to have himself increasingly portrayed as above both Party and state, in the interests of reconciling conflicts between the two. No doubt the present day 'Hitler Wave' has helped to perpetuate the acceptance of the above stereotype in the minds of the general public.

In retrospect, however, it is apparent that during the 1960s and early 1970s, historians went too far in their anxiety to dispel this myth. As they increasingly turned their attention towards the actual structures and daily life of the Third Reich a picture began to emerge of a society dominated by violently competing interests, rather than by the rule of one man. In 1969 it was possible to write a book called *The Limits of Hitler's Power*[2]; no phrase exemplifies this explanatory model better than Schoenbaum's now familiar term, 'institutionalized Social Darwinism'.[4] During this process Hitler seemed at times almost to disappear entirely from the centre of the stage; simultaneously the whole idea of a smooth running state vanished with him and in its place appeared a new model of the Third Reich as a system chiefly characterized by its inefficiency and lack of planning. Thus the notion of a unified movement advancing inexorably from one pre-determined goal to another became progressively more difficult to sustain. Admittedly the attempt to portray the Third Reich as a mixture of rival centres of power, or to use Broszat's term, 'polyocracy', did not prevent the appearance of a spate of biographies. Not all of these latter studies are, however, content to repeat the earlier picture of Hitler's Germany simply as a society under the rule of one man, but even in the newer accounts of National Socialist rule there remain considerable differences of opinion as to the precise part played by Adolf Hitler. Here we are of course concerned not with his personality as such (See Chapter One) but with his *function* in the Third Reich.

One German historian has pointed out that 'Hitler no more stood at the head of the Party than he did at the head of the State, but he was in principle over both.'[5] If this were so it would be fallacious to look for any actual system in the Third Reich since government would have been personal. The appropriate simile used in this account is that of a net, where the strands were not of equal length nor of equal thickness, and may have changed their interrelationship from time to time, but which had one thing in common: the ends were all in the hands of Adolf Hitler.[6] This rather tortuous analogy does at least probably get nearer the truth than any schema showing how the Third Reich was run. A Gauleiter with access to Hitler could be politically more important than a cabinet minister who was unable to see his chief of state for years on end. The concept of a clearly regulated and accountable division of responsibility is therefore of little use in helping us to understand the Third Reich. Relationships were continually changing owing to changes in personnel in both Party and State. No diagram could ever accurately portray the organizational structure of Hitler's government.[7] His role both as a source of power and as an integrating factor in the country was underpinned by his use of referendums, which in effect acclaimed him personally, as Meinck has demonstrated.[8] Significantly, popular dissatisfaction against the regime, as evidenced in its own secret reports, show that Hitler was invariably excepted as a person from general criticism.[9]

The degree of personal loyalty which Hitler received from the nation as a whole, at least until the later stages of the war, was paralleled by the personal homage he received from the Gauleiters. Typical was Gauleiter Sprenger who said, when he heard that Himmler had been made Minister of the Interior, he would continue to act according to the decrees of the Führer rather than obey Himmler directly.[10] Indeed such loyalty was institutionalized by means of the Party itself: 'Hitler successfuly bureaucratized the Party Organization by convincing his corps of functionaries that their own successful role as his agents depended on their ability to accept that obedience to the dry, unpopular executives with whom Hitler staffed Party Central Headquarters, was an integral part of service to Hitler the person.'[11] Moreover liaison between these executives themselves at Munich 'was guaranteed neither by locale nor institution, but in the last resort only through personal contact with Hitler'.[12] Competition for Hitler's favour took place at an even higher level, as witness the battle between Todt and Keitel, each striving to ingratiate themselves with Hitler during his rearmament programme.[13] This no doubt explains perhaps why Haffner should see the Third Reich as a Hitler creation, the conscious result of his decision to take the road to politics. 'After his discovery of his hypnotic capacity as a public speaker, Hitler took the decision to become the Führer.'[14] Such a line of argument would, however, seem to suggest an uncritical acceptance that Hitler's supposedly absolutist control of the Party during the 1920s was automatically transferred to the state after 1933.[15]

Hitler never seems to have believed that of himself. Indeed, he is alleged to have said to Hermann Rauschning, 'I am no dictator and never will be a dictator...There is no such thing as unlimited power, and I should never dream of pretending it to myself. The word dictatorship is misleading, there is no such thing as dictatorship in the accepted sense.' There has in fact been a growing readiness to agree that dependence on Hitler as the fount of authority was perfectly compatible with a degree of autonomy for the different power groups under the Führer. Although they were subject to his will in those issues where he did directly concern himself, they were able in other areas to appear to some extent as independent political units. Hüttenberger offers a definition of this phenomenon as 'A condition of government which has no generally recognized constitutional foundation, but whose development is characterized by a random growth of power groups and the relationship between them at any one moment.'[16] Historiographically, an important part of the debate now centres around the battle between this whole concept and the view of the Third Reich as a coherent monolith, which persists in many biographies and school books. Kühnl goes so far as to argue that most people uncritically accept the Third Reich as the centralized dictatorship of Adolf Hitler without paying enough attention to the implications of the connections between the different power groups.[17] Secondly, however, historians who now accept the concept of polyocracy in general are by no means united as to how this came about. Thirdly, there is controversy about the precise composition of the various power groups involved and the relationship between them, which will be examined first.

As early as 1942 Neumann was suggesting in his book, *Behemoth*, that Germany was ruled essentially by four different groups, consisting of the Party, the Wehrmacht, the bureaucracy and big business,[18] which is a variant of the familiar concept of an alliance of the NSDAP with the traditional elites of Germany.[19] Whilst Hüttenberger accepts that there were four power centres involved, he does not agree over which four. His classification is based on the one hand on two forces both 'saturated' by the Party, that is, the NSDAP Political Organization at Munich and the SS/SD/Gestapo complex, and on the other hand the German Labour Front and the *Reichsnahrstand*.[20] In Saage's version, the NSDAP and the SS are again presented as two categories, with big business and the Wehrmacht as the third and fourth, in which respect he follows Schweitzer.[21] In Broszat's view a triangular power structure supported the Third Reich, comprising the Party, the 'State' and Hitler's own personal authority?[22] In a sense these are all, apart from *Behemoth*, refinements of Fraenkel's original concept of the 'Dual State', which he used to describe the division of power between Party and State?[23] The problem of using these terms as a form of shorthand is that they conceal the rivalry between the different elements making up both. As Broszat recognized, however, no formal categorization could do justice to the complexity of the system, with its shifting balance of power?[24]

Whilst historians have not reached full agreement on the exact classification of power groups, their attempt to analyse these relationships necessarily highlights the way in which the structure of government in the Third Reich actually developed, rather than remaining a merely static system. In their attempt to do justice to this movement historians may have fallen victim to the error which Bollmus warned against, namely, 'an artificial rationalisation in retrospect of the style of management of Hitler and his many functionaries.'[25] Schweitzer for example, in criticizing the 'totalitarian' theory of the Third Reich, concluded that the system was best described as 'partial fascism' until 1936, because of the victory of big business over the SA and 'middle class socialism' two years previously. Only in 1936 does he see the transition to what he regards as 'full fascism', which is when the Party triumphed over industry or, in personal terms, when Goering replaced Schacht as the effective head of the German economy?[26] Schweitzer's analysis, which emanated from his interest in German industry, was reinforced by Horn, who was primarily concerned with the political system. He concluded that the growing consolidation of the regime changed the weight of the unequal alliance between Party and State to the benefit of the former?[27]

The idea of a close relationship between industry, and indeed agriculture, and the NSDAP as the basis for the regime predates modern research, in that left wing theorists were already pointing to this in the 1930s?[28] There were, however, differences between such writers in spite of Western attempts to lump them together. Similarly whilst in the GDR the current Stamokap theories describing the Third Reich assume that Hitler and the Party were no more than the tools of monopoly capitalism, a rather more sophisticated Marxist interpretation has been developed in the work of T. W. Mason. His argument about the 'primacy of politics' in effect affirms that the regime achieved a degree of autonomy particularly from 1936 onwards, in which incidentally he sees the roots of the economic crisis of 1938-1939.[29] The idea of the political executive which initially wins support of 'monopoly capitalism in crisis' for its policies, but which then becomes progressively independent the longer the regime lasts has been given the convenient label of 'Bonapartist'. This is in keeping with Marx's own analysis of the Second French Empire and the development of the concept of 'Bonapartism' by August Thalheimer in the early 1930s.[30] Neumann suggested that although originally the Party went into an alliance with groups which included industry, the increase in the power of the political executive, especially in the Second World War, set free tendencies which in the long run would actually have destroyed the bourgeois capitalist order. Such a variant seems to take the Bonapartist theory a stage further.[31]

However sophisticated these explanatory models may be, their very profusion and refinement convey a strong scent of neo-scholasticism. Tawney may have been incorrect when he described Marx as the *last* of the schoolmen. Often the style used in this type of analysis seems to parallel that of the middle ages and threatens to reduce the entire debate to one about terms rather than things. Thankfully this is less true of the various attempts to discuss how consciously Hitler pursued a policy of 'divide and rule'.[32] How far did his known tendency to create competing organizations both before and after seizing power spring from a natural aversion to taking firm decisions, and how much from a determination to leave himself as supreme arbiter above the quarrels of Party and state? Otto Dietrich, Hitler's one-time press adviser, argued that 'he systematically undermined the authority of all higher political organs in order to increase the absoluteness of his own power.'[33] This raises the query as to how far one man could possibly control or manipulate such a complex government. It may have been the case that Hitler was the apprentice rather than the sorcerer, and indeed for Rauschning the Führer 'maintained his position of supremacy but lost his freedom of decision'.[34]

Nonetheless, the most common historiographical view is that Hitler deliberately fostered competition between his subordinates in order to avoid the emergence of a rival to his own dominance. As Dietrich again put it: 'Hitler was a miser unwilling to share his powers, who consistently, cunningly and stubbornly isolated himself from the influence of all those whom he suspected of even the shadow of opposition to his will.'[35] Diehl-Thiele's work on Party-state relations tended to reinforce this notion by citing among many other instances the creation of the *Volksturm* in 1944, when the new organization was put politically under Bormann but militarily under Himmler. Hitler must surely have been conscious of the rivalry this would cause.[36] Mason further suggests that Hitler constantly demanded too much from the leaders of the armed forces, industry and the civil service as a deliberate technique of government.[37] One of Hitler's Gauleiters, Lauterbacher, affirmed his own belief in an interview in 1967 that the Führer could have put an end to the ensuing chaos at any time he wished, and concluded therefore that the very fact he chose not to do so was in itself evidence that there was some degree of intention behind the way in which rivalries were fostered.[38] For Bollmus, however, this kind of Social Darwinism had dangerous implications for Hitler's own position. By allowing his strongest subordinates to fight among themselves, he was actually favouring the eventual victors among them, and thereby increasing the chance that they would compete with him for the overall leadership.[39] Taken to its logical conclusion his argument would mean that Hitler was as much a prisoner of the system as its initiator. Others have maintained that the very lack of clarity in the vertical organization developed by the NSDAP was one of the most important prerequisites for strengthening the Hitler myth and his own personal power.[40]

What these explanations have in common is the presumption that at least Hitler was a 'strong ruler' in conventional terms, but there is also a school of thought, of which H. Mommsen is probably the best known exponent, which depicts him as a 'weak dictator'. Like other modern historians Mommsen lays heavy stress on the administrative anarchy within the Third Reich but differs from them by suggesting that this simply arose from Hitler's inability to take decisions.[41] He not only denies that Hitler was an absolutist, but refuses even to concede to him any great capacity as an arbiter of conflicts in the Third Reich, when he argues that 'Instead of functioning as a balancing element in the government, Hitler disrupted the conduct of affairs by continually acting on sudden impulses, each one different, and partly by delaying decisions on current matters.'[42] Goebbels himself, admittedly during wartime, seemed to support the view that the Third Reich was a weak dictatorship in his diary entry of 16 March 1943, when he wrote: 'We live in a state where areas of authority have been unclearly divided...the consequence is a complete lack of direction in German domestic policy...From this developed most of the quarrels between the real leaders and ruling authorities.' Petersen also suggests that as well as the difficulties inherent in the system over which Hitler presided, his own personal shortcomings as a decision taker played a crucial part. This 'arose more from a sense of inadequacy and a truly characteristic hesitancy, than from simple lack of interest.'[43] Rich, by contrast, felt that the Führer really did lack interest in administrative detail, citing as evidence his instructions to the head of the Reich Chancellery, Dr. Lammers, shortly after assuming power, that he was not to be bothered by routine matters.[44] It has even been argued by Broszat that ultimately a situation was reached where 'the secretary to the Führer (Martin Bormann) had taken over the government.'[45]

The trouble with such theories is that they do not give enough weight to Hitler's ability to make his own decisions tell, particularly in those areas where he actively intervened. Hildebrand has therefore made a resolute defence of Hitler's dominance in the field of foreign policy and clearly disagrees with the notion of Hitler as a 'weak dictator'.[46] Nonetheless such historians accept the idea of chaos within the Third Reich, even if they differ over the precise areas of activity where it applied, as well as over the question how far it was actually intended by Hitler. Here we ought to point out that it is completely consistent with Hitler's known hatred of bureaucracy and civil servants that he should have been not merely indifferent to administrative confusion, but that to some extent at least he should have welcomed it for more profound reasons. Firstly, the whole ethos of National Socialism was to put emphasis on the spirit rather than on the letter of institutions, thus giving full rein to the individual leader at all levels. Secondly, as Kettenacker points out, allowing the existing state to degenerate into a series of conflicting offices was part of Hitler's overall attempt to destroy old forms and create a new society.[47] Whether that is in fact true, or whether we are reading intention into what happened accidentally can only be cleared up by examining areas of conflict between the existing state structures and the Party as a kind of administrative parvenu, anxious to assert its claims as the governing instrument of the new society. Such was clearly the intention of many NSDAP leaders. As Wagener, of the economic department of the Munich Headquarters, said: 'The Party is the instrument of power with which one must conquer the government and afterwards control it. The Party is therefore of primary importance.'[48]

In general terms Wagener must have been ultimately disappointed with the progress made by the NSDAP after 1933 in attempting to take over power, the limitations to which can be confirmed even at the local level. On 1 January 1937 there were 707 *Landrat* offices in Germany, of which only 201 were occupied by men who had been Party members prior to the National Socialist accession. A further 345 posts were held by 'March converts', that is opportunists who had only joined the movement after it came to power, and of the remaining offices 135 were in the hands of non-National Socialists, with 26 places vacant.[49] The general picture is born out in a study of parish chairmen *(Bürgermeister)* in the district of Memmingen in Bavaria, carried out by Frölich and Broszat. Of the 24 *Bürgermeister* who stayed in office between 1933 and 1936 only 7 were old Party members; of the 17 who had joined since 1933 10 had previously not even been members of any political party. Additionally, 10 *Bürgermeister* of the Bavarian People's Party were able to hang on to their appointments until 1936. Such figures demonstrate the danger of reading too much into the mere statistics of Party membership in the Third Reich and show that at parish level the NSDAP's breakthrough was more apparent than real. This applies equally to the members of parish councils in the same district, who numbered 243 in July 1945, of whom 77 had still not joined the NSDAP.[50]

The failure of many Party members to attain administrative posts was in part also due to their unsuitability. As Gauleiter Wagner pointed out to Ley in April 1941, it was enough during the period of struggle prior to 1933 for a Party district leader to be a good fighter, but different qualities were now needed to govern Germany.[51] In addition the disappointing degree of progress made by the movement may well reflect Hitler's ambivalence towards it as a governing institution. No doubt this derived from his recognition of the limitations of many 'old warriors' as administrators. Yet his attempt to frustrate Party control of the state in the transitional period does not of course imply that Hitler wanted a strong central state for its own sake. In other words Hitler regarded his seizure of power as the starting point for a revolution, but not for an immediate one. He therefore saw a strong state as an obstacle in the long run because it would have taken away the revolutionary fervour of the movement.[52] As Hitler had said in *Mein Kampf,* there could be no state authority as an end in itself. Mussolini's concept of the state as eternal and the Party transitory, would have been an obscene idea in the Third Reich.[53]

Although the Party as a whole subscribed to this view there were nonetheless significant exceptions. In the first place, many members were determined to find good jobs in existing state or local administration as a reward for the years of struggle and this strongly held desire prevented Hitler at first from sweeping away the old forms of authority overnight. Secondly, notwithstanding Hitler's own personal views certain senior members of the NSDAP did believe in the maintenance of state authority as an end in itself, of whom the most important was Frick, the Minister of the Interior.[54] The latter, who as a career civil servant was certainly in favour of a strong central state, called the 30 January 1934 Law for the Reconstruction of the State the 'Magna Carta' of the Third Reich.[55] It is important here to grasp precisely what the real difference between Frick and Hitler amounted to. According to Mommsen what the former wanted was a politically homogeneous leader corps imbued with Nazi ideals.[56] Surely the point here, however, is that he wished this body to have its powers defined by a properly written constitution, based on a strong central state. Hitler too desired a leadership cadre with National Socialist beliefs, but unlike Frick he did not wish it to be tied down by the constraints of formal rules. Krebs, who was Gauleiter of Hamburg between 1926 and 1928, averred that Hitler had a conscious determination to ape the unwritten constitution of Britain, of which Krebs said he made no secret.[57]

This is important as another illustration of Hitler's predilection, not self-evidently for parliamentary democracy but for an organic political system giving full flexibility of movement to a leadership corps, an ideal which manifestly found expression in his instructions to the Gauleiters about the Reich law of April 1933; the law installed Reich Governors in certain regions of Germany, posts normally given to Party members. Whereas the legislation was perhaps understandably seen by Frick as another centralizing measure, because it ostensibly transferred power from regional to central government, the practice was very different precisely because Hitler gave the posts to Gauleiters. Indeed he implied that their power and future influence depended to a considerable extent on what they personally made of their office. This law, like that of 30 January 1934, merely replaced one form of regional authority with another, because Gauleiters were by definition regional leaders. When Frick complained about this development Hitler came to an ambiguous decision, namely that the Reich Governors were under the Minister of the Interior, but only in exceptional circumstances. Such a ruling had the advantage of appeasing Frick without putting any real restraints on Gauleiter encroachment on state authority in practice, since what constituted 'exceptional circumstances' was never clearly defined. It is characteristic of Hitler that after receiving complaints from state authorities of Party interference in March 1934, he drafted a speech which was intended to clear up the entire issue, and yet in the end this was never delivered.[60] Ultimately Frick remained dissatisfied, as in 1941 he was still trying to restore the authority of the *Landrat* as a state office vis-à-vis the Party.[60]

It is clear that the Führer, like most other National Socialists, had little liking for state authority as such. The statement of February 1934 that 'We command the state, the state does not command us', was no empty phrase, as was confirmed by the ultimate fate of the civil service in National Socialist Germany. Dislike of the faceless bureaucrat was almost an article of faith for Germany's new leaders, and in this respect Frick is a conspicuous exception.[62] In the National Socialist scheme of things it was up to the political leader to provide the charisma and the value system of the new state, whilst civil servants were reduced merely to carrying out the administration necessary to implement these ideals in practice. The regime also needed the civil service after the *Machtergreifung* because, as has already been argued, there were simply not enough qualified administrators within the Party. Moreover, as Mommsen has pointed out, the civil servants themselves were ready to collaborate with the regime for two reasons. Firstly, the National Socialist accession had been carried out in a semi-legal fashion and secondly the bureaucracy was ready to submit to a degree of rationalization.[63] No doubt its reaction was partly due to a desire to preserve its own existence, but probably also derived from its belief that there was a certain routine by which change should be introduced. Mommsen feels that the law of 7 April 1933, whereby the purge of the civil service was legalized, is the point at which the NSDAP met the bureaucrats halfway.[64] As he argues, it did mark a retreat from the exercise of arbitrary power, and as such was a concession by the Party; at the same time, since it in effect sanctioned the National Socialist takeover, the civil service had come to endorse the regime, which Mason also accepts.[65]

If, however, the civil service thought that it had achieved a permanent *modus vivendi* with the government it was soon to be disappointed. In the first place the whole system of polyocracy in the Third Reich broke their career structure, in the sense that new ministries and new bodies were constantly being created; the normal practice of promotion by seniority became as a result very difficult to apply. Secondly, the constant, unregulated Party interference in administration, as well as Hitler's habit of issuing personal decrees without consultation, caused a steady erosion of civil service prestige in general.[67] This does not contradict the point already made concerning the disappointment in Party circles about their failure to take over the government of the Third Reich en bloc. It was precisely because the Party was not successful in this aim that it was obliged to infiltrate the state mechanism, thus upsetting the state servants without necessarily always removing them. The nadir for the civil service seems to have come by 1941, when Frick was so concerned about its low morale that he actually asked Hitler to make a public statement thanking the bureaucrats for their efforts.[68] No written answer to this request has ever been found, but in his *Table Talk* on 1 August 1941, Hitler said that he had had to refuse, which in effect re-affirmed his contempt for them. The example of the civil service confirms, on the whole, that 'polyocracy' is a valid explanatory model to use for the system of government in the Third Reich and it is almost certain that further investigation of other areas at the top of the administration will confirm the general picture.

In the case of the judiciary it has been argued that in the Third Reich it was actually given some room for movement, in the sense of not being continually under pressure from the new regime, but that this freedom was rarely exercised. Why did the judiciary make itself the instrument in this way? Was it because it simply had a tradition, like the bureaucracy, of service to the state? Ideology was arguably of less moment than the need to continue with this tradition.[69] Additionally, Weinkauff has suggested that already in the Weimar period judges were coming under the damaging influence of what he calls positivistic law, a development which mentally prepared them for National Socialist justice. The latter thesis has not, however, found wholehearted support.[70] Nonetheless Broszat has provided ample evidence of the way in which the judiciary attempted to collaborate with the regime in a process of self-coordination, rather like the civil service in general, in order to preserve intact the principles of justice at law.[71] The effort to preserve the *Rechtsstaat* is clearly manifest in Justice Minister Gürtner's attempt in 1935 to get a number of SA men brought to trial for the atrocities which they had committed in a concentration camp in Saxony.[72] Yet ordinary courts soon lost power to the instruments of terror, particularly the SS and Gestapo, and simultaneously to the so-called social honour courts. The process was immensely speeded up during the war when 'National Socialist justice' superseded the old *Rechtsstaat.*[73] Although Hüttenberger is correct in this statement, there is no doubt that the practice of compromising with the new regime had begun much earlier. The sanctioning of a retroactive execution of the Reichstag arsonist, van der Lubbe, probably represented the first milestone along the path to unregulated terror. Another example is the way in which increasingly from 1934 the concentration camp functionaries shook themselves free of any legal supervision. After that year the SS officers ceased to supply information on those prisoners who had been 'shot whilst escaping.'[74] So Gürtner found it more and more difficult to achieve his aim as the National Socialists strengthened their grip on the institutions of Germany. The tacit acceptance at the end of the Röhm affair that Hitler had been entitled to act on his own initiative during a time of 'national emergency' represents another stage in the process whereby the judicial establishment gradually gave way to the pressures of the National Socialist state.

At the same time, although Anderbrügge has shown how ideology played its part in influencing new legislation (see p. 42), it would be incorrect to assume that the old *Rechtsstaat* simply gave way to a state based on a body of coherent *völkisch* National Socialist doctrine, as many Party jurists had hoped it would prior to 1933. Indeed the very embodiment of such ideas, the so-called People's Court, found itself supplanted in the last resort by the SS and Gestapo. The President of the Academy of German Law, Hans Frank, had propagated romantic ideas 'that the *völkisch* Führer state would restore Germanic principles of law and the independent German judiciary.' Yet his deputy could say in August 1935 that Gestapo arrests were 'completely incompatible with the National Socialist conception of security at law...(and) in conflict with the natural regard for law of the Northern races', which he argued encouraged the belief 'that the activity of the secret state police,like the Russian Cheka, was outside the law and purely despotic.'[75] By 1941 the legal confusion was such that Bormann wrote to Lammers complaining that the Gauleiters were no longer able to understand the national legislation. They therefore saw themselves forced more and more to take individual decisions as to whether or not the Reich law should be applied.[76]

In both areas, administration and justice, Hitler fitfully intervened, often directly and successfully, in the sense of having his own personal decisions implemented, but it is clear from the Bormann letter that in general terms the Social Darwinist principles which underlay polyocracy could equally prevent any regular, clear cut and consistent exercise of power. There are problematic areas where the latter proposition is not necessarily true, for example foreign policy, in spite of Francois Poncet's observation in November 1933. As French Ambassador to Germany he was well placed to note that 'In the domain of foreign affairs, there no longer reigns any more than in other areas of government, that order, unity and discipline which the Third Reich brags it has brought with it. There is not merely one Minister, nor is there only one Foreign Office. There are half a dozen.'[77] Yet the polyocracy in foreign affairs did not apparently prevent Hitler from implementing his own ideas, as will be seen in a later chapter.

Historians have not, however, been content merely to examine the top levels of the administration in the Third Reich in their quest to discover whether it was in practice a centralized or polycentric dictatorship. Regional and local aspects of this struggle between Party and existing bureaucratic institutions need to be examined too. This is a relatively new historiographical development since the normal practice was invariably to look at the seizure of power from the centre; what studies we did have of Party-state conflict at regional or local level tended to come from the period of Party growth prior to 1933. We are now being fairly well-provided with evidence on conflicts away from the centre of the stage, mainly by West German scholars. The question is: to what extent was friction at lower levels simply the reflection of that at the centre of the German administration? It must be faced that this problem has rarely been considered in what are frequently just *descriptions* of polyocracy in practice lower down the administrative ladder. In contrast to the studies of the Ministerial bureaucracy, those of the provincial administration make less attempt to develop a separate conceptual framework. It seems tacitly to be assumed that the model developed to explain higher level conflicts will necessarily be applicable lower down. This is not to deny the value of the accumulation of empirical data for various areas of Germany after 1933. It may well be that disputes up to Gauleiter level were much more the outcome of a hunt for office than was the case at the centre, and were devoid of any constructive theories or proposals. Perhaps this was because the obstacles to Party encroachment on the state were obviously generally less formidable in the localities. The worm's eye view of Germany in 1933 could often give an impression of total anarchy, as witness the following quotation: 'The authority of the state is being endangered by the universal and unjustified interference of political functionaries in the machinery of normal government...Everybody is arresting someone...everybody is threatening someone with Dachau...Uncertainty about authority has set in right down to the smallest local police station.'[78] This particular view of Bavaria has been confirmed by the work of Klenner, who points to a very complicated battle waged there between the summer of 1933 and the following spring. The chief protagonists were the SA, the Gauleiters, Himmler and conservative elements round the Reichsgovernor Ritter von Epp. What complicated the matter still further was the shifting nature of the relationships between the various groups involved.[79]

In Prussia the stituation was still more involved because of the incongruence between the geographical borders of the Prussian provinces and the National Socialist Party organization; there were 21 Gauleiters in the 12 Prussian provinces.[80] This arose from the decision taken by Gregor Strasser, then Party Organization leader at Munich, to make the National Socialist administration geographically consistent with the electoral constituencies under the Weimar Republic.[81] What this could mean in practice has been graphically shown in the Prussian province of Saxony. The Oberpräsident was an SA man but in each of three counties under him there was a different Gauleiter, all of whom were more radical than he was, which made it virtually impossible to take a unanimous decision. This state of affairs lasted until July 1944.[82] Those Gauleiters who also secured the post of Oberpräsident in Prussia created a new provincial counterweight which could actually frustrate the central Prussian government. This is one instance where the prestige of a Party office invested what was hitherto held to be a moribund institution with a new authority.

In Bavaria the position of the Gauleiters was somewhat different. Frick wanted to make them local government officials *(Regierungs-*

*präsidenten)* so that they would be subordinate to him as Minister of the Interior, but Hitler refused to back him up and gave the Gauleiter the freedom either to accept this office or to reject it; some at least took the latter course.[83] In this instance central control was frustrated as effectively as by the Gauleiters in Prussia, albeit in a somewhat different way. An even more extreme example of high-handedness on the part of a Gauleiter was provided by Josef Bürckel, in the Bavarian Palatine, who passed a law according to which Party district leaders were entitled to claim 'voluntary' financial contributions from all civil servants in the area, up to 20 per cent of their salary.[84] Their power has been underlined by Milward, when he pointed to the difficulties which Hitler experienced with many Gauleiters, after January 1942, because of their opposition to the total war policy which he was then attempting to execute.[85]

The wealth of empirical data now available on the conflicts in the administration of the Third Reich from the highest to the lowest level has not, however, brought agreement amongst historians as to whether the resulting system of polyocracy was produced by a conscious policy of 'divide and rule' on the part of Adolf Hitler, or was the unintended outcome of what Mommsen called a 'weak dictatorship.' The question still remains as to how and why this system of government arose. A study of the civil service by Jane Caplan provides powerful support for the Mommsen thesis. As she saw it, 'the disintegrating effect of the regime on the institutions and practices of politics...was both unplanned and unintentional. In other words the tendency did not derive from any deliberately subversive purpose, but rather seeped into the processes of government through the regime's neglect, or ignorance, of the conditions of long term policy making and institutional practice.'[86] Interestingly enough, whilst a modern historian like Caplan stresses the inability of the regime to cope with these administrative conflicts, and the resulting 'anarchy', some contemporary observers seem to have been struck by the great skill with which the Führer and his subordinates adjusted and regulated the administrative mechanism in order to preserve efficiency of government. Thus in 1938 Boerner could say that 'The higher unity of the new order, the state in the larger sense, is erected upon a carefully cultivated organizational and functional dualism. To insure that this dualism does not in practice lead to a friction destructive of the system, a constant process of adjustment and delimitation of authority between the two organizations is necessary', which he traced through three stages of development as far as the Party was concerned after 1933.[87] One obvious reason for the divergence of views between Boerner and Caplan, with all the implications that this holds for the concept of weak dictatorship, is that the latter has the advantage of having access to documents not available in 1938, as a result of which the general concept 'Party' can now be broken down into its various constituent elements. Historians before the war saw the anthill as it were from the outside, but defeat in 1945 uncovered the interior and made them increasingly aware that the constant movement was less orderly and planned than had at first been imagined. We are in any case today more conscious that any complex modern state will inevitably become 'polycratic', in the sense that this is normally used of the Third Reich, although the facade of unity which the regime was able to preserve until after military defeat temporarily obscured this. We are then left with explaining the peculiar degree of intensity of the institutional conflicts in Hitler's Germany, which must in part at least be related to the wider problem of the way in which the Party grew during the 1920s and Hitler's role in this and its arrival in power.

Modern historical research has demolished the old concept of Hitler marching at the head of a tightly organized, unified column, whose members all subscribed to exactly the same ideals, the corollary of which was the widely accepted concept of the monolithic state after 1933. To begin with there is now a much greater recognition of the important geographical variations within the Party.[88] Additionally, Armin Mohler has pointed to the fact that quite irrespective of region, there were five main types of National Socialists; namely, the other *völkisch* groups, neo-conservatives, Freikorps elements, youth associations based on the leadership principle and supporters of the Rural People's Movement, a radical organization in North West Germany.[89] In addition the plurality of socio-economic interest groups who joined the movement ensured that, as Meinck has pointed out, the Party was so internally divided before it came to power that there were bound to be clashes afterwards.[90] The transition to office and the way in which it was carried out accentuated the existing tendency towards rivalry, for example leaving the Political Organization Headquarters at Munich in a far worse position than the S.A. The latter had a crucial and active role to play, as did the Gauleiters, whilst the Political

Organization was put in a curious kind of limbo. Not surprisingly, such an organizational structure did not make for unity of purpose after 1933 for the loss of the Munich HQ's control over the Party was not compensated for by any comparable gains in the state.[91] Even propaganda, as we have seen, was taken over by a state ministry. Goebbels, along with other prominent Party leaders, was the sort of strong personality who had been of absolutely crucial value to Hitler in actually bringing the movement into power, in which his capacity for organizing propaganda had played no small part.[92] In every way such powerful personalities had made themselves indispensable to Hitler during the 1920s and were bound to become important centres of authority in Germany after 1933, provided that they continued to show great loyalty to Hitler as a person. The fate of Gregor Strasser and his absence of support had already in 1932 illustrated this point. Since Hitler, as has been pointed out earlier, almost invariably returned whatever personal loyalty he received from his subordinates, they were given all the more scope to feud with one another.

This could lead, as in the case of Himmler, to the accretion of enormous personal power, to the extent that he lost count of the number of offices he held. The remarkable patronage exercised by such a 'four square and upstanding' man did not make him a rival to Hitler, merely to other Party and state functionaries. Mommsen's description of the SS in fact provides a perfect illustration of how at every level the polyocratic administration rested on personal loyalty. 'The SS was a miscellaneous collection of very different political groups and at the same time a loose assortment of organizations and associations, linked only by a personal relationship to Himmler, with overlapping areas of responsibility and which quite often tried to follow policies independently of one another, only reluctantly yielding to the ultimate authority of the Reichsführer SS.'[94] Just as the network of Hitler's personal relationships was the cornerstone of the Third Reich, of which Himmler was a member, so he himself at a lower level held together the threads of a similar number of intimates.[95] The key to understanding the government of the Third Reich is a thorough grasp of the importance of personal loyalty at all levels.

The whole debate about the nature of the dictatorship in Germany has been refined by research into the government of the German-occupied territories. That the Third Reich would export its internal polyocracy had become evident even before the Second World War broke out.[96] The dismemberment of Czechoslovakia in 1939 was accompanied by a characteristic scene, described by Heinemann: 'impetuously accompanying the German armies occupying Bohemia and Moravia, Hitler spent the evening of March 15 in Prague Castle, where his experts proceeded, in noisy and somewhat confused fashion, to work out a constitutional form for the new administration.'[97] No amount of such forward 'planning' could, however, prevent the ensuing and characteristic rivalry between Neurath, the official Reich Protector, and the 'motley crew of Nazi opportunists who were attracted to this new area.'[98] Many of these 'carpet-baggers of occupation' arriving from Berlin had no experience of Czech affairs at all. Moreover the Sudetenland deputy, Karl Hermann Frank, had already with the aid of SS groups and Sudetenland administrators established his own power base in Prague before Neurath had even arrived.[99] It required enormous effort on Neurath's part to stave off at least the worst aspects of the racialist policies of the SS, SD and Gestapo, which therefore came into full operation only after his removal in the autumn of 1941. He could not, however, prevent his rivals from frustrating his own plans for a genuine cooperation beween Czechs and Germans.[100]

At least within the Old Reich, the conflicts inherent in the Social Darwinistic value system of the National Socialist government had been kept within some kind of reasonable limits, both by the constraints of public and world opinion, as well as by the residual authority of the pre-1933 state organs which survived the National Socialist takeover. In the newly conquered territories a 'man of will and ambition', to use Hitler's words, could virtually write his own rules. The clashes were now largely limited to three main protagonists. Two of these were National Socialist groups who had best survived in the struggle inside Germany before 1939, namely Himmler and the SS on the one hand and the leading Gauleiters on the other. These inevitably brought with them the practice of administration with which they were already familiar inside Germany, that is to say a combination of ad hoc measures and a racialist value system. They now found themselves unavoidably at odds with the third power centre, the Wehrmacht. It seems reasonably clear that Gauleiters such as Koch and Terboven regarded National Socialist hegemony in Europe very much as an opportunity for personal empire building. This in itself makes it difficult to conceive of any single 'New Order'. How could Social Darwinism, so clearly in evidence during National Socialist occupation, be combined with long-term planning? Stamokap historians have also pointed to the competing interest groups who were actually framing the occupation policies behind their desks in Germany. Their interference reinforced the anarchy created by the conflicts of authority between the groups actually in occupation of foreign territory.[101] East German historians have therefore characterized the New Order as 'a striking mixture of unrestrained adventurism, unscrupulous barbarity, fantastic speculations on a continental and intercontinental scale, sober General Staff work, and carefully calculated capitalistic greed for profit.'[102] In North Europe alone the competing agencies in the struggle for booty included the Four Year Plan Office, the Reich Group for German Industry (an employers' association), the Foreign Office and the central offices of the Party itself, among others. Not surprisingly no central guidelines were ever issued for the area.[103] As this evidence suggests, a great deal of the struggle subsumed under the heading 'New Order' centred around competing economic interests, a theme to which we will return in Chapter 6.

How involved the purely political rivalries could become can be seen from the example of Josef Bürckel, who as a result of the victory of 1940 now found that the former French province of Lorraine had been added to his existing domains in Germany. In pursuit of his policy of 'Germanization' he suddenly expelled one hundred thousand of the more obdurate French-speaking Lorrainers, in the middle of delicate negotiations which the central German government was conducting with the Vichy regime in France.[104] Here was a classic demonstration of how polyocracy could be exported as a result of conquest, and how the characteristic high-handed Gauleiter behaviour could now find a freedom of expression to a degree hitherto unexampled inside the Reich. Extraordinary as Bürckel's behaviour may seem, it was actually exceeded by those Gauleiters in East Europe where racial ideology added yet another dimension to their empire building. This particularly applies to Erich Koch in the Ukraine, and to a somewhat lesser extent to Hinrich Lohse in the Baltic region. Both these men were nominally placed under Rosenberg's Ministry for the Occupied East, but neither of them had the faintest intention of following any of his instructions, as Rosenberg himself recognized even prior to their appointment. In the Ukraine in particular a four-sided battle developed in which the power centres were respectively: Koch; his chief, Rosenberg; Himmler's SS, which had control over the policing of the occupied territories; and the Wehrmacht.[105] A similar situation has been documented for the General Government in Poland, where Himmler in his capacity as Reichscommissar for the Strengthening of German Folkdom struggled with the *Reichsnährstand* (RNS) which was charged with maximizing agricultural production in the area.[106] It was therefore obviously in its interests that Polish peasants should be reasonably well treated, since food output was in the final analysis dependent on their goodwill. Himmler, however, as part of his duties as Reichscommissar, wished to carry out a resettlement programme in the General Government for the benefit of ethnic Germans, which entailed displacing existing Polish farmers. His actions in this respect, particularly in Zamosc, caused a blazing row with the RNS and the latter attempted to enlist the aid of Goering to frustrate Himmler's plans; it attributed the increase in partisan activity in the area directly to the ill will which Himmler had caused. It should be stressed that pragmatic considerations seem to have been uppermost in Himmler's mind in this instance, since he stated that the ethnic Germans were more productive as farmers than the Poles, whereas the *Reichsnährstand* pointed out that food for the German war effort was required now and displacing Polish peasants, whatever the improvement in the long run, would entail an immediate drop in production.[107]

Underlying such local quarrels were the long-term goals of the SS and its leaders, which went far beyond immediate political issues. Fest argued that Himmler did not merely see the SS as a police force or as an instrument of control in general, but as a cell in a new conception of imperial government as the instrument of domination for the whole of Europe. Typical of such dreams was Himmler's notion that after the war a new state of Burgundy would be carved out of France and handed over totally to the SS, with its own SS ambassador in Berlin. Equally characteristic were the thousands of man hours devoted to drafting schemes for the permanent colonization of the East based on model villages and towns, to be defended by SS settlers *(Wehrbauern)*.

On inspection therefore, the 'New Order' dissolves into a maelstrom of competing interests, as does the whole concept of the

Third Reich as a monolithic dictatorship. It is of course possible to try to reconcile the two apparently conflicting portraits of Hitler's Germany by suggesting that centralized dictatorship and polyocracy were not necessarily in opposition as government systems. Heiber, for example, has described the Third Reich as 'anarchy under authoritarianism'.[109] In fact it must be an oversimplification to subsume the entire system into one of two logical categories, a kind of 'either, or' as the Germans would say. Furious and conflicting activity did indeed exist in many areas of German society after 1933, but there are surely two points to be made here. The first is that this state of affairs does not preclude the possibility that centralized control also occurred in Hitler's Germany. An obvious example would be the conduct of foreign affairs, for which four competing authorities were set up but where Hitler remained firmly the supreme arbiter.[110] The second point is that there has been a marked tendency in recent work to overreact against the traditional version of the Third Reich as a monolithic society.

Whilst newer research has destroyed the concept of a monolith it equally suggests that the idea of 'weak dictatorship' is unsatisfactory as an overall explanatory model of the Third Reich. The Röhm affair illustrates how Hitler could run the entire gamut of the exercise of power. When the SA leader complained in October 1933 that too many people in the Party thought the real revolution was over when in fact it was not, Hitler allowed him to set up SA Commissars in Prussia inside Goering's own domain, and these also competed with the Party in general. This apparently shows Hitler as weak and indecisive, but the point has been made that he was probably riding with events until an opportune moment arrived to settle the problem. As we now know this came on the night of 30 June 1934, when the SA leadership, including Röhm, was annihilated on Hitler's orders.[112] Clearly then, the Führer could and did intervene decisively at key moments and had no trouble in persuading the cabinet to accept him as the final arbiter. If the term 'weak dictatorship' has any validity at all, it must refer to the *effects* of the whole Hitlerian system on the conduct of affairs in Germany. In other words, how efficiently were these managed in practice? Here there is a very obvious divergence of views. The concept of 'institutionalized Social Darwinism' as the basis of an incompetent system was dimly perceived, as we have seen, as early as 1933, and was powerfully reinforced by the work of Schoenbaum and his successors. The merit of such an approach was that it demonstrated that a dictatorship may indeed be far removed in reality from the efficiency to which it pretends. This obviously occurred to Bollmus, who raised the question as to how this apparently chaotic situation could be reconciled with what was actually *done* in the Third Reich. His answer, namely that the 'achievements' of the Hitler state were wholly negative, for example the destruction of the Jews, or a war of aggression, and that the regime could offer nothing constructive, is not wholly convincing.[113] In the first place it fails to explain how National Socialist Germany very nearly won the war by 1943, having been a virtually bankrupt and weakly armed state only ten years previously. The process of German rearmament concealed a multitude of activities involving economic reconstruction, which can hardly be described as merely negative, whatever its eventual goal. Secondly, it does not pay enough attention to the *idea* of a New Order in Europe; even if Hitler's vision had not focused precisely on this subject, nonetheless he was convinced that out of the wreck of war a different society would be created. In effect the Bollmus thesis virtually resurrects Rauschning's old concept of a 'revolution of destruction' and the Bullock notion of Hitler as a nihilist.

In the last resort no single model can really do justice to the fluctuating shifts in the power groups of the Third Reich and their interrelationships, in the sense of providing a mono-causal account. The determined search for such an all-embracing explanation is perhaps a reflection of the loss of direction experienced by academics once they had thrown overboard such historical ballast as the 'totalitarian' model and the 'sole dictatorship', which no serious historian now accepts as an overall picture of the Third Reich. The chief problem remaining is whether the administrative chaos existed as a conscious result of Hitler's own approach to government, namely 'divide and rule', or whether it came about simply through an unplanned organic growth of institutions, as Jane Caplan has more recently suggested. It may well be that the two views are not incompatible in the sense that Hitler's own predilection was to allow his subordinates a great deal of latitude. This was perfectly consistent with the historical growth of the Party prior to the accession of power and with its Social Darwinistic ethos. What Hitler may not have anticipated, however, was the degree of confusion which this attitude would cause in a modern industrial state. Therefore it still remains open as a historical question exactly to what extent many of his policies were determined by his conscious volition, and how much their execution was affected by the administrative chaos which undoubtedly existed. On one level it is difficult to quarrel with Hüttenberger's conclusion that 'Research in the last decade has increasingly conveyed to us the picture of an extremely complex government mechanism, built upon several power centres which frequently fought against or at least blocked one another, but which were all generally accepted as being subordinate to Hitler, the all powerful leader.'[111] Yet surely the most promising approach to the problem is to integrate the serious studies of Hitler the man with the findings of the school of structural history. It will then be apparent that there is no necessary division between an analysis of Hitler himself and of the society which he governed. The Führer can then be seen in the centre of a complex web based ultimately on relationships between personalities rather than on abstract theories of government.

# 4 Hitler's social revolution?

'We hold no brief for equality, we want classes, high and low, up and down.'[1]

Until the 1960s most historical writers tended to stress the neo-feudal aspects of National Socialist thought. This, in conjunction with the barbaric terror employed by the regime led to the general concept of Hitler's Germany being simply a step backwards in time. Characteristic of this approach was the book by the American journalist Edgar Mowrer, published in 1933, *Germany puts the clock back*. This belief is understandable in the light of contemporary National Socialist speeches and writing. The preamble for the *Erbhofgesetz* (the law which entailed peasant farms), for example, stated that the object of the legislation was to preserve the peasantry under the safeguard of Old Germanic inheritance custom.[2] Not surprisingly many historians came to the conclusion that 'Nazi thinkers quite consciously tried to model the New Order along feudal lines.'[3] Insofar as some academics have also simultaneously tried to present the Third Reich as a totalitarian society this may be held to have shown some confusion of thought. After all, the concepts of 'feudalism' and 'totalitarianism' are mutually exclusive. Moreover, it has not always been clear what was meant by feudalism. Some saw Hitler's political aim as the revival of a kind of universal state like the Holy Roman Empire. In *Behemoth* however his very nationalism (hardly itself a feudal concept) precluded any revival of the medieval Reich, such as that of the Ottonians or Hohenstaufens.[4] For many, feudalism seems to have been represented even by the *Führerprinzip,* carrying with it the concept of 'an honourable self-subordination by mutual contract' as the only true basis for Germanic political organization.[5]

Such an explanation of the Leader principle is certainly one-sided. For example, it leaves out questions about the whole relationship of the concept to the Social Darwinism of the nineteenth century. But here our concern is chiefly with the impact of National Socialism on the actual structure of German society, rather than with historical parallels. That these were all too often misleading is obvious enough when it is considered that not until the 1960s was it seriously asked whether National Socialism may have acted as a modernizing force. Once this hypothesis was put it became easier to see that theory had often been confused with the practice of National Socialism. As Schoenbaum's book demonstrates, beneath the cover of Nazi ideology 'the historic groups continued their conflicts like men wrestling under a blanket.'[6] It was, however, Dahrendorf who argued most persuasively that a genuine social revolution did take place in Hitler's Germany in the sense that those who exercised power often came from a lower social class than that which had traditionally governed the country.[7] Dahrendorf's modernization thesis implies that much as Hitler may have hated the pluralistic society, the changes introduced under his regime as well as the impact of World War II, helped pave the way for the democratic West Germany of today. This obviously conflicts strongly with the idea of National Socialism as nothing more than medieval barbarism reborn.

The whole discussion is bedevilled by the lack of any clear definition of the concept of 'revolution' as applied to National Socialist Germany. Indeed many historians, not all of them Marxist, have referred to the *Machtergreifung* as a counterrevolution. Was Hitler a conservative revolutionary, to use the term applied to Bismarck? The trouble with this sort of terminology is that it does not really explain anything. The following example serves to make this point, where Mosse is discussing the genesis of fascism: 'The bourgeoisie could have a revolution as an outlet for their frustrations, and at the same time rest assured that order and property would be preserved.'[8]

What then in fact does such a 'revolution' consist of? Bracher does not advance our understanding by arguing that we must take more seriously the concept of 'revolution of the Right', which was used at the time. Indeed his whole article on this theme is almost a model of how to empty the idea of 'revolution' of any consistent concrete meaning, whilst at the same time affirming that as a political phenomenon it certainly did take place. 'The very nature of Hitler's thought and action was clearly ambivalent: romantic-irrationalist *whilst* technocratic-modernizing, backward and future orientated elements are closely combined.' Yet, 'I would, however, be reluctant positively to identify it with modernization, even if unintentional.' The argument is further clouded by the later passage: 'The modernization thesis tends to move too far away from the concrete phenomenon of National Socialism and particularly Hitler'.[9] What is meant here by 'concrete phenomenon'? It is, to say the least, doubtful if ritual obeisance by historians to the terminology of sociology and political science will itself advance our understanding of the Third Reich.

Hitler's self-imposed task surely was to restore order to a troubled and divided society, as he believed Cromwell had done for England (see p. 49). This analogy admittedly broke down when the additional factor of Marxism in twentieth century Germany had to be confronted and destroyed. It is above all T. W. Mason who has directed our attention to the importance of the 'Legacy of 1918'[10] both for Hitler's appeal to the electorate, alarmed as it had been by the experiences of the 1918 Revolution and by the whole concept of class struggle. Yet however true this was in a social sense, it was not necessarily so in a political one. For Hitler the restoration of stability and the elimination of the class struggle were two sides of the same coin. It was precisely this point which the German establishment failed to grasp when attempting to 'use' Hitler prior to and subsequent to the seizure of power.

Some sections of German society were certainly under the impression that Hitler was the instrument whereby the Kaiserreich could be restored in all but name,[11] but as Trevor-Roper pointed out in his introduction to *Hitler's Table Talk*, Hitler's attitude towards the pre-1918 social order was one of extreme distaste.[12] Indeed, he actually congratulated those who had undermined the old order on the grounds that they had done Germany a good turn.[13] This is where a more careful analysis of the concept of counterrevolution is needed, in the sense that restoration of political authoritarianism does not necessarily imply social conservatism. For this very reason the idea of a *Volksgemeinschaft*—which is after all how Hitler characterized his new social order—must be taken more seriously than it has sometimes been. Indeed, the notion of *Gemeinschaft* as a tightly bound, organic rural community dates back at least as far as the thesis of Tönnies, in his *Gesellschaft und Gemeinschaft*, published in 1879. For Schoenbaum, however, it seems to have little value other than as a device for political persuasion.[14] This is not to deny that the National Socialists were fully aware of the political advantages of propagating the notion of the united ethnic community, where class divisions as exacerbated by Marxism were overcome by the stronger ties of blood and race. This was above all their first concern, as evidenced both by the preamble to the Labour Law of February 1934, which set up the German Labour Front (DAF), and by Hitler's well known speech to the German generals in February 1933. A further factor in his mind was the belief that German hegemony in Europe could not be restored until the internal divisions in German society had been overcome. He made this point specifically in his now famous address to the Industrieklub on 27 January 1932.[15] Additionally, most leading National Socialists seem to have developed the 'front-line' complex. In other words service in the community of the trenches in the First World War led many of them to believe that the cure for all Germany's ills lay in the reconstitution of the comradeship and unity of that period, which should now embrace the whole of Germany society. This was also in itself an appropriate means to end the divisive effects of Marxism in Germany.

In this respect it is necessary to consider the whole development of the National Socialist Party and its electoral appeal prior to 1933, as an important element in the formation of the concept of *Volksgemeinschaft*. Indeed the whole idea would scarcely be comprehensible unless reference were made to the expectations which the Hitler movement had awakened in certain sections of the German electorate at that time.

It is axiomatic that Hitler came to power by turning the NSDAP from approximately 1927 onwards into a party of electoral mobilization. Yet as early as July 1932 it was clear to the British Embassy in Berlin that Hitler was rallying only certain sections of the German voters behind him. This is illustrated by the telegram to the Foreign Office after the election to the effect that Hitler had exhausted all his reserves. In other words a substantial proportion of potential voters on the right and centre of the German political spectrum (with the exception of those adhering to the Catholic Centre Party) had already been brought into the National Socialist camp. Obviously 'mobilization' was at best only partial. This perception has been the starting point for the continuing investigation of Hitler's electoral support. The latter, rather than Party Membership, was crucial in the last resort, since during the depression many would-be supporters of

Hitler were unwilling or unable to pay the subscription. In any case Party membership in 1933 stood at about 2.5 per cent of all German adults and is scarcely sufficient in itself to support a detailed class analysis. No doubt this is why so many historians have adopted widely varying views on the matter. On the one hand the importance of Hitler's claim that the NSDAP was the only movement above all classes and parties is accentuated. At the same time it has almost become a truism that National Socialism owed its electoral success mainly to support from the middle classes.

Few have contributed more to this notion than S. M. Lipsett, who argued that the typical National Socialist voter was a small-town, middle-class Protestant, who had in many cases previously voted for a regional party. This has been described—perhaps a little harshly—as 'electoral folklore' because although not devoid of an element of truth it is too general to be of real value in explaining the electoral growth of National Socialism.[16] To begin with, it does not necessarily follow that there was any consistency in National Socialist voting support since, as Childers argued, 'The retroactive application of the 1930-1932 paradigm to the Nazi electorate of the mid-1920s is based on the implicit and erroneous assumption that its constituency (sic) was sociologically static.'[17] In short, the class basis of National Socialist voters prior to the Depression did not necessarily remain unaltered during and after it. Kühnl has argued that one of the criteria for calling a government 'fascist' was that it should rely on mass support coming primarily from the old and new middle classes; Geiger agreed that the National Socialist movement in Germany recruited mainly from the middle class groups hit by the crisis.[18] It is true that the 'middle classes' were an important factor, but as ever the problem of definition remains. It must be asked whether a valid distinction can be drawn between the 'old' and 'new' middle classes, where the latter represented salaried, non-manual workers. Contemporary sociologists suggested that the old middle classes were made up of the self-employed, regardless of economic sector. Both Broszat and Winkler have more recently stressed the important of artisans, small businessmen and peasants in providing mass support for National Socialism.[19] Such sectors of the old middle class could more readily see themselves as potential victims of any economic depressions, or as Sauer has argued in a wider framework, they could be regarded as the 'losers' in the process of industrialization, or modernization. 'Facism is a revolt of the declassés...they (the lower middle classes) indeed suffered, or feared they would suffer, from industrialization...peasants, who opposed the urbanizing aspects of industrialism; small businessmen and those engaged in the traditional crafts and trades that opposed mechanization or concentration.'[20] Winkler agreed that the extent of the economic crisis threatened small businessmen too, more than ever before, and suggested that overall the middle classes were victims not so much of the fear of revolution as of evolution; in his view social declassification, or even the apprehension of it, produced anti-capitalism as well as anti-socialism.[21]

Of these various social groupings, the peasantry offered perhaps the greatest possibilities for the Party, according to Bracher, since they wished to win back both material prosperity, once the Depression had started, and social prestige.[22] Since Hitler in *Mein Kampf* already stated that he saw in a sound peasant stock the best protection in all times against social and political evils, it would have been surprising had he not responded to growing rural anxiety. Indeed Childers claims that the change of direction of the Party around 1928, in order to concentrate very largely upon the agrarian sector, exactly followed the increasing uncertainties of the countryside.[23] The Party was stronger in the urban areas in the 1920s and it is interesting to note here that it has become almost an article of faith in the historiography of the Third Reich that in 1928 the failure of the so-called 'urban plan' caused the movement deliberately to institute a reorientation towards rural areas.[24] In fact there has been little hard evidence provided for this belief and it was not until March 1930 that the Party even produced its own programme for agriculture.

Hitler ought to have had more success with propaganda directed towards the old middle classes threatened by the advance of industrialization, than with any aimed at the new middle classes, who in most cases owed their living to a modern industrial society. This category comprehends such professions as teachers, lower-ranking civil servants and white collar workers in general. Clearly the possibility is not precluded that many of the latter might have moved to support for Hitler once they lost their jobs in the Depression, which produced more and more 'losers' in an absolute sense. These presumably would then swell the ranks of those in Sauer's model whose discontent was based on their decline in relation to other contemporary socio-economic gropups. Indeed this point was picked up before the Second World War, in an essay by Emil Lederer, who talked of the fear of the new bourgeoisie of becoming declassé; in their own self-image they were emphatically not part of the proletariat and reacted strongly to any possibility of downward social mobility.[25] An even earlier observer had remarked on the heightened insecurity in 1933.[26] Whether this is true or not, it is undoubtedly correct that, as one section of the new middle classes, teachers as a group were over-represented in the NSDAP, perhaps due to the susceptibility of the profession to the economic crises and to the cuts in public expenditure which accompanied them.[27] It was noticeable that many intellectuals who subscribed to the idea of Nordic superiority came from what has been described as the academic proletariat, who felt themselves to be victims of capitalism because it had not brought material gains commensurate with their education.[28] Similarly Heiber has drawn attention to the solid National Socialist gains amongst students from 1929 onwards,[29] at a time when most of these came from higher or middle class backgrounds.

In general, however, Barkai is correct in arguing that research into class structure of NSDAP support has too often been based upon abstract models.[30] Once Germany felt the lash of depression sociological analysis of the differences between 'old' and 'new' middle classes simply became too schematic. In the prevailing atmosphere after 1929 such a distinction became increasingly academic. In addition discussion is further bedevilled by the difficulty in obtaining evidence for class support for the National Socialists from an analysis of their actual membership. At a time of acute financial distress many peasants and workers simply did not feel able to afford a Party subscription, which makes it difficult to read too much significance into the fact that these sectors were underrepresented in the ranks of Party *members*. The most obvious example was provided by the *Nationalsozialistische Bauernschaft*, founded by Darré in 1931, precisely for those members of the peasantry who could not pay the full Party dues, which means that they were not included in the statistics of paid up supporters.

Such considerations did not of course apply to the Party leadership itself, and so there is validity in the point that *its* social structure was different again, in that Party leaders tended to be drawn from somewhat higher ranks of society than the usual members.[31] Böhnke's study of the NSDAP in the Ruhr for the period prior to 1933 also distinguishes logically between the membership and the leaders but nonetheless, sociologically, places them both in the same category when he writes that the NSDAP was a 'bourgeois party, whose profile was stamped by members of the middle classes and whose leadership was overwhelmingly middle class.'[32] The 'electoral folklore' about the 'middle class' basis of the National Socialist movement's appeal has therefore been remarkably persistent and the challenge to it has been a relatively recent one.

To be fair one of the reasons for the acceptance of this belief in the first place was Hitler's own apparent conviction, by 1931 at the latest, that he could never hope to win the mass of workers for the NSDAP.[33] Calic estimated that in March 1933 Hitler gained only ten per cent of the working class vote of which a good part came from the unemployed. It may well be the case also that since most of the earliest analyses of fascism were made by left wing writers, the role of the working class in the growth of the NSDAP was not properly recognized. Yet there was contemporary evidence which suggested that as early as September 1930, between 15 and 20 per cent of NSDAP votes came from workers.[34] Now that such facts have been rediscovered it is not surprising that what we have referred to here as the electoral folklore about the middle class support for National Socialism has been increasingly challenged. Schulz suggests that from 1929 to 1930 onwards the NSDAP was increasingly attracting working class support.[35] According to Falter electoral defectors from the SPD helped to swell the National Socialist vote in the elections of 1930 and 1932; he suggests in fact that the SPD lost 5 per cent of its vote to the NSDAP at each of these elections.[36] In this connection Erdmann's point is interesting, namely that the NSDAP, although in his view a largely middle class party, did nonetheless contain more workers than any other contemporary non-Marxist party.[37] Any statement that the Party made no breach in the ranks of the working classes until March 1933 is therefore suspect and may well reflect considerations of party politics.[38] The curious thing is that many historians were apparently ready to stigmatize the NSDAP as a catch-all party, which was prepared to promise anything to everyone in order to gain their votes, whilst at the same time academics have overlooked the very solid degree of working class support the Party must have enjoyed prior to 1933.

The point here is not to embark on yet another examination of NSDAP support by class analysis, which has often confused the issue, but to suggest that electoral backing prior to 1933 signposts the way in which the concept of an ethnic community was beginning to take hold in the popular imagination. If the NSDAP is compared to contemporary parties, based very often upon class support, as in the case of the SPD or KPD, or on economic interest, as in the case of the middle class parties, or on regional interests, then it is apparent that the movement must be seen essentially as a broad one, indeed virtually the only one which could genuinely lay claim to representing the whole 'community'.[39] Mühlberger's recent study of Westphalia confirms this in its conclusion: 'Despite the imbalance between middle class and working class representation in the Party, the NSDAP was a genuine *Volkspartei*. It secured support from all social classes in German society and was not just simply a middle class movement or class party.'[40] On the whole the best summary seems to have been that afforded by a contemporary observer, the American journalist Lochner, who concluded that the NSDAP was supported above all by the middle class and sections of the working class.[41]

The ability of the Hitler movement to transcend social barriers in Germany was not at first paralleled by any similar success in breaking down denominational differences between Protestants and Roman Catholics. Indeed it has been argued that from 1930 onwards the NSDAP became more and more a Protestant party, for which various reasons have been adduced. In spite of this there appears to be some evidence that in the March 1933 elections there was a significant breakthrough for the movement in Catholic areas.[42] This is clearly not to say that German Catholics flocked to Hitler, but rather further to support the argument which has been developed so far. Although it received strong middle class support from 1930 onwards, 'The NSDAP, with its ideology of the *Volksgemeinschaft* and its super- nationalism, was able to win support from all sectors of the population, white collar and manual workers, peasants and civil servants, self-employed and housewives, young and old, Protestants and Catholics, people in border areas or in the middle of Germany, entrepreneurs and unemployed, to such an extent that more than any other political group of those years it had the air of a people's party.'[43]

Oddly enough the success of the NSDAP's appeal to the electorate has not been given full weight in explaining the relative ease with which the movement eventually took over power, which has too often been dealt with largely in terms of the backstairs intrigues of the powerful German elites. In this connection it has to be remembered that because of his wide electoral appeal Hitler was already the leader of the largest party in Germany in July 1932. At this point, under the British system, he would have become leader of the government automatically. Seen in this light then, it has to be remembered that, as well as the provisions of the Weimar constitution, certain elements in the German establishment actually delayed Hitler's accession to power by not seriously negotiating with him earlier. It is at least as important to emphasize this point as it is to underline the number of Germans who did not help to elect Hitler. In the final analysis, under any system of universal suffrage, how many votes are required before a Party can consider itself as elected? Nearly one German in every three, male or female, voted for Hitler in July 1932.[44] That he had already, as it were, created the basis electorally for a *Volksgemeinschaft* obviously must have some relevance to the speed with which he was able to consolidate his power in Germany in the early months of 1933. This is not to overlook the role which terror played in the process, but it does seem reasonable to suggest that wide sections of the German public welcomed the National Socialist takeover precisely because the Party was seen as the 'German movement.'[45]

Such considerations obviously have relevance to the role played by the traditional elites, which in view of the foregoing may well have been exaggerated by certain historians, who fall into two separate and to some extent opposed categories. Firstly, the Stamokap theorists have a vested interest in laying great stress on the support which Hitler received from big business and the landed interests. Secondly, there are those who have tended to take the reminiscences of Papen and Schacht at their face value and have assumed that their cooperation with Hitler was of overriding importance in bringing him to office. Both groups share, however, the conviction that behind Hitler stood what are usually referred to as the traditional elites of German society: big business, landowners and the military. It is such an assumption which has led so many historians to dismiss the concept of a *Volksgemeinschaft* out of hand as nothing more than a swindle, designed not for the benefit of the German people, but rather to ensure that what are seen as the ruling classes remained firmly in the saddle, whoever was nominally Chancellor. This theory must rest upon the logical inference that it was the German establishment who put Hitler into power for their own reasons.

As in the case of the 'middle classes', however, divisions also existed within the ranks of the traditional German elites. Many of these had also suffered from the process of industrialization, particularly the large landlords. Sauer sums up their whole attitude by saying: 'The upper-class losers tended to react in a non-fascist way but were potential allies of fascist regimes.'[46] When, however, did they actually become allies of the Hitler movement? According to Schweitzer big business and the landowners remained apart until 1931 and then on the eve of the Third Reich came together in one power bloc in order to overcome the Depression with the aid of the political dictator. Saage, however, says this was problematic since, if such an upper class bloc existed, why should it need Hitler?[47] One obvious rejoinder is that Hitler had the mass following. Perhaps the version produced by Radkau is rather more sophisticated, in that he believes that it was the rivalries and the doubts within the ruling classes, rather than their unity, which helped Hitler into power.[48] All these versions, however, tend to reinforce the concept of Hitler as in some way or another being brought into office by the upper classes, which is almost the counterpart to the 'electoral folklore' about the middle classes. The different sectors of the establishment need some brief separate consideration in order to determine to what extent this thesis has validity.

As yet there is little direct evidence that the agrarian landlords in Germany did generally turn to fascism, and this is at least partially explicable by the relatively high degree of protection against foreign competition which the larger landed proprietors already enjoyed before 1933. In the first place, they were the chief beneficiaries of *Osthilfe*, and secondly the price of grain in general fell less between 1929 and 1933 than did prices for other agrarian products, mainly produced by the peasantry. Whilst, however, they had perhaps less economic reason to turn automatically towards National Socialism there were other factors at work here. They had a robust dislike for the more egalitarian elements of fascism.[49] Additionally, many obstinately clung to their loyalty to the Kaiserreich and the monarchy.[50] If all this is true, then the whole concept of a power bloc between agrarian and industrial interests which helped Hitler simply dissolves. In this respect Winkler's complaint that not enough attention has been given to the role of the big landlords in bringing Hitler into power may well be the reverse of the truth.[51] A Marxist writer such as Kühnl could be correct in his assumption that it was not what he referred to as the feudal landlords who assured Hitler's success, but the most decisive elements of industry.[52] A powerful factor influencing those theories which stressed the role of the agrarian establishment are the events of January 1933, centring on the so-called *Osthilfe* scandal. Most accounts have followed Bullock in postulating the existence of a secret report, then due to be published, which would have exposed how the Junkers had been exploiting *Osthilfe* for their own benefit. As yet no firm evidence has been provided for the existence of such a document. It is true that a Reichstag committee agreed to set up an examination of *Osthilfe* administration, but this body did not cease to sit merely because Hitler replaced Schleicher. In fact its report, which more or less whitewashed the Junkers, appeared in April 1933. Since the advent of the new regime did not change the composition of the investigating committee there is no reason to suppose that the change of government made any difference to their report. Why then should the Junkers have bothered to throw Schleicher out?

As far as big business is concerned, the extent to which it facilitated Hitler's rise to power, particularly in the matter of finance, has obvious implications for the *Volksgemeinschaft* after 1933. If Hitler was in fact their puppet, then it is clear that he could not have introduced any profound changes in the structure of German society inimical to their interests. Turner has shown that many historians have been badly deceived by the industrialist Fritz Thyssen's claims to have been Hitler's paymaster in his memoir, *I paid Hitler*, a title which countless academics ever since have taken at face value. The truth is that big business had come to display a hesitant attitude towards National Socialism by the close of the 1920s. The reaction of such businessmen as Emil Kirdorf tended to be a deviation from the norm, in that if the political record of big business is examined, 'it quickly becomes evident that these pro-Nazis are conspicuous precisely because they were exceptions.'[53] Most of the money flowing into the Party's coffers during the 1920s came not from industrialists but in the shape of contributions from its own members, clearly shown by the statistics provided by Schulz.[54] Three times the amount given by German industrialists was provided from the Party's various membership contributions, collections, sales of brochures and so forth.[55] This does not mean to say that funds from big business, including those which came from outside the borders of the

Reich,[56] were an unimportant asset to the early movement. Moreover, the exceptions could be important, according to Hallgarten, who argued that 'the interest the United Steel Group took in his cause enabled Hitler to overcome the Party crisis of the Fall of 1932, when the Nazis almost succumbed to the von Papen policy of exhausting them by a series of expensive election campaigns.'[57]

The point about Hitler's financial backing is that it explains neither his electoral success, except in the most obvious sense of supporting his propaganda, nor how he actually came to power in January 1933. If money alone could buy political power, how can one account for the steady decline of the DNVP, although it too continued to receive substantial funds after 1928?[58] Similar considerations apply to von Papen, who was strongly aided by industry against Hitler.[59] Is it then the case that big business simply followed public opinion, in the sense that it took an active supporting interest in the NSDAP only after it had become the most important and aggressive factor in German politics, as a result of the electoral success largely achieved without its help?[60] It seems fairly clear that most big businessmen were simultaneously both attracted and repelled by the National Socialist movement. Although accepting its aggressive nationalism and anti-Marxism many feared that the National Socialists might actually live up to the second part of their name.[61] It was partly in recognition of these fears that Hitler, at the request of Kirdorf, wrote a special pamphlet for industrialists in 1927.[62] In spite of such efforts the ambivalent attitude of most businessmen towards National Socialism persisted.

This confirms the argument implicit here, that the question—'who supported Hitler?' is still very far from being definitively answered. As late as November 1932 a petition from industrialists and bankers to Hindenburg asking him to appoint Hitler as Chancellor had only some 30 names on it.[63] This is hardly conclusive evidence of large scale business manipulation to get Hitler into office, which is why Turner has emphasized that most businessmen pinned their hopes initially on Brüning and then even more on von Papen. According to Turner big business was not actively involved in the intrigues in the weeks prior to Hitler's appointment. He does not, however, absolve industry from all responsibility for the destruction of the Republic since it was interested in von Papen's concept of a new state, which would in any case have been anti-democratic.[64] Only in December 1932, when Schleicher was in power, did businessmen begin seriously to turn towards Hitler, because the former's social programme and demand for union support aroused their distrust. Possibly of equal importance was the fact that their initial misgivings about the socialist element in Hitler's movement were considerably diminished by the resignation of Gregor Strasser, also in December 1932.[65] According to Hallgarten this was crucial to the context in which the meeting between Hitler and von Papen at the house of the Cologne banker, Schroeder, finally took place on 4 January 1933. By then the group around von Papen (the *Herrenklub*) was ready to listen to compromise suggestions coming from those who had already gone over to the NSDAP.[66] Even at this late stage, however, sections of German industry were still prepared financially to support other right wing parties, as I. G. Farben did in the case of the DNVP and the DVP in March 1933. Its financial support for Hitler at the same election has to be seen against this background.[67]

The fitful development of the relationship between National Socialism and big business which recent Western research suggests is not accepted by Marxist historians, although it must be recognized that the work done by many liberal academics has often been in response to the 'agent theory' formulated by left wing historians. In the simplest form of this theory, i.e. Stamokap, monopoly capital was forced to make a political intervention in the acute crisis in Germany by the middle of 1932, not only as a step in the development of capitalism but as part of the class struggle, the installation of Hitler being an integral part of the process.[68] In opposition to Turner and Hallgarten, however, Zumpe makes little effort to distinguish between the sectors of industry in her use of such undifferentiated phrases as 'monopoly capital' or 'finance capital'. In this respect, and giving due credit for all the new empirical information she has produced, Zumpe's analysis is to some extent a retreat from the insights of an earlier Marxist, Sohn-Rethel. He suggested in the 1930s that Hitler's main support had come from what he called the 'deficitary elements' of the bourgeoisie, that is to say those sectors of business most hit by the economic crisis: 'The transition to fascism in Germany rests on the political victory of the declining elements of the bourgeoisie, gatherered in the Harzburg Front (the 'Fronde of the idle debtors' as contemporaries referred to it) over the profitable elements behind Brüning.'[69] To some extent Mason takes up the suggestion that the prerequisite of collaboration between the industrial leaders and National Socialism was precisely the fact that the unity of the former had fallen apart under the world economic crisis. His point of departure is that by late 1932 heavy industry had come to believe that the reconstitution of the Germany economy would be possible only under the NSDAP.[70] The differences between Turner and others, and Marxist historians have been most acerbic since Abraham's book, *The Collapse of the Weimar Republic.* However, they would both disagree strongly with Lochner's surely quite untenable suggestion made in 1955, that of all sections of German society big business bore the least responsibility for Hitler's successful seizure of power.[71]

It should be emphasized that a great deal of historical research on German big business after 1933 is concerned with its role in the economic management of the Third Reich, which will be dealt with more fully in Chapter Six. What we are concerned with here is the relationship between the various social classes within the *Volksgemeinschaft.* The fact that we do not accept Hitler and the NSDAP as being the conscious agents of big business does not of course preclude the possibility that the regime functioned in a way beneficial to the interests of some elements of the pre-1933 German establishment. After all, Hitler destroyed the organized labour movement in Germany virtually as soon as he came to power. Moreover his racial doctrines favoured free enterprise, representing as it did the operation of social Darwinism in the field of economics, and thereby helped to secure the continuance of existing property relationships. Historians such as Mason and Schoenbaum have tended to assume that the *Volksgemeinschaft* was nothing more than a cosmetic operation because it did not involve a restructuring of German society. In fact it may well be that the idea of a *Volksgemeinschaft* which Hitler dangled before the eyes of the electorate was not necessarily perceived as entailing dramatic social change. On the contrary, many supporters were expecting from Hitler nothing more than the preservation of their existing status; in other words they saw in him an insurance policy against proletarianization. It is logical therefore to discuss initially the political imbalance between the upper and middle classes after 1933.

Historiographically there has been a significant consensus about the disappointments of those actually described as artisan socialists, who had been attracted by the idea of a corporate state. What these groups apparently wanted from National Socialism included an end to department stores, the nationalization of the banks and the securing of small business and agrarian property rights. Thus for Fischer the story of economic development after 1933 appears to consist quite simply of middle class anti-capitalism being frustrated in the interests of big business and rearmament.[72] Here he is in effect echoing the thesis of Schweitzer, namely that big business was successful in defeating artisan socialism after 1934. Bloch underlines this with his suggestion that the real winners of the Röhm purge were industrialists and bankers, in that the artisan socialism for which the SA stood had now been definitively overcome.[73] There is indeed strong support from historians for the notion, as Schoenbaum puts it, that ideology stopped at the door of the boardroom. By this he means that big business was left relatively untouched in contrast to the disappointment felt by the lower middle classes. In this connection the expectations which had been aroused in the latter sector prior to 1933, in respect of their own autonomous trade associations inside a corporate state, were not met. What the artisans got in fact in June 1934 was an obligatory guild, but only under state supervision.[74] In organizational terms this meant defeat for the Combat League of the Commercial and Industrial Middle Classes (KGM), set up under the Party aegis by von Renteln in December 1932, the object of which was to mobilize small business for National Socialism inside the planned corporate state. In May 1933 this association took a step forward with its assumption of the leadership in the businessmen's association, the German Industrial and Trade Congress. In the same month, under the influence of the KGM, a National League of German Artisans was formed, followed by formation of the League for German Retail Trade. This latter joined with other organizations to make up the Association of German Trade, again under von Renteln. The omens were now looking good for small business, especially as in June 1933 the NSDAP set up its own office for corporative reorganization of German industry.

The honeymoon was, however, abruptly terminated in the following month, when the new Minister of Economics, Schmitt, temporarily suspended all corporative reorganization and on 7 August the KGM was summarily dissolved.[75] Ohlsen therefore concludes: 'The forbidding of further corporative development and the destruction of the KGM made the true power relationship of the facist system evident and led at once to a further weakening of small business.'[76] According to some historians this development began before the seizure of power, although they are not in agreement as to precisely when. For Lebovics, it had already begun in the late 1920s, when Hitler was making overtures to big business.[77] Meinck, however, follows the more generally agreed line that it was not until 1931-2 that Hitler really began to get through to industrial leaders, but that this was then crucial for the defeat of the corporate elements in the Party after the accession to power.[78] Thus the propaganda slogan, 'Security instead of competition', encouraged the belief that middle class interests would be protected in the Third Reich through the medium of a corporate state.[79] A regional study of Thuringia tends, however, to reinforce the impression that increasingly after 1933, middle class interests were subordinated to those of big business.[80]

At first sight this appears to confirm Ohlsen's assumption that the period immediately after 1933 sounded the death knell of the aspirations awakened in the old middle classes by Nationalist Socialist propaganda prior to the actual takeover, which would preclude the existence in any real terms of a *Volksgemeinschaft* for these sectors of German society. There are, however, a number of serious objections to such a thesis. In the first place, the view that the interests of artisans and tradespeople suffered a definitive setback from 1934 onwards is simply too schematic. For purely technical reasons, it is mistaken to assume that only big business profited from rearmament. National Socialist measures were aimed at favouring *viable* concerns of whatever size, which actually involved many small businesses in the rearmament programme. Whatever may therefore have happened to the corporative state, the very way in which the rearmament programme itself was carried out gave the National Socialist government a social basis in parts of the old middle class, as well as in big business.[81] Here we have to run the risk of underlining the obvious (because so many have argued the opposite), namely, that to assume a dichotomy of interest between big business and smaller scale entrepreneurs is mistaken. Some historians who have contributed to this thesis have not always given full weight to the way in which industry operates in a modern state: most obviously, large numbers of smaller specialist concerns live by serving their larger counterparts through the manufacture of components and accessories.

What is true of the rearmament programme is also true of the work creation scheme launched by the regime soon after its inception. Many of the projects under this general heading were of considerable benefit to artisans, and they should not be seen merely in terms of serving the interests of big business. Indeed, Wolffsohn suggests that the work creation programme had a definite integratory function for the entire nation.[82] Even the rationalization introduced by the National Socialists had positive benefits for the majority of businesses, since the more viable were protected and therefore naturally enjoyed a larger volume of trade through the disappearance of their weaker competitors. Moreover this whole process has to be seen in the context of general economic recovery, from which the middle classes were also beneficiaries. Whereas in 1934 there were 673,000 Germans earning from 3,000 to 12,000 marks annually, by 1938 this total had more than doubled to over 1.5 million.[83] This rising tide of prosperity, after the experience of depression and crisis of the late 1920s, helped to offset lingering disappointments about the failure to establish a corporate state.

Similar arguments apply to that other pillar of the old middle classes, the peasantry, since it too failed to receive the self-governing professional representation which it desired. The general consensus of historical opinion on the *Reichsnährstand* (Reich Food Estate—RNS) is that it was an instrument of state control, particularly from 1939 onwards, rather than a genuinely autonomous professional organization.[84] Winkler on the other hand affirmed that the RNS as an organization was popular with the peasantry precisely because it did give them political weight in the Third Reich.[85] This is, however, somewhat doubtful in view of the fact that after initial recovery in the agrarian sector, which Hitler promised in March 1933, peasants found themselves increasingly disadvantaged in comparison with the other sectors of the economy, as work creation and rearmament produced a boom in German manufacturing and construction industries. This is best illustrated in the following figures. The annual percentage increase in the total income of the agrarian sector from farm sales over the preceding year was 17.5 per cent in 1933-4 and 16.9 per cent in the following year. By 1935-6, however, the annual increase had fallen to only one per cent and incomes remained relatively constant thereafter, at least in peacetime.[86] Such statistics do not encourage the supposition that the farming community enjoyed any particular political weight in the Third Reich. At the same time we should not overlook the importance of their initial period of prosperity, secured through the institution of higher and above all fixed farm prices, which as in the case of artisans and small businessmen gave a material base, initially at least, to the

*Volksgemeinschaft*. Hüttenberger argues, however, that by the end of the 1930s this euphoria was beginning to disappear, which he took as evidence that the NSDAP had not been able to formulate a successful policy for the middle classes.[87]

Here again academics seem to be demanding rather more from the Third Reich than any government of a complex industrial state could reasonably be expected to provide. What regime has ever been able to execute a programme acceptable to all sections of the middle classes over an extended period of time? More generally, as Hitler himself put it in a cabinet meeting as early as 8 February 1933: 'The Reich government has to capture 18-19 million votes. There is no economic programme in the whole wide world which could satisfy such a huge mass of voters.'[88] It could, however, at least be argued that he had successfully preserved most of the middle class from the dire fate of falling back into the ranks of the working class, or proletarianization. On this basis alone, it must be incorrect to continue to affirm that the middle classes were betrayed by the regime after 1933. Both in material terms and in regard to social status, their position in society was if anything enhanced. This point remains important despite the qualification that both industrial and agrarian middle classes were awarded more social protection only until 1936, when all other interests were subordinated to the priority of rapid rearmament. Did they, however, assume automatically that the strains induced by the tempo of rearmament would necessarily constitute the peacetime norm in the Third Reich for evermore? After all, the Four Year Plan was supposed to end by 1940. Another point of great significance here is the way in which prior to 1933 National Socialist propaganda constantly assured the different sectors of German society that the crucial precondition for any individual economic recovery was that it should take place within the context of a general national reconstruction. This propaganda line was perfectly consistent with the slogan 'common good before individual gain', which the regime constantly hammered into the minds of the population after 1933. It may well be that the middle classes were prepared to subordinate their special interests provisionally for the sake of Germany.

There remains a view, particularly prevalent on the Left, which holds that because the interests of the working class were thrust aside, all propaganda about a *Volksgemeinschaft* was nothing more than a cosmetic arrangement. This is really an argument about the extent of working class support for the Hitler regime. A leading British historian of the German labour movement, T. W. Mason, has made the point that terror was used very much on a class basis, in that it was employed against workers and not against the bosses.[89] Mason's thesis is that Hitler was convinced that Germany's defeat in 1918, due to revolution at home, had been caused by the failure of the Kaiser to destroy Social Democracy when the Great War broke out. Hitler was determined not to repeat this error, although according to Mason he had no idea in 1933 as to what precise tactics to adopt in order to avoid doing so. It needs emphasizing, however, that Mason recognized Hitler's grasp of the fact that ultimately the working class could only be won over by its conversion to a new *Weltanschauung*, and that limits were set to the terror, not least by the economic needs of the regime. He does of course accept that within this framework Hitler's main desire was to smash the hold of Marxism over the organized labour movement in Germany. On this basis the *Volksgemeinschaft* becomes merely a vehicle for social control.[90] This proposition has received support from Müller, who sees Hitler's leading motive in founding the 'Strength through Joy' movement as the need to build a resolute people, without which no 'great policy' would be possible. Such considerations have led Müller to suggest, without any further evidence, that Hitler was primarily concerned with workers simply as an instrument to achieve his expansionist aims, and not with any improvement in their social and economic position.[91] In the sense that expansion provided new markets for German capitalism this is closely related to the 'agent theory' of Hitler as the front man for the traditional interests of the dominant classes in Germany. Such a belief was expressed by left-wing contemporaries as early as 31 January 1933. In a speech to the SPD Party Committee Rudolf Breitscheid said that the party now found itself facing a class confrontation in its purest form: on one side stood the working class, and on the 'other side the united reaction, under capitalism, supported by the brown hordes of Herr Hitler.'[92]

What complicates this issue is, first of all, that a number of workers did actually vote for the movement. Additionally, inside the ranks of the Party there was a quite numerically strong group concerned with workers' problems precisely because they were themselves from the working class. Their activity centred around the National Socialist Works Cell Organization (NSBO), which had been founded to enable the movement to defeat Marxism on the shop floor. At the same time it was necessarily forced, in order to be credible to the workers, to represent their interests. In short, an instrument designed ultimately to overcome the class struggle was itself, at least intially, obliged to participate in it, for example by taking part in a number of strikes.[93] Almost ironically the NSBO acquired such a 'Leftish' reputation that Strasser was assumed by many businessmen to be a socialist simply through association with it.[94] There is evidence that even after 1933 certain of its members took their claims to be representatives of the working class quite seriously, since at that time Ley, then at Party HQ in Munich, banned the organization from intervening in economic matters. Indeed by the end of 1933 disciplinary measures by the Party against the NSBO brought many of its members into concentration camps as 'Marxist criminals'.[95] Yet for all this, as the Eastern bloc historians have argued, the organization as a whole had been the main instrument in destroying the Free Trade Unions earlier that year.[96]

The fact that the Socialists referred to their organizations as the Free Unions did not preclude the possibility that non-Socialist organizations might also represent the interests of the working class, which according to Turner was exactly Hitler's point of departure. In this account, Hitler understood how trade unions arose but did not accept them as the SPD did, since he felt that they had to be depoliticized. His concept of a worker's organization was therefore not as a vehicle for class struggle, but as an organ for vocational representation, whose proper function was to strengthen the national economy.[97] Whether this thesis is valid or not, Hitler certainly presented himself as the honest broker between industry and labour in May 1933.[98] It is also surely significant that other non-Marxist trade unions continued to exist after 1933, even though they had made clear their opposition to Hitler in the 1920s. This was the case with the Catholic Workers' Association, which lasted until 1942, at which point it still had 34,000 members.[99] In itself such evidence is not conclusive. On one level it might well furnish support for the idea that Hitler was not against unions as such, so much as against those under the sway of Marxism. Equally, it might suggest that he was merely engaging in a form of window-dressing as part of his 'honest broker' policy, particulary since in this instance the numbers involved were so small.

The point to be made here is that Hitler's determination to break the hold of Marxism on the working class cannot be seen simply as an attempt to exclude German workers from the *Volksgemeinschaft*. On the contrary, it was the pre-requisite for their integration through conversion. As Hitler said in an interview in January 1934, he chose the word 'worker' for the movement because he wanted to win it back for the nation.[100] Crucial in this whole area is the Hitlerian concept of the 'nationalization of the masses' (see p. 47). As Mosse has pointed out, the mass appeal of National Socialism inevitably pulled workers into its politics of government by acclamation, and should not therefore be seen as being limited just to 'marginal people', such as the old middle classes.[101] His thesis has found support in the argument that the regime set great store by the role of the Labour Front in winning over the workers, especially for the period 1933–6.[102] Even the autobahn programme was utilized for nationalist propaganda, apparently with some success, among the construction workers themselves.[103] At the very least this needs to be set against the picture we already have, both from Austria and Germany, of illegal workers' parties which quantitatively outweighed the resistance of all other groups to the regime.[104]

Although propaganda appeals were part of the *Volksgemeinschaft*, Hitler realized by the end of the 1920s that any new *Weltanschauung* had to have an element of material advance in it.[105] This was of course perfectly compatible with the way in which the NSDAP understood the term 'socialism'. For example the National Vocational Competition *(Reichswettgewerb)* in February 1935 was presented in this light: 'Socialism is the designation for that obligation to bring everyone to the place to which he is naturally suited...' The Vocational Competition was the appropriate vehicle to express this.[106] The Party press echoed the sentiment on the anniversary of Hitler's accession, in 1939, by writing that in the National Socialist State, 'the worker increasingly finds...the possibility is given to him to reach that place in the factory which corresponds to his own performance.'[107] Of course 'socialism' in the Third Reich was by no means a rigid or well-thought out concept, but was frequently stretched to embrace varying aspects of German society. For Goebbels the goal of socialism in Germany was a people of free and responsible property owners, whereas Ley described it as comradeship and loyalty, honour, even blood and race.[108] This is not, however, to say that there were no actual positive achievements to accompany the rather vague ideology. As Goebbels pointed out in April 1935, the 'Winter Help' (*Winterhilfe*) scheme actually did relieve the distress of poor people.[109] The crux of the matter here is not the financial aid so much as the obligation imposed on the better off members of society to aid the poor on the grounds of national and racial affinity.

The real significance of social welfare in the Third Reich was first underlined in the work of the British economist, Guillebaud, who placed considerable emphasis on its importance in strengthening support for the regime among the working classes. As a contemporary observer it was clear to him that many Germans did not regard the *Volksgemeinschaft* merely as a swindle. Strangely enough this insight was lost by many later historians. Doubtless the failure for so long to consider the labour and welfare measures of the Third Reich derived from the obsession of so many researchers with charting the advance of the German economy towards the Second World War.[110] This approach ignored the solid economic benefits accruing to the working class, at least for the period up to 1939. The group of workers with the lowest income, up to 1,500 marks per annum, grew by 167 per cent between 1932 and 1940. This statistic indicates the number of previously unemployed who had now found places, the majority of these probably being unskilled workers since these would have been more likely to have been unemployed during the Depression. At higher income levels the number of Germans earning between 1,500 and 2,400 marks shows very large increases, whilst the group between 2,400 and 3,600 marks nearly doubled. Such statistics provide a striking contrast to those of a contemporary left wing commentator, whose own far less favourable figures finish in the year 1936. Since even Mason admits that workers were better off after that year, it seems to be the case that Sohn-Rethel's evidence, whether by accident or design, stops just when workers were beginning to improve their position.[111] In this connection one has to remember how dramatically Hitler solved the unemployment problem—by whatever means. There were at least six million unemployed when he came to power in 1933, a figure reduced to 74,000 by July 1939, at which time there were more than a million job vacancies. These facts have led a contemporary West German historian to suggest that in spite of the wage freeze the real income of workers actually increased, although he does make the point that results varied between individual sectors of the economy.[112]

To those historians who in spite of such evidence continue to regard the *Volksgemeinschaft* as nothing more than window dressing, the question must be put as to what extent the concept of an ethnic community necessarily rests on the benefits it actually affords to the working class. That material gain could in many instances buy working class allegiance to the regime is demonstrated by the secret reports compiled by the SD during the war, which suggested that at least the better paid workers followed Hitler to the end.[113] Propaganda and material prosperity cannot alone change class relationships, however, and it is precisely this which has been emphasized by Schoenbaum, who has queried National Socialist sincerity in regard to the whole notion of *Volksgemeinschaft*.[114] Above all he found no evidence that the National Socialists had been able to reconcile what appeared to him to have been two contradictory propositions. The first of these was the *Volksgemeinschaft* itself, where everybody had some claim to equality by virtue of being German. Secondly there was the notion of *Leistungsgemeinschaft* (roughly, 'from each according to his ability'), which Schoenbaum takes as implying inequality among Germans. But, according to Guillebaud at least, many Germans did accept the *Volksgemeinschaft*. To a real degree it appears that National Socialist welfare measures functioned as a means of social integration. The social facilities offered by the DAF surely had some impact on working class perceptions of the movement. As already pointed out even the Winter Help campaign was more than a propaganda stunt, in that it appeared to break down barriers by encouraging a feeling of social obligation among better off Germans towards the needy members of the *Volksgemeinschaft*. The same might be said about the propaganda effects of the *Eintopf* meal, based as it was upon voluntary, shared sacrifice for the good of the whole community.

The interesting feature of such positive social facets of the regime is precisely the fact that they coexisted with more blatantly dishonest and brutal attempts to pretend that both sides of industry had exactly the same aims. As early as 18 May 1933, Goering pointed out in the Prussian Landtag that industry needed stability and therefore that the responsibility for running the plant should be left with the existing leadership.[115] Thus Kühnl tends to see in industrial relations inside the Third Reich nothing more than an expression of the elementary economic interests of entrepreneurs. As he puts it: 'Employers, above all big employers, were able to advance their social interests in the Third Reich at the expense of wage earners and of the lower middle classes.'[116] Further evidence for this point of view is provided by the fate of the DAF, the foundation of which reinforced big business suspicion of the regime, which had already been aroused by the existence of the NSBO. However, Hitler subsequently excluded the DAF from any share in the formulation of wages policy, which seems to have allayed the fears of industrial leaders. In November 1933 the head of the employers' association stated in a circular to his members that since the position of the DAF had been cleared up, entrepreneurs could happily take part in the construction of a true *Volksgemeinschaft*.[117]

What this conceals, however, is that the idea of an ethnic community could actually be turned against those businessmen who failed to live up to the social obligations which the whole concept placed upon them. In the Spring of 1933 two factory owners were actually imprisoned for failing to keep the prices which had been agreed between the metal workers and their employers and approved by the Trustees of Labour.[118] Social responsibility clearly then *could* work both ways although there were comparatively few examples of this kind of action in defence of working class interests. In effect the National Socialists were offering the German working classes a package deal. Against the forfeiture of any share in political decision-making and the loss of free trade unions was balanced extended social welfare measures and a part of the enhanced political standing of the German nation in Europe. How attractive this arrangement was to workers was clearly connected to some extent with the progress of foreign policy and ultimately of the war itself, since German victory would have brought great benefits to all members of the *Volksgemeinschaft*. Victory would clearly have strengthened the latter, as it does any kind of regime.

Here we have to raise the second of our original points about *Leistungsgemeinschaft*, namely that the inability to reconcile this with the *Volksgemeinschaft* asks too much of any government. What contemporary society did achieve these aims in the post-Depression era? Too many historians, in assessing the social policies of Hitler's Germany, seem to be employing as their criterion an ideal society which has never existed in practice. Was it to be found in Britain under the National Government, plagued by mass unemployment and huge inequalities of wealth? Was it to be found in France, or in Spain, torn apart as they were by political divisions in the 1930s? Was it to be found in Stalin's Russia? More interesting by far, however, than such 'horizontal' comparisons is the question as to what extent it can be said that the *Volksgemeinschaft* was perhaps an agent of modernization in Germany, as Dahrendorf's work implies?

The problems which historians have encountered in characterizing the social composition of the Third Reich can only really be resolved within an analysis of German society based upon a much longer time-scale. It has been pointed out that the role of the aristocracy within the Prussian civil service had already considerably diminished by the 1920s.[119] The process of social mobility had been accelerated by the experiences of the First World War, for all the emphasis which scholars sometimes put on the survival of elites from Wilhelmine Germany. Indeed Hitler's own career might be seen as illustrative of this trend, in view of his somewhat obscure social origins, and this is equally true of many leading National Socialists. 1933 was therefore one more milestone in the continuing process by which social prestige and political power slipped further from the hands of the pre-1914 Establishment in Germany. This directly conflicts with the Stamokap view of Hitler as the agent of capitalism and Junkerdom. In fact, pulling South East Europe—with its agrarian exports—strongly into the German economic sphere after 1936 was a direct setback to Junker interests.[120] Further stages along the route by which the agrarian leaders lost power must include both the effects of the Second World War and the land reform in the Soviet zone of Germany in 1945.

Dahrendorf's modernization thesis points to an interesting conclusion, namely that the obsession of earlier historians with the neo-feudal aspects of National Socialism concealed the real issue. Instead of being diverted by the question, 'Hitler's social revolution?', we need to analyse Hitler's part in the continuing German social revolution of the twentieth century. Therefore to attack Dahrendorf by saying that the 'Third Reich neither destroyed the old social structure nor did it extinguish class consciousness' is misplaced.[121] For Kettenacker Hitler's seizure of power was essentially to be seen as the revolution of the German lower middle classes, which expanded greatly during and after the war. Displaced by the inflation of 1923 they thereafter felt politically neglected by other parties. He concludes that although the National Socialist period was not intended to be a time of social revolution it did nonetheless have a more modernizing effect than the events of 1918.[122] This remains true even in spite of the anomalous elements in the Third Reich, notably the peasantry, many of which were fixed like 'flies in amber' by the law of hereditary farm entailment. With these and the important exception of women too, social mobility was at the very least not held back in the Third Reich.

In making the remark at the head of this chapter Goebbels surely did not mean to promise that Hitler would effect sweeping social changes to the benefit of the people who voted for him; this a fundamental and widely held misunderstanding about the whole concept of the *Volksgemeinschaft*. Nor is there firm evidence to suggest that Hitler's supporters expected radical *social* changes when he came to power; they were more than content to be saved from further decline or at least to have their existing position in society preserved. Hitler's *Volksgemeinschaft* would not be recognized as a true social community by a liberal or Marxist but it was apparently tolerable nonetheless to wide sectors of the German population, for whom Hitler did not cease to be a sounding board after he came to power in 1933. To what extent the middle classes, for example, were disillusioned by the failure to achieve a corporate state is still unknown, since historians have yet to present convincing evidence to support the general assumption that there was widespread disappointment among them prior to 1939. Similarly in the case of the working classes complaints about shortages of food or raw materials or long hours are endemic in modern society and do not necessarily imply any desire to change the political regime. It is therefore misleading in many respects to play down the pointers to stability and concentrate on the evidence for dissatisfaction, as Herbst has said of Mason's work.[124] The outbreak of war in 1939 did, however, eventually produce a sharp drop in the standing of the Party. Indeed it might well be argued that this is precisely where the *Volksgemeinschaft* became a confidence trick. The bare fact that German society clearly did not disintegrate during the hostilities would not in itself be a sufficient answer to Marxists, who would no doubt argue with some truth that the failure to achieve a genuine social revolution in their terms was the very factor which had led to the war, with all the strains this placed on the ethnic community.

# 5 Foreign policy: ideology in action?

> 'The foreign policy of a people's *völkisch* state must first of all bear in mind the duty of securing the existence of the race which is incorporated in this state. And this must be done by establishing a healthy and natural proportion between the number and growth of the population on the one hand, and the extent and resources of the territory they inhabit on the other.[1]

No other aspect of the Third Reich has attracted quite so much attention from historians as its foreign policy. Since this culminated in the outbreak of the Second World War the fascination is perfectly comprehensible. Unavoidably, it has been the centre of controversy between scholars. The earliest trend in studies of National Socialist foreign policy centred almost exclusively on the immediate origins of the war. Lewis Namier's pioneering study, completed in 1946, was the first serious attempt to cope with the flood of source material which became available after the war had ended. The proceedings of the International Military Tribunal at Nuremberg, which Namier admitted had led to a modification of his own earlier views, figured prominently. The significance lies, however, in the title of his major work, *Diplomatic Prelude*. It set the tone of the discussion of National Socialist foreign policy for the next ten or twelve years. The subsequent publication of captured German documents, specifically to throw light on why war broke out, reinforced this trend because they consisted almost exclusively of diplomatic exchanges and discussions.

Until the early 1960s, with a few notable exceptions, this somewhat narrow view of the origins of the Second World War and of National Socialist foreign policy in general still obtained in academic circles. The most prominent exponents of it were Trevor-Roper and Alan Bullock. Both shared the belief that Hitler's foreign policy after 1933 pursued long term goals which had been conceived as early as the mid-1920s. For Trevor-Roper it was axiomatic that 'Hitler between 1923 and 1934 had clearly made known unchanging aims.'[2] F. H. Hinsley and A. J. P. Taylor, among others, could not agree with him. Both of these historians had already suggested that the execution of Hitler's policy was by no means as planned or clearcut as the Bullock/Trevor-Roper school had argued.[3] For F. H. Hinsley, Hitler's attack on the Soviet Union was determined not so much in the framework of a long developed policy of *Lebensraum*, but had to be seen rather as an extension of the war against the United Kingdom.[4] This seemed to imply that Hitler was an opportunist in foreign policy, a concept which was placed firmly in the forefront of historical discussion of the subject by Taylor's now famous work, *The origins of the Second World War*, published in 1961. Although highly praised in many quarters, the storm of abuse with which this book was originally greeted revealed that raw nerves had been touched. In part this was due to the inability of many to accept the underlying thesis, namely that the elaborate plans which historians attributed to Hitler existed only in their own minds.[6]

The concerted attack on this aspect of Taylor's book diverted attention from its major contribution, which was to lift the whole discussion of the war's origins to a different plane by placing Hitler's activity in the years immediately prior to its outbreak in the fuller context of the European diplomatic scene. For all that, the work was undoubtedly flawed because Taylor's treatment of the then available evidence was cavalier. He concluded, for example, that Hitler's limited armaments expenditure may have meant that he was not preparing for war at all, whereas, as Milward has argued, this meant only that he was preparing for more limited war.[7] Equally, Mason has criticized Taylor's excessive reliance on one source of German rearmament statistics, namely those provided by Klein.[8]

In retrospect Mason's criticism can be seen as part of a distinct turning point in the whole discussion of the Third Reich and the origins of the Second World War. The purely diplomatic study, of which Taylor's book was perhaps the climax, was increasingly abandoned in favour of a wider approach. Curiously enough, the process was triggered off in part by the publication of a book about the origins not of the Second World War, but of the First, by the German historian Fritz Fischer. Although this study was also in most respects concerned with diplomacy, it put greater emphasis on the primacy of domestic policy, in effect reinforcing the earlier theses of Kehr.[9] Above all Fischer focused attention on the whole issue of 'continuity' in German foreign policy in the twentieth century. The main points of the Fischer thesis are that the First World War was not simply an accident but was to a considerable extent the outcome of trends in pre-1914 German foreign and domestic policy. Secondly, he pointed to the widespread support among the German population at large for the policy of annexations, particularly in the East, as exemplified by the Treaty of Brest-Litovsk. The book towards the end raised explicitly the whole question of the originality of Hitler's aims in the Second World War. This doubtless accounts at least in part for the fact that Fischer's book caused far more controversy than the earlier account by Hans W. Gatszke, who had already documented the annexationist programme for the West in the First World War.[10]

Thus the almost simultaneous contributions by Taylor and Fischer helped to revitalize the debate over National Socialist foreign policy. Taylor places the Hitler era firmly in the context of the existing state of international relations by showing precisely what limited room for movement Germany in reality possessed. In that sense the 'horizontal perspective' of contemporary Europe in Taylor was complemented by the way in which Fischer attempted to locate the foreign policy of the Third Reich inside the 'vertical' frame of reference of twentieth century Germany. This argument of course could hardly be without its effect on the notion of Hitler as a long term planner. For both historians Hitler's policies are seen as the outcome of his intentions, although less so than in the case of either Trevor-Roper or Bullock. The latter portray Hitler as dominating the centre of the stage whilst both Taylor and Fischer assume that he was obliged to listen to some of the other actors. The debate about Hitler's 'intentionalism' in foreign policy has subsequently been further refined in the work of a group of West German historians, notably that of Jäckl, Hillgruber and Hildebrand. The first of these has stressed the overwhelming importance of Hitler's racial ideology and the part which it played in forming his foreign policy principles, thus in effect continuing and elaborating on the work of Trevor-Roper and, still earlier, of R. K. Ensor.[11] Hillgruber and Hildebrand considerably extended the discussion of the continuity of Hitler's aims by proposing that he was bent on world domination, for which *Lebensraum* in Eastern Europe was nothing more than an essential prerequisite.

In all these versions, Hitler's intentions remain as the fulcrum of the debate. The historiography of the foreign policy of the Third Reich has now, however, been paralleled by a development which gives far more attention to the notion of 'functionalism'; that is to say that National Socialist foreign policy was much more the outcome of the internal dynamism of Hitler's Germany than the result of rational planning. Prominent here are Broszat and Mommsen. A variant of this thesis is to be found in the work of Mason, who emphasizes the economic crisis of 1938-9 which, coupled with the essential nature of National Socialism and the exigencies of the international system, pushed Hitler towards war in 1939. He summarizes the process under the heading of a 'flight forwards', in terms of an attempt by the regime to escape the class conflict and internal muddle of Germany after 1933.[12] In order to resolve the issues which have been raised by the discussion concerning 'intentionalism' or 'functionalism' as the main ground for the foreign policy of the Third Reich, historians have been compelled to examine more closely how National Socialist ideas developed in the 1920s prior to the accession to power. Additionally they have tried to set the execution of such ideas within the framework of international relations between 1933 and 1945, a sequence we can now trace.

Owing to the detailed refinement of Trevor-Roper's work by historians since the 1960s it is increasingly plausible to maintain the existence of politically intelligible goals in National Socialist foreign policy. According to the intentionalists Hitler may have varied tactically but not strategically. This presupposes that Hitler actually developed what may reasonably be described as a 'programme'. Much energy was expended on attacking this notion in the early stages of the debate, because the advocates of the programmatic explanation of National Socialist foreign policy were wrongly seen as presenting a 'blueprint' for Hitlerian aggression. In fact Jäckl, Hillgruber, Hildebrand, Kuhn and others were uncovering what they regarded as the most important driving forces of National Socialism.[13] *Mein Kampf* has therefore been confirmed, as Ensor and Trevor-Roper had argued, as the major source for early National Socialist foreign policy.[14] What the research has further stressed, however, is the importance of ideas and material existing prior to and after *Mein Kampf*.[15] The major constituent elements in this 'programme' seem to have been Hitler's racial ideology, the concept of living space with which it is linked, and his varying attitude towards the United Kingdom and the Soviet Union—the two powers which he came to regard as central to his calculations.

The connection in Hitler's mind between racial views and foreign policy is illustrated in the opening paragraph of *Mein Kampf*, where he justifies the unification of Germany and Austria, even if it proved to be economically disadvantageous, on the grounds that people of common blood should form one political unit. The durability of Hitler's views on this subject is demonstrated by his emphasis on the importance of what he called a 'racial core' of some 110 million people in the centre of Europe as a factor ensuring Germany's ultimate victory in war.[16] One of his leading henchmen expressed the idea even more emotively in June 1942: 'Here lies our duty as a people on this Earth. For thousands of years it has been the mission of this blond race to rule to Earth and to renew its wellbeing and culture.'[17] The very fact that the speech was made in occupied Europe underlines the connection between National Socialist racialism and the concept of living space: indeed the latter has been seen as the ultimate expression of NSDAP racial ideology by many Anglo-Saxon and West German historians.[18] For some, however, Hitler's quest for living space in the East has been seen as one facet of his distaste for urban and industrial life,[19] which of course is consistent with his determination as expressed in *Mein Kampf*, to bring German living space into what he called a sound and healthy balance with its population. This is not to say that he was clear originally as to the location of this room for expansion, since initially he seems to have fluctuated between Eastern Europe and overseas colonies as target areas.[20] That the search for living space as the primary goal of Germany's foreign policy was not confined to the leader of the NSDAP can be seen from the views of Backe in the early 1920s. (See p. 40).

Many historians would, however, want to say that the emphasis on living space was merely a cloak which served to conceal Hitler's real aim, which was to root out communism.[21] Erdmann has pointed out that after 1929 references to living space in Hitler's speeches were much less frequent than previously, whereas the emphasis on anti-Bolshevism was intensified.[22] Certainly a great deal of the research on Hitler's early programme has shown that his anti-Bolshevism played a crucial part in finally determining his priorities if, as he argued, the choice lay between overseas colonies and Eastern conquest. The fact that he also regarded the Bolshevik victory of 1917 in Russia as a significant advance by international Jewry on its march to world domination was clearly a further factor in Hitler's mind. It may well be that any 'alliance' with Russia, which some historians have implied was a possibility for Hitler immediately after 1918, was never in fact acceptable as a policy.[23] The problem has been for those engaged in studying early National Socialist foreign policy to determine the date at which Hitler finally opted in favour of an alliance with Great Britain against Russia, which was certainly expressed in *Mein Kampf*.[24]

A further factor in the evolution of Hitler's early 'programme' was his need to overcome opposition within his own ranks, particularly that coming from the group round Strasser and Goebbels in the 1920s. Many of the Party followers were in fact themselves Anglophobes.[25] The Locarno Treaties of 1925 played a certain role here in that Strasser apparently interpreted the agreements as a device by the British and the French to enlist Germans as cannon fodder against the Soviet Union. More particularly, Strasser became interested at that time in an alliance between what he called the have-not nations, which included Germany and the Soviet Union.[26] The fact that there were such differences of emphasis amongst the early National Socialists over foreign policy has been remarked, but the significant point is that ultimately Hitler's line prevailed, and indeed the foreign policy sections of *Mein Kampf* have been seen as deliberate refutation of Strasser's ideas.[27] Similar points could be made about Italy: Hitler had argued for an alliance with her from as early as 1919 and had held firmly to this, even though he had to overcome opposition within the movement to his readiness to abandon the German-speaking population of the Tyrol in the interests of such an alignment.

The point here is not to trace in all its labyrinthine detail the work which has been carried out since the 1960s on Hitler's early foreign policy, but rather to underline the current consensus; namely, that by the mid-1920s he had already worked out certain maxims, even before he had had any close contacts with those leading industrialists whom Stamokap historians still wish to contend were the driving force behind his policies.[28] Hitler's general principles derived from a combination of ideological assumptions and from reflections on the fluctuating international relations prior to 1933. A third dimension has, however, been introduced into the discussion of the National Socialist 'programme' by the work following Fischer's thesis that there is a clear continuity in German war aims, which was mentioned earlier in this chapter.

If there were such a continuity, then Hitler's 'alliance system' would have derived in part from his anxiety to avoid the errors which, as he saw it, had caused Wilhelmine Germany's defeat. The

Treaty of Brest-Litovsk had appeared to crown Germany's Eastern dominance, which failure in the West had then snatched from her hands. The need to return to the situation obtaining at the time of this treaty has been shown to have been an important constituent of Hitler's whole Eastern policy. Such reminders of the objective strategic realities facing the Germany created in 1871 have been an important corrective to the tendency to treat Hitler's policies as radically new. This is perhaps what Fischer was getting at when he wrote about the 'continuity of illusions'.[29] In this respect Taylor's views are close to those of Fischer, in his assumption that the object of the Second World War was really to restore the German hegemony in Eastern Europe, lost after Brest-Litovsk.

The problem about the controversies over the 'continuity' of German foreign policy is that with the exercise of a little ingenuity almost anything can be fitted into this concept. Fischer has also pointed for example to the persistence of 'Mitteleuropa' in German thinking both during the First World War and after it. The reconstitution of the Central European Economic Association in 1927 is thus automatically seen by him as proof of his thesis. In this he is not alone, but the diligent search for such evidence has undoubtedly led to a schematic and at times over-rigid approach to what constitutes 'continuity'.[30] It cannot be denied that this brings out similarities between Hitlerian and traditional German policies. An interesting example of the approach is afforded by K. Lange, who in 1959 traced the concept of *Lebensraum* right back to the Pan-German League of the 1890s.[31] On the other hand, the model fails to show that there may also have been quite important differences. Paradoxically many of those academics most concerned with stressing the continuity of German policies have helped to demonstrate how National Socialism actually broke with the past.

This is very evident in the way in which West German historians above all have further developed the concept of a National Socialist foreign policy 'programme' by referring to Hitler's '*Stufenplan*'. If the existence of National Socialist aims developing through 'stages' could be demonstrated, then obviously this would provide evidence that German foreign policy in the 1930s was an expression of Hitler's *intentions*. Of what did this 'policy by stages' *(Stufenplan)* consist? The core of the belief is that Hitler had grasped that the goal of Eastern conquest, although assuring Germany's position in Europe, could not possibly be his final aim; rather it would necessarily lead after the elimination of the Soviet Union to eventual struggle for world domination with the other major power, the United States of America. In this process Britain would either voluntarily join the German side as Hitler hoped, or be forced by military defeat into his camp in a general war between Germany and the United States. Again, the discussion has long passed the stage where opponents of such an explanation simply interpreted it to mean that Hitler had a detailed timetable pinned to his study wall. What the advocates of the *Stufenplan* are doing is examining the internal logic of Hitler's original programme, and extrapolating to the situation it would produce. Above all the work on the *Stufenplan* confirms the directional thrust, as it were, of National Socialist foreign policy, even if the question of timing is necessarily unresolved.

Aigner has affirmed that: 'All the observations and considerations come to one thing in the end, whether Hitler actually was the ice-cold, rationally planning man, as he liked to see himself, and as the supporters of the world domination theory see him.'[32] It may, however, be truer to say that the real advantage of the newer work on Hitler's 'programme' has been that it has provided perspectives with which the historian can re-examine the international relations of the 1930s with a fresh eye. Whilst it is inappropriate in this study to resort to a detailed narrative of the diplomacy of the 1930s to make this point clearer, we can at least ask how Hitler once in power coped with the major enemy of his programme and with those countries whose friendship he had concluded was most valuable. Hitler's attitude to Britain and the Soviet Union immediately after 1933 seems to have been remarkably consistent with the views he had formulated during the 1920s. For Britain, this meant that Hitler angled for an alliance, in which context he himself saw the Anglo-German Naval Agreement of March 1935.[33] On the other hand meticulous studies of Hitler's attitude towards Britain demonstrate that despite the treaty he began to ask himself as early as 1935 whether Britain could be drawn into his alliance system through its own volition, or whether it would have to be forced into it by him.[34] The events of the next two years helped to clarify his priorities because they showed the difficulties in bringing both Italy and Great Britain to his side simultaneously.

The Italian-Ethiopian war and the end of the Stresa Front, together with renewed Italian-French tensions, helped to push Germany and Italy closer together, as did the outbreak of the Spanish Civil War. It goes without saying that these events inflicted serious strains on Anglo-Italian relations. As late as August 1936, however, Hitler was still showing pronounced signs of flirting with the United Kingdom in his now celebrated instruction to Ribbentrop to 'bring back England' during his ambassadorship in London. Ribbentrop's failure no doubt played its part in the further change of emphasis in Hitler's remarks about Britain in 1937. Since it was a world power it continued to be a major concern of Hitler after that year, but increasingly as an unavoidable opponent and not as an ally.[35] Further support for the theory that 1937 was decisive in this respect is afforded first by Hitler's speech on 13 September, when he suggested publicly that, 'Neither Britain nor France wanted to see any favourable readjustments of power in Europe benefitting Germany or Italy.[36] Such evidence also highlights how unwise Taylor and some of his followers have been in attempting to discount the importance of the so-called Hossbach meeting of 5 November 1937, largely because they treat it in isolation. Hitler's reference there to the British and French as 'hate-inspired opponents' was perfectly consistent with his changing attitude. Those academics who base their approach firmly on the notion of intentionalist action in Hitler's foreign policy have received further reinforcement from his speech at a National Socialist training school in Sonthofen on 23 November 1937, only four days after the visit of Lord Halifax. The general tenor of Hitler's remarks that day suggests that the offer of peaceful revision of the territorial settlement conveyed to him by Chamberlain's emissary simply did not go far enough to suit the Führer's expansionist goals. Hitler was intent, after 1937 at the latest, on pushing German claims, if necessary against British opposition. His remark that the German Reich was a revolutionary force in the international situation is further evidence of this.[37]

Historians seem in fact to have uncovered two main strands in Hitler's policy towards Britain from the mid 1930s. On the one hand his desire for an agreement persisted but was increasingly subordinated to the realization that he might have to move without British acquiescence, and indeed even perhaps in face of its active opposition. How important 1937 was to the development of Hitler's tactical awareness of the British position is confirmed by his insistence that year—against the advice of his experts—on ordering a battleship fleet which would have been ready by 1944. It was for this reason that Hitler made his now celebrated reallocation of resources in January 1939, giving priority to the Navy not merely over exports but over other branches of the services as well (the so-called 'Z' plan).[38] Hitler's reorientation found echoes inside the Naval leadership itself. It cannot be coincidental that Raeder heard at the Hossbach meeting on 5 November 1937 a diatribe against Britain as the 'hate-inspired enemy' and that in the very next Naval war games in the summer of 1938 she figured as the main opponent for the first time.[39] As to the time-scale, from autumn 1938 onwards the Navy began to develop a plan to ensure that it would be in a position by 1943 to carry out a full surface war against Great Britain. This is not, however, necessarily proof that Hitler blundered into war earlier than he intended in 1939. He clearly felt that the existing fleet was adequate for the immediate task of helping to drive Britain from the continent, for which no large-scale surface navy was required.[40] Moreover even if in 1943, at the end of the proposed 'big fleet' build up, the German Navy had been inferior to those of the United States and Great Britain, this should not be taken to imply that Hitler did not intend any challenge to them in the long term. Some historians have fallen into the trap of assuming that because such a policy, seen in the cold light of statistical comparisons, seems unrealistic, Hitler could never have harboured such intentions. The answer surely to this is that the whole idea of National Socialist expansionism when viewed in the context of German resources and in that of the international situation in the twentieth century was equally 'unrealistic'.[41] The history of Great Powers is full of such 'unrealistic' assumptions. In addition, as we emphasized in an earlier chapter, Hitler had a strong gambler's streak in his personality and such plans were quite consistent with his 'va banque' tactics in foreign policy.

In this respect the '*Stufenplan*' which West German historians have inferred from National Socialist utterances and from the logic of the situation has proved to be a useful analytical tool. It frees us from the shackles imposed by the 'opportunist' framework, in which Hitler was seen as drifting, or sometimes racing, from one short campaign to another. We can now see that despite the economic difficulties of 1939, Hitler was already expecting long-term opposition from the major sea powers, Great Britain and the United States. As Dülffer puts it: 'Behind the Blitzkrieg against Poland there were already clear implications of further acts of aggression; far from being mere vague schemes, these were already being concretely planned'.[42] Once war with the Western powers had become a reality Hitler had no longer any need to conceal his real aims, which is why to break off a narrative of German foreign policy in 1939 can be so misleading, as Bullock pointed out in reply to Taylor.[43] What is interesting here is the newer evidence demonstrating clearly that Hitler was indifferent in the first half of the war to any peace initiative based on the assumption that the German Reich would merely remain a great power among several in the postwar order. This suggests that to talk of Hitler's plans for world domination is far from misguided and that the war can legitimately be seen as a stage towards it.[44] In this connection further proof is furnished by Hitler's remarks on the 27 November 1941, when he met the foreign ministers of Denmark and Finland. The occasion was the extension of the Anti-Comintern Pact and Hitler took the opportunity of talking to his guests about the coming task of making Europe self-sufficient, so that it would be capable of carrying through a conflict against the United States and Great Britain.[45] This all combines to reinforce the main argument of Dülffer's work on the German Navy, which is that naval planning was a central feature of Hitler's strategy and not a side issue as was so often implied in earlier discussions of Hitler's Blitzkriege.[46]

It seems then most likely that Hitler finally identified England as an enemy primarily because he could not achieve its support. In a real sense it is more accurate to say that his 'programme' was thwarted rather than abandoned—to his considerable frustration, as witness his disgusted remark that the trouble with the English was that they thought history came to an end in 1918. What he meant by this was that the British continued to behave as though Germany's defeat in the First World War had ensured the continuance of the British Empire for ever. In doing so they failed to grasp, as Hitler saw it, the need for a strong continental ally whose friendship would enable them to concentrate on their overseas possessions. His exasperation with the British came out again in August 1939, when he said plaintively: 'Everything I do is directed against Russia; if the West is too stupid and blind to grasp this, I shall be forced to reach agreement with the Russians, to attack the West and then, after its defeat, turn against the Soviet Union with my combined forces.'[47] Hitler's admiration for the way in which the British had acquired their Empire blinded him to the fact that the price he expected for aid in its defence was simply too high. As Albrecht Haushofer put it in a letter to Hess in August 1940, however eager the British were to retain their Empire they would nonetheless rather see the Americans take it over than do a deal with Hitler.[48] All of which underlines the question raised by Hildebrand as to how well informed Hitler actually was about the United Kingdom.[49] His obsession with the British alliance arose from the fact that he failed to understand London and its policy. Hitler was enraged by their obstinate inability, as he saw it, to perceive where their own true interests lay. The consequence for him was that he could never secure whole hearted concentration upon what he seemed to regard as the great overriding task of National Socialism. 'Germany, secure in her rear, could then have thrown herself, heart and soul, into her real task, the mission of my life, the raison d'être of National Socialism, the destruction of Bolshevism.'[50]

How central this latter theme remained to Hitler's thinking has been brought out more and more even in studies of Germany's relations with other European states in the 1930s. Abendroth for example has argued that Hitler's intervention in the Spanish Civil War can be seen as a logical outcome of his overall foreign policy, in that it was designed to prevent the building of a Communist bloc in Western Europe, apart from the more familiar explanations given for Hitler's policy in Spain.[51] Similar considerations informed Hitler's readiness to encourage Italian influence in the Mediterranean and to work for the Anti-Comintern Pact between Germany, Italy and Japan. As we have already pointed out, to follow all these problems through in a detailed narrative would lie well beyond the scope and intention of this book. The same can be said of the relationship between Germany and the East European states, although this will receive further consideration in the following chapter, insofar as they were related to Germany's foreign trade policies. It is the debate about Russia, Hitler's other major foreign policy interest, which chiefly concerns us here.

As in the case of newer work about Germany and Britain, so in that of German-Russian relations, the so-called 'programmers' and 'Stufenplanners' have rendered valuable service in making sense of what to contemporaries seemed the twists and turns of German policy towards the Soviet Union in the 1930s; these began with a breach in Soviet-German relations, apparently reinforced by the German-Polish treaty of 1934, and ended with a mutual German-Soviet treaty of non-aggression in August 1939. Underlying these events however, was a constant ideological line against the Soviet Union which the great majority of historians have always accepted. This found concrete expression even in the memorandum with which Hitler introduced the Four Year Plan into Germany in 1936, with its emphasis on the need to develop Germany's resources in the face of the build up of the Red Army. As Meinck has pointed out the introduction of the Four Year Plan coincided with violent anti-Soviet outbursts in the government-controlled media, which could hardly have been accidental.[52] It is therefore quite consistent, both with what we have said about German-British relations and with what Hitler planned for Russia, that he refused to listen to Raeder's advice in the summer of 1940 to the effect that he should concentrate on the Mediterranean in order to defeat the British Empire there.[53] This might well give credence to the DDR historian Zumpe's assertion that the decision to attack the Soviet Union had already been taken by July 1940.[54] How fixed was Hitler's determination to deal with the Soviet Union once and for all is confirmed in Cecil's work, which contains the interesting point that prior to June 1941, German intelligence had intercepted Soviet Government telegrams to its own mission in the Far East, to the effect that Stalin was interested in getting a new agreement with Hitler.[55] This was undoubtedly due to his direct interest in getting Germany further involved in the struggle with the West. Hitler's subsequent invasion of the Soviet Union confirmed that he did not wish to be diverted in this manner. When Raeder tried again after 1942 to involve Germany in a more concerted naval strategy with Japan, against the British and Americans, Hitler remained obsessed with the immediate struggle against the Soviet Union.[56] In smashing Russia Hitler would not only be overthrowing world communism but also acquiring *Lebensraum*.

At the same time his undoubted determination to deal with the Soviet Union is not sufficient evidence for concluding that here, rather than on the world stage, lay his ultimate ambitions. On the contrary, in the Second World War, as in the First, German domination of East Europe and Russia was regarded as the precondition of world power.[57] Hitler in any case must have become aware in other ways of how difficult it would be for a National Socialist dominated Europe to coexist indefinitely with the United States. The 'New Plan' of 1934 had by the following year already generated friction over trade relations in South America.[58] By 1939 a senior civil servant of the Four Year Plan staff had composed a memorandum on Germany's economic position in the world and the difficulty of exports, the first point of which concerned American hostility towards German trade in South America; it was even suggested that the Americans were trying to pull the British into an anti-German trading bloc.[59] If anything such considerations support the idea of a *Stufenplan* which would result in the ultimate clash between Germany and the U.S.A., not only the two remaining Great Powers but ideologically opposed too.

Having earlier considered the problem of 'continuity' in the formulation of Hitler's programme, it seems logical here to consider that factor in relation to its execution. To what extent was Hitler the heir of Germany's past, and to what extent did he break new ground? Rather than retracing the often rather tired debates about 'continuities' and 'discontinuities' in German foreign policy, it would seem more fruitful here to look closely at the *outcome* of Hitler's actions. Could the 'New Order' be deduced from Germany's past policies and actions? There are those who have argued that the plans for the reorganization of Europe were the counterpart to Allied propaganda about the Atlantic Charter, but this is to confuse propaganda with reality.[60] It has also been said that a great deal of the New Order in practice could have been carried out by any German Nationalist regime. Goebbel's appeal was to German nationalism when he directed the press in 1941 to stress that the Third Reich was fighting in the Soviet Union for its own future and not for a new Europe.[61] This was underlined by Hitler's own remarks at a conference with leading functionaries of his regime on 16 July 1941, where he made it absolutely plain that the Germans, as opposed to Europe in general, were to be the beneficiaries of Eastern conquest.[62] This at least explains the otherwize puzzling refusal of Hitler, initially at least, to accept help from Italy and Japan in attacking the Soviet Union. If this were the whole story, Hildebrand would have been literally correct in his earlier assumption that 'Hitler's programme integrated all the political demands, economic requirements and socio-political expectations in German society since the days of Bismarck.' In a more recent study Hildebrand does not, however, imply this since he emphasizes the near autonomy of Hitler's foreign policy goals, which suggests that they could not have derived wholly from past models.[63]

This is not to say that the Führer had any fully formed ideas, right up to the end of the war, on the eventual shape of postwar Europe.[64] The very different occupation policies carried out for different areas of the Continent throw doubt on the general term 'New Order', as we have already argued earlier in the book. It must, however, be strongly emphasized that different peoples were treated differently according to their alleged biological worth. In the last resort Hitler's obsession with his extreme racial ideas about world Jewry and Bolshevism constitute the true break in Germany's history, above all in his determination to execute his programme at all costs. The treatment meted out to the East European peoples under National Socialist occupation is a ghastly proof of the way in which the new regime broke with Germany's past, as Frank's diary shows.[65] As in the case of the elimination of the Jews, there is no historical debate on the fact of this activity, which was consistently practised throughout the region.[66] There has been controversy about the Wehrmacht's role in the executions in the East. Yet Streit and others have now made it quite clear that far from restraining the excesses of National Socialist liquidation policies, the Army actually supported and indeed in some cases initiated them. The Army had already been infected by National Socialist indoctrination.[67] In any event it is difficult to imagine the German Army of the First World War behaving in a similar way towards Russian prisoners. The extreme racialism underlying the New Order in the East has been emphasized by the contrasting picture of National Socialist occupation policies in the West and North Europe afforded by the greater number of studies now available of those areas.[68]

What we have said so far has provided a great deal of support for the intentionalist explanation of National Socialist expansionism and above all for Hitler's obsessive concern with foreign policy. What, however, has been the effect on the study of National Socialist foreign relations of the functionalist school of thought, which we introduced earlier in this chapter? The debate concerning 'intentionalism' or 'functionalism' has no necessary connection with that over continuity. The idea that the foreign policy of pre-1914 Germany was primarily dictated by domestic considerations has been made familiar firstly by Eckhart Kehr and latterly by Rosenberg and Wehler. That this might also be true of National Socialist Germany was argued by Mommsen, who suggested that the foreign policy of the Third Reich was a kind of internal policy projected outwards.[69] In Broszat's argument, the institutional and domestic development inside the Third Reich sowed the seeds of the regime's own destruction. In short, the dynamic force generated by the internal conflicts of Germany after 1933, rather than any fixed long term goals, was ultimately the determining factor of Hitler's foreign policy too: 'The disruption of the unified bureaucratic state order, the growing formlessness and arbitrariness of legislation and of decision making, and of transmitting decisions, played a part in speeding up the process of radicalization which was every bit as important as any ideological fixity of purpose.'[70] For Mommsen, 'It is questionable... whether National Socialist foreign policy can be considered as an unchanging pursuit of established priorities.'[71]

The problem with this framework of reference is, firstly, that it does not fully address itself to the direction and timing of National Socialist foreign policy decision taking, and secondly, that it fails to do justice to the continuity of purpose which the intentionalists have emphasized. Their elaborate mapping out of the Hitlerian route seems to be flatly dismissed in the functionalist judgement that 'Hitler's foreign policy aims, purely dynamic in nature, knew no bounds; Joseph Schumpeter's reference to "expansion without object" is entirely justified. For this very reason, to interpret their implementation as in any way consistent or logical is highly problematic.'[72] Broszat reinforces such a view by writing that 'The Hitler regime was certainly capable of generating astonishing energy, but it had long been incapable of the rational exercise of power.'[73] Valuable as the functionalist school of history is as a corrective to the at times over-schematic approach of the intentionalists, it does tend to overlook a real continuity of purpose in National Socialist foreign policy. Above all it fails to do justice to the fact that Hitler *did* come very close indeed to achieving the programme which he had originally outlined. Both Mommsen and Broszat are too acute as historians not to experience some unease when confronted with the undoubted mass of evidence compiled by such academics as Hildebrand, Dülffer, et alia. Mommsen's escape route is to lapse into a certain degree of unclarity, as witness the following: 'In reality, the regime's foreign policy *ambitions* were many and varied, without any clear *aims* and only linked by the *ultimate goal*'[74] (our italics). What exactly is the difference between 'ambitions', 'aims' and 'goal', in the field of foreign policy practice? Moreover, where would all these derive from if not from what can reasonably be described as a 'programme'? Broszat, on the other hand, finds a different way out of his dilemma by conceding that 'Hitler's obsessive preoccupation with specific ideological and political principles proved to be a decisive driving force behind National Socialist policy.'[75]

What the functionalist argument leads to here is the unavoidable conclusion that the period of the Third Reich must be seen as a break with the past, since it is the nature of the regime which determines the foreign policy. In this they agree with Jacobsen, who has taken the period 1933 to 1945 as an interregnum in the conduct of German foreign affairs.[76] An undoubted advantage of the functionalist explanations of foreign policy is that they help to focus on the institutional rivalry endemic to the Third Reich, from which foreign policy was not exempt. Their work helps for example to show how mistaken was the idea so recurrent in writing on German external relations after 1933, that the German Foreign Office somehow continued to 'conduct' foreign policy until it was 'coordinated' in 1938. As a widely cited book on the Wilhelmstrasse commented: 'Until this time (1938) the German Foreign Office's functions and its personnel had remained substantially unaffected by the five years of National Socialist rule.'[77] In view of our present awareness of the structural realities of the Third Reich, the question of 'composition' and 'personnel' cannot be seen as the most important issue, given the fact that rival institutions and offices existed which also attempted to influence 'foreign policy.'[78] This awareness provides an extremely valuable corrective to the way in which intentionalist arguments tend to minimize the contribution of Hitler's followers to the conduct of foreign policy. There were after all plenty of people in the Third Reich in high office who would have been content with the traditional great power policy, amongst whom may well have been numbered Hitler's foreign ministers, Joachim von Ribbentrop. Far from being the rather foolish incompetent portrayed in Fest's book, Ribbentrop has been shown by Michalka to have had fully worked out ideas of his own on foreign policy.[79] This casts an interesting light on the regime, but in the end the fact that Hitler's views prevailed suggests that his long-term goals and principles ultimately did provide the driving force for the Third Reich's expansionism.

Both the functionalists and the intentionalists affront Stamokap historians by appearing to exculpate what they term the German monopoly bourgeoisie.[80] Their view is probably best summarized in the recent declaration by a joint East German and Soviet historical commission to the effect that in foreign affairs Hitler was the agent of monopoly capital.[81] It is not the case, however, contrary to so many assertions in Western accounts, that Stamokap historians simply offer blanket explanations. On the contrary they too have developed in recent years a more sophisticated approach to the whole problem. It is now recognized in much of the recent periodical literature of the Eastern bloc that the dialogue over foreign policy decisions went far beyond the leaders of monopoly capitalism, in that NSDAP leaders, civil servants and the Wehrmacht are also seen to have participated.[82] This is an interesting reversion to the ideas of Franz Neumann, who consistently argued in *Behemoth* that the decisions of the regime were the product of compromise between the foregoing leading groups.

Stamokap historians do not take this explanatory model very far, in that they shun a serious examination of the areas of possible conflict between economic expansion on the one hand, and military conquest on the other.[83] There may well be an overlap between military conquest and economic gain, but there can be no question of an automatic identity of interest. Logically, they also overlook the ideological rationale behind much of the New Order, in their desire to see it as an 'overall system' for the exploitation of foreign wealth in the interests of German capitalism.[84] As we have already pointed out, however, this does less than justice to the variations within the German-occupied areas. Equally, the analytical framework of the Eastern bloc historians does not on the whole allow for a systematic probing of the significance of the differences between prominent leaders in the Third Reich. The divergence of views between them and Hitler is usually reduced to a question of the scale and timing of preparations for the war.[85] This does not make a great deal of sense of Schacht's apparent readiness to re-integrate Germany into the normal patterns of world trade, in the context of Halifax's offer of November 1937. Even the chief figure in the Stamokap demonology, I. G. Farben, was apparently entertaining doubts in 1938 about the course of German trade, since one of its leading functionaries appeared to be suggesting in a public speech that Germany should move away from autarky, a view apparently similar to Schacht's.[86] A fuller account of the relationship between Party and industry as it concerned foreign policy will be given in the following chapter. What seems curious in the last resort is that Stamokap historians often turn out to be intentionalists, in that foreign policy is seen as the implementation of worked out goals, only in this instance those of monopoly capitalism using Hitler as its agent,[87] which hardly explains the death of six million Jews. Indeed Stamokap historians seem to prefer not to explain National Socialist racialism except as an epiphenomenon. This is a serious weakness in the Eastern bloc's analysis.

It is of course untrue to suggest that there is no difference whatever between Marxist historians in their attitude to the Third Reich. Indeed this is perhaps why Mason's work—which is in the Marxist tradition—has become so controversial not only in the West but in East Germany as well. He has upset Stamokap historians with his suggestion that the regime eventually freed itself from the constraints of the capitalist paymasters, developing in effect a 'Bonapartist' theory (p. 156). To continue the debate on foreign policy, Mason sees Hitler's expansionism as a means of avoiding class conflict at home, which resulted from the strain imposed on Germany by the economic policies followed by the regime. Mason has not been content to discuss this merely in a generalized form, but has developed sophisticated arguments relating to the timing of the war.[89] Thus the mounting international crisis of 1938-9 is seen in Mason's work chiefly but not exclusively in terms of the pressures exerted by the economic crisis within the Third Reich. Since, however, the accent of his research is on Germany's economic position in these years, the plausibility of his theory must in the final analysis depend on whether there actually was a crisis situation or not, a point which will be taken up in the following chapter. Mason therefore shares to a very real extent the functionalist belief that National Socialist foreign policy represented the outcome of the internal structure of the regime, rather than the implementation of goals *sui generis*. Indeed he has gone on record as suggesting that Hitler had no concrete war aims or idea of his future Reich as an imperialist structure, but rather waged a war of plunder, the proceeds of which were intended to sustain it until victory was assured.[90] The radical implications of Mason's work for 'war planning' are also duly considered in the following chapter.

Looking back, it is interesting to find that Neville Chamberlain, invariably dismissed in so many earlier accounts as a rather naive old gentleman who was no match for the Führer, actually said at a sitting of the Cabinet Committee on 27 March 1939, twelve days after the German entry into Prague, that the goal of British policy should be 'to check and defeat Germany's attempt at world domination.'[91] He correctly assumed that Hitler's ambitions did not end with the absorption of Bohemia. In this respect his insight was more penetrating than that of the American State Department, which in 1943 stated that it was impossible to deduce from the writings of Hitler and other Nazi leaders that the regime was bent on world power.[92] The important question raised by these judgements is whether the National Socialist period of office represents a continuation of German history or constitutes a break. As to the former, it depends to which 'continuity' reference is being made. Hildebrand has discussed the regime in terms of the traditional Prussian foreign policy, which he contrasted with that of England.[93] On the other hand it should not be overlooked that Hitler was an Austrian, which has led Hammer to raise the possibility that he was really continuing the foreign policy of the Habsburgs.[94] Or again, was National Socialist expansionism the second chapter in the continuing story of Germany's striving for European hegemony or world power in the twentieth century, a dominance which previous empires, such as the British, the French and the Spanish had sought in earlier [illegible] bid for world power can no longer itself be seen as [illegible] break with Germany's past. At the same time there [illegible] in that past to prepare it for Auschwitz, even allowing [illegible]dence of anti-semitism in Central European history. [illegible]ical ideology of National Socialism transformed all [illegible]als in its desperate efforts to provide a final solution to what it perceived as the 'cancer of Jewish-Bolshevism'. As Hitler put it, 'I have been Europe's last hope. She proved incapable of re-fashioning herself by means of voluntary reform...to take her, I had to use violence.'[95] Fortunately for Europe, the material superiority of the alliance which Hitler conjured up against himself made the realization of this task impossible. In the final analysis the brute facts of economic life defeated a gamble based on ideology and the political dynamism of the regime.

# 6 The economics of the Third Reich: ideology, management, planning.

> 'If I recognize any dogma in economic matters, then it is that which maintains that there is no such dogma in this field and that actual experience counts for more than theory.'[1]

The whole question of National Socialist foreign policy has been complicated by its obvious connections with the economy of the Third Reich, although many historians have doubted Hitler's ability and interest in economic matters. Such a view was fairly orthodox until the early 1970s. Notwithstanding the earlier work of Kroll, credit for reviving the idea that National Socialist economic thoug[illegible] ought to be taken more seriously should be given to Heyl[illegible] reappraisal of Hitler in this respect stimulated the discussio[illegible] in a rather general fashion. For Heyl, Hitler was far from [illegible] sort of economic simpleton who believed that Germany's problems could be solved for all time by a policy of plunder.[2] Despite this pioneering article the real work of submitting National Socialist economic views to a systematic analysis was done by Avraham Barkai, in a short article written in 1975. His contentions were further developed two years later with the publication of a full scale work on the economics of National Socialism.[3] At the time Turner was also pleading for more attention to be given to the economic views of the movement, whilst in fact concentrating his attention on Hitler.[4] The combination of these historians helped seriously to undermine the hitherto existing consensus, based as it was on three major premises. The first of these was that whatever economic ideas the movement may have had stemmed largely from Gottfried Feder; since he was known to be a crank this necesarily prejudiced historians against any serious review of National Socialist economic thought as it existed prior to 1933. Secondly, such a view received powerful reinforcement from the proceedings of the postwar trials at Nuremberg, where the prevalent opinion was that National Socialists had known nothing of finance or economics and had therefore relied simply on Schacht's 'wizardry' to pull them through. Thirdly, there was a tendency to accept the Bullock/Carr picture of territorial conquest and plunder as a substitute for economic policy. In fact this could be seen as a part of a wider preoccupation of the historians of National Socialism with the whole question of the so-called 'war economy' which was believed to have existed in Germany in the 1930s.

The newer works suggest that despite the undoubted importance of the rearmament programme in the Third Reich, National Socialist economic ideas in general went beyond this and arose at least partially from theories developed prior to the takeover in 1933. As Barkai would have it 'National Socialist economic policy, to a not inconsiderable extent, if not exclusively, was dictated by ideological and political precepts of which rearmament and war were an integral part.'[6] However important preparation for a possible war may have been after 1933, it cannot alone explain the economic policy of National Socialism. Kroll suggests that National Socialism represented economically a complete revulsion from liberalism and that its outlook was basically mercantilist, the real aim of which was to get the economy under political control, which it would probably have done under any circumstances.[7] Recent historians have been more inclined to attempt to map out—as in the case of foreign policy—to what extent the Party had developed a coherent economic programme before it actually came to power.

Barkai therefore logically began with a consideration of Feder. As his book emphasizes, no fewer than ten of the 25 points in the original Party programme dealt with economic problems, however generally.[8] Notwithstanding Feder's later ignominious decline, Barkai points out the appeal to the early movement of the rather vague, indeed ridiculous distinction between 'creative' and 'parasitic' capitalism, a concept which had the advantage of being 'anti-capitalist' without alienating necessary business support. The important factor here is not the fate of Feder nor—as in the realm of foreign policy—the absence of real precision in the economic plans, but the establishment of certain basic principles, within the framework of which the National Socialists would be able to look for more detailed solutions to problems when the occasion arose. It cannot be said too often that Hitler in particular did not believe in committing himself irrevocably to a detailed blueprint on any subject, since he wished to give himself room for movement when he came to power. Nonetheless such freedom of choice was exercised essentially within the boundaries of the general principles already formulated.

Even the opponents of Hitler in the NSDAP, some of whom wanted to concretize the doctrine to be followed, were helping to set the parameters of the Party's economic policy. Already in the 1920s it was evident that views within the movement were not being determined by economic criteria alone. Gregor Strasser for example was anti-capitalist partly because of his belief in the efficacy of 'war socialism' (state intervention in the German economy between 1914 and 1918), but partly also because capitalism was perceived by him as Western and international, that is to say anti-German.[9] Even if the conventional wisdom has it that Hitler defeated Strasser's attempt to make the programme more precise in 1926, in economic as in other matters, the latter's economic thought continued to be influential within the NSDAP, as will shortly be seen. General evidence for this point is provided by the similarity between many of Hitler's own ideas and those of Strasser. The Führer was apparently at the time already pondering the connection in the economy between collectivization and individual enterprise. Because he saw production as 'creative' it should he felt be left to the entrepreneur, although some branches, such as trusts and transport, should be socialized. Admittedly this was in a conversation with Goebbels and Hitler may well therefore have deliberately overstated his belief in socialization. The fact remains that there is nothing in the foregoing with which Gregor Strasser would have disagreed.[10] It may also well be that at this stage, whatever historians have said about Feder, Hitler was still somewhat under his influence.

With the prospect of power and as the Depression raged in Germany, the NSDAP was inevitably compelled to make more specific pronouncements on economic matters, partly at least to avoid losing credibility with the voters. An important source for Party thinking at this time is the memoirs of Otto Wagener.[11] According to Wagener, who had worked in the economic policy section of the Munich Party Headquarters, by the middle of 1930 Hitler was already aware of the need to revise the economic sections of the original Party programme. As he looked for what has been referred to as a 'third way' between liberalism and state socialism he remained, however, true to his Social Darwinistic ethos of opening up opportunities for the 'gifted' individual, if necessary through some re-allocation of existing property. This latter point he seems however to have abandoned two years later.[12] At that stage many earlier historians tended to assume that the Party theorists had also been jettisoned as part of the process whereby Hitler pragmatically sought power. This was consistent with the view that later Schacht was the key economic mastermind. Our contention here is that this is incorrect. The fact that at the beginning of 1932 Hitler expressed dissatisfaction with the 'socialist' tendencies of Strasser and Wagener by ordering Wilhelm Keppler to set up an advisory body of experienced businessmen, the so-called Keppler Circle, is not to be taken as evidence that the ideas of his apparently discredited colleagues had ceased to be important.[13]

Both Strasser and Wagener put forward programmes in 1932.[14] That of the former was based on a speech he made in the Reichstag in May 1932 and was distributed as their platform material by the NSDAP, to the tune of 600,000 copies, at the time of the July elections of that year.[15] What were the main ideas of Strasser's so-called 'Immediate programme'? The point of departure, as the title suggests, was the need to overcome unemployment, to be met by a combination of state credit, rural settlement in East Germany and the nationalization of private monopolies—all of which would permit the creation of new jobs.[16] Hitler did not withdraw official approval of the 'Immediate programme' as it stood until the autumn of 1932, no doubt partly in the face of opposition from Schacht and the Keppler Circle. Nonetheless a minority of historians have recognized the fact that Strasser's ideas continued to be influential in the economic thinking of the movement, and indeed in the management of the German economy after 1933. Kroll goes so far as to suggest that Schacht's 'New Plan' of 1934 in itself owed something to Strasser.[17] Whilst Barkai felt that Kroll exaggerated Strasser's influence he too urged that the latter's ideas 'pointed the way towards the economic policy after the seizure of power.'[18] In Wagener's case his own economic plan in 1932 contained the outline of later legislation, notably that concerning the Law for National Labour as well as wage and price controls and the institution of Trustees for Labour.[19]

In effect therefore Hitler was objecting to attention being drawn to specific detail, which he well knew could be electorally embarrassing. He was not, however, in any way averse to thorough discussion of economic principles within the Party. In view of the newer economic studies considered here, it is no longer possible to maintain the concept of the NSDAP as a party of economic illiterates who were bailed out by Schacht.[20] The National Socialists had already worked out plans for the future reorganization of German agrarian marketing by 1931, necessitated by the collapse of the liberal-capitalist order. Their response was part of a wider discussion about Germany's economic future during the World Depression. Indeed so lively and varied was that debate that it now seems literally incredible that historians should have overlooked the possibility that the NSDAP must have been pulled into the reassessment, especially through their conviction that the world crisis in itself confirmed the bankruptcy of liberalism.[21] If Barkai is correct, the NSDAP in fact showed considerable readiness to experiment economically, in so far as it was the only major party in Germany prepared to assimilate the ideas of the economic reformers, or as they came to be known, 'Keynesians before Keynes'. Ironically one of the 'reformers' from which Strasser derived many of his ideas, Friedlander-Prechtl, was himself part Jewish.[22] It is worth remembering too that re-thinking in Germany—as indeed elsewhere—necessarily involved businessmen as well as theorists: Czichon has argued that on the eve of Hitler's accession German industrialists could be divided intellectually into three groups. Firstly, there were what he called the right-wing Keynesians, whose political representative was von Papen, secondly the 'Left Wing Keynesians' led by Krupp, for whom Schleicher was the political mouthpiece and finally, the National Socialist industrialists, including Thyssen and Kirdorf.[23] Whatever their differences these came to recognize ultimately the necessity for more extensive state-financed economic expansion to haul Germany from the depths of the Depression.[24] As we have seen, such ideas also formed an integral part of the Strasser programme and demonstrate again the extent to which the collapse of the world economy forced almost everyone to re-think their economic ideas.

Part of the overall re-examination of possible strategies involved the notion of autarky, which has received considerable attention, to the extent that many historians have presented it as being virtually Hitler's only economic idea. Typical of this trend is the stress in Turner on the Führer's anti-urban prejudices, carried to the point where a restructuring of the whole German economy, with a new importance being given to agriculture, would free the country altogether from the need to export, thus insulating it from the crisis-ridden outside world.[25] Certainly the whole subject occasioned vigorous argument amongst economists and 'reformers' who were predicting the demise of the self-regulating economy and demanding more active state intervention, preferably within a closed trading area.[26] Powerful weight was added to the debate, as Gessner has reminded us, by the agrarian pressure groups who perceived in the world crisis the ideal chance to reactivate the propaganda directed against an export orientated trade policy, which they had been attacking since before the First World War. In its place they argued for 'healing' the German economy, by which they meant that the German public would be forced to buy German food, even though it was much dearer than foreign products.[27] So insistent had the demands of the self-sufficiency lobby become that Lederer made in September 1939 what he himself recognized at the time was a vain effort to swim against the tide, by exposing the fallacy that Germany could ever survive being cut off from the rest of the World. As he pointed out, 73 per cent of Germany's trade was with the industrialized world, the loss of which would prove lethal.[28]

Notwithstanding the certainty of many historians about Hitler's own penchant for autarky, there is evidence that he was also conscious of the political pitfalls which the concept concealed. In Radkau's view, by 1930 at the latest Hitler knew that an overt policy of autarky would bring him into conflict with substantial parts of German industry.[29] At the same time he could hardly remain unaware of the pressure within agrarian circles for protectionism, not to say self-sufficiency, at a time when he was angling desperately for their vote. In private Hitler also expressed doubts about the prospects of going it alone, since in late 1932 he allegedly told Strasser that autarky was 'pure nonsense'.[30] This remark almost certainly related to Germany within its existing frontiers since if it were literally true it would contradict his foreign policy and the subsequent expansionism in Eastern Europe, in search of what has usually been referred to as a *Grossraumwirtschaft*—or an economic order on a continental scale. It is therefore more helpful to relate the concept of autarky to the actual development of Germany's foreign trade after 1933 and to the 'New Order', as we shall do later in this chapter.

What needs to be emphasized here is that Hitler and the NSDAP could not avoid thinking about economic problems, since like their predecessors they necessarily had to be concerned with the question of how Germany's long term future could be secured and the immediate unemployment problem solved. The first question had already been raised before 1914 and was naturally made more acute by the loss of the First World War and the Depression. One school of thought, which had pondered developments since the onset of industrialization in Germany in the later nineteenth century, had always concentrated on the relative disadvantage of their country in comparison with other leading powers. The British and French had huge overseas empires, the United States and Russia disposed of vast areas of their own land. How was Germany, a latecomer on the political scene, to ensure its economic future when denied any of these advantages? Obviously the loss of her colonies after 1919 exacerbated the general feeling among Germans of being what Hans Grimm called 'People without space'. Under such conditions economic factors intruded ever more on the sphere of policymaking and in general the solutions canvassed were frequently anti-liberal in tone. Krüger is therefore correct to stress in context that 'Hitler was simply an extreme exponent of this movement, and whatever may have been said up to now of his lack of understanding of economic principles, he not only grasped the problem, but it was fundamental for him and further helped to influence his thought and action.'[31]

A greater awareness of such formative influences has not been without its impact on the debate over key areas of National Socialist economic management after 1933, as the case of work creation schemes illustrates. In keeping with the earlier historiographical obsession with rearmament in the Third Reich many have stressed the close connection between this and work creation projects from 1933 onwards. More recently Wolfram Fischer has again argued that it was impossible to separate these schemes from armaments production plans, in his discussion of the so-called 'New Plan' of 1934.[32] It is ironic, however, that an East German historian has latterly drawn our attention to the fact that the 'New Plan' cannot be seen just as a means of rearmament but has to be judged within the context of unemployment and the breakdown of German capitalism.[33] Indeed, the crucial importance for Hitler of solving the unemployment crisis should be given the greater emphasis here, since it would be the yardstick by which the populace of Germany would judge his regime in the all-important short term. So Kroll is correct to remind us that Hitler may not have solved unemployment primarily through rearmament projects.[34] At the very least it is difficult to draw firm conclusions on this matter as can be shown by reference to the part played by autobahn construction in the government's work creation schemes.

Overy's work provides strong evidence for doubting the wisdom of automatically assuming that road-building projects were simply part and parcel of the general rearmament process. He demonstrates that the 'automobile revolution' together with road construction had a role to play in assisting Germany's general economic recovery after 1933.[35] More specifically he argues that 'The strength and rapidity of the recovery can be explained with reference to cars and roads rather than to tanks and aircraft. Business confidence was restored, not with threats of foreign war but with the promise of modernization and financial security, for which achievement motor transport could lay a considerable claim.' In statistical terms the Wehrmacht brought only 15,700 lorries between 1934 and 1936 from a total of 126,000 produced. Apart from its economic benefits the autobahn building was an immensely important propaganda coup for the government and in itself played its part in bolstering business confidence.[36]

In sum, between 1933 and 1936 there was a substantial growth of economic activity in Germany which resulted in massive reductions in unemployment. Moreover the boom was fuelled by a programme of public works and state expenditure along the lines suggested by Strasser in the middle of 1932, for which Schacht therefore cannot be given the sole credit. To this extent it is also misleading in general to talk about *Schacht's* New Plan. Exchange controls, which were also a feature of the programme, had been introduced as early as August 1931 and I. G. Farben among other firms had already begun to develop independently the sort of barter agreements which have likewise been invariably discussed in the context of the 1934 legislation.[37]

It is appropriate at this juncture to remember that Germany's problems could not be solved by domestic work creation schemes alone, important as they may have been. Exports were also crucial and the only real prospect of a solid improvement in the economy lay in their expansion, at a time when this was extremely difficult to achieve.[38] That Hitler was aware of this further belies the conventional picture of him as having no economic ideas; he clearly grasped the importance of the issue in a speech he made in April 1933 to the government's economic committee. The occasion for this seems to have been the coming World Economic Conference to be held in London, which prompted the Führer to summarize his thoughts on the Depression. He attributed the disaster to the errors made in the previous 20 years by the developed countries, which had permitted the formerly non-industrialized areas of the globe to build up a manufacturing capacity. He even seemed to be toying with the idea of limiting capital goods exports from Europe by international agreement in order to retard the industrial development of overseas countries.[39] Although this latter suggestion was never executed Hitler preserved a desire to ensure that underdeveloped countries should remain the suppliers of raw materials to industrial Europe, a concept which is totally in tune with the National Socialist economic line of neo-mercantilism. With this in mind we can now turn our attention to the less developed areas of Europe where Germany did heavily involve itself, namely those of South East Europe. A whole range of interesting issues has been raised by historical research into the continuity of German trade aims in this region and the precise relationship between the New Plan and German foreign policy.

Milward is quite correct in pointing out that 'German international economic policy in the 1930s has almost invariably been interpreted as an integral aspect of an aggressive foreign policy, designed to satisfy the major international political ambitions of the National Socialist government. The changes which occurred after 1933 in Germany's economic relationships with other countries are always presented as deliberate, positive changes of policy.'[40] On one view the New Plan has been represented as part of a systematic attempt to exploit South East European markets by means of a series of bilateral trade agreements.[41] Further, the latter treaties have often been seen within a still wider framework, namely in terms of the deliberate creation by the Third Reich of a so-called 'informal Empire' in South East Europe, seen as the first step towards the erection of a *Grossraumwirtschaft*. In time of war Germany would thus hope to be provided with a blockade-proof economy based on a secure hinterland. This explanation has been reinforced by the work of historians seeking to establish the continuity of Middle European associations in German politics through and beyond the 1920s. Needless to say the Stamokap interest in economic imperialism has also resulted in greatly increased discussion of the National Socialist regime's 'Griff nach Südosteuropa.' According to this interpretation the exploitation of the region was both thorough and complete.[43] Whilst many Western historians by contrast have contended that

German penetration of South East Europe was by no means total by the end of the 1930s only a minority of writers, including Milward, have suggested that these states rather than Germany were the main beneficiaries. 'That the formation of the Reichsmark block should be seen as "Nazi exploitation" or "penetration" of South Eastern Europe is a remarkable tribute to the ability of National Socialism to explain all events, however unwelcome, as being in accord with the new *Weltanschauung*'.[44]

Schroeder is one who stresses the continuity of policy between the Third Reich and the late Weimar Republic in respect of the 'informal Empire' which politicians and businessmen had already begun to build up under the impact of the Depression.[45] Volkmann agrees in substance with this view[46] and as Milward again puts it: 'All the main principles of bilateral trading agreements with underdeveloped Europe were worked out in the Republic before 1933. Schacht's Neuer Plan in 1934 merely systematized into deliberate policy a set of trading devices which were already widespread.'[47] As a matter of fact this point echoes the earlier findings of Guillebaud. Milward further wishes to say that it is an error to assume any necessary positive connection between foreign trade patterns in the Third Reich and the basic aims of foreign policy. 'There is little geographical congruence between the Reichsmark trading block and any future *Grossraumwirtschaft* or *Lebensraum* which Hitler or the Nazi Party may have intended.'[48] The weight of evidence suggests that Milward is right to stress that there was no clean break in foreign trade when the National Socialists took over in 1933 but in Barkai's work the autarkic block which began to emerge in outline during the 1930s was also a logical outcome of the movement's economic theory, irrespective of the difficulties which actually arose in practice. This is in the final analysis a real difference of emphasis in comparison with Milward even though both agree as to the actual patterns of German trade after 1933.

During this debate concerning the relationship between foreign trade and foreign policy in the Third Reich and how effectively the first supported the latter, it has been underlined that there is no evidence to support the belief that directives from Hitler personally played a part in the development of trade relations after 1933. The implication here is that the Führer was not interested in the question. Radkau's conviction of this stems from his analysis of the trading patterns around which the New Plan was fashioned, in that

Germany's best customers prior to 1933 were the ones most disadvantaged by the new arrangements.[49] Two considerations are left out of account by such an explanation. The first is whether Hitler had any choice in the matter, bearing in mind the constraints of the world economic crisis in general. The second relates to his speech of 1933—which has already been cited—where he clearly rejected previous trading patterns. This suggests again that if he had an entirely free choice it would have been exercised in the direction in which circumstances were already conspiring to push him. In effect this is another way of saying that the regime's ideological and political goals ultimately took precedence over short term economic ones. Such a context must therefore be kept firmly in mind in any examination of the actual difficulties arising from the execution of the New Plan.

It would have been strange had there not been problems as the regime strove to cope with the Depression and to move towards the longer term conclusions which it seemed to dictate, namely that Germany should break away from the fluctuations of an international order based on liberal-capitalism and the cycle of boom and slump which this seemed to entail. In the short term, pending the realization of a *Grossraumwirtschaft*, bilateralism was the only possible solution. The absence of any viable alternative, as we have already argued, has been overlooked by critics of bilateralism. Secondly, such policies were consistent with the general principles in respect of Germany's economic future which had already been formulated by the movement prior to the accession to power. It is in this area that Barkai's work is particularly valuable, not least because it helps to clarify the range of choices which the regime purportedly had in 1936. Was there really the option, which Kroll and others have suggested, of switching back to consumer-led economic development at the expense of further state intervention in the economy?[50] Was this really feasible for a movement which was in principle so totally opposed to the international economy as the liberal theorists of the nineteenth century understood it? Even prior to 1914 the latter had shown distinct signs of strain as the world's leading industrial countries found themselves competing for diminishing export opportunities.[51] It is not altogether surprising that with the 'formative influence' of the world Depression behind him, Hitler did not exercise the 'choice' of attempting to reintegrate Germany into the world economy in 1936 but continued along the apparently logical path of sealing Germany off as far as possible from the uncertainties of international trade.

At this point the debate about the nature and efficiency of National Socialist economic management again becomes inextricably tied up with the whole issue of rearmament and more particularly with the question as to whether the Third Reich could be described as having introduced a 'war economy' even prior to 1939. Otto Nathan's study in 1944 was actually subtitled 'Germany's mobilization for war' and even its revised edition in 1971 continued to argue that Germany centrally planned and directed the economy for war during the 1930s.[52] From this line of study developed the widely accepted concept that the most appropriate designation of the economic system of Hitler's Germany was a 'war economy in peacetime.' Erbe's highly influential study in 1956 did a great deal to perpetuate this framework of reference.[53] Kroll's book, published in the same year as Erbe's, reinforced what was now becoming orthodox opinion when he maintained: 'The crucial determinant of economic policy was the aim of forcing through rearmament at a hectic tempo in order to be able to wage war.'[54] These studies were valuable in their application of Keynesian models to the Third Reich's economy and provided a first attempt at a comprehensive statistical and analytical account.[55]

Klein's study *German economic preparations for war*, appearing in 1959, was the first serious revision of the 'war economy' thesis. His material, drawn largely from the US strategic bombing surveys, illustrated that the extent of German arms expenditure prior to 1939 had been far less than most Western observers had supposed (or indeed than Hitler himself had claimed). Klein accepted that warlike preparation was taking place in Germany after 1933 but concluded from his figures on arms expenditure that it must have been for a limited conflict. This would have had the considerable advantage, he argued in effect, of not demanding too much by way of sacrifices from the German public in peacetime.[56] In other words Klein provided the valuable service of illuminating the economic background of Blitzkrieg as a strategic concept, whereas until then it had always been taken merely as a tactical manouevre. Such a notion was further developed by Milward in the middle of the 1960s, who was concerned to show that Hitler was preparing for a more limited series of short wars.[57] Historiographically speaking Carroll's book is very much part of this process of revision insofar as it argued that a 'war economy' did not exist before 1938 at the latest.[58] The implication of the work of Klein, Milward and Carroll is that 1939 represented no sudden change for the German economy. Whereas the earlier studies had maintained that a war economy existed in peacetime, the work of Milward in particular suggests that a peace economy was carried on into wartime, in that there was initially a high volume of consumer goods being produced after 1939, in contrast to the United Kingdom.[59]

Central to a great deal of the above general discussion about the nature of the German economy has been the Four Year Plan of 1936. This has often been seen as a turning point, not least because it apparently marked Hitler's first vigorous personal intervention in the economy.[60] Thus in 1957 Simpson could argue that in the period 1936 to 1937 Schacht was engaged in a struggle to retain his influence in the Third Reich and to prevent the execution of what Simpson referred to as the 'new program'. This supposition seems to have rested on the somewhat surprising conclusion that until 1936 Schacht had been unaware that the National Socialists were 'bent on a program of drastic rearmament'[61]. However, Schacht was present at the ministerial discussion of the state of the economy on 2 May 1935, where the effect of posssible inflation on rearmament was the main topic of discussion. Although greater stress was certainly placed on making Germany less dependent on outside raw materials,[62] this is not enough in itself to support the idea that the Four Year Plan marked a watershed in the German economy. There were admittedly important differences of emphasis between Schacht on the one hand, and Goering on the other about the tempo of arms production, which terminated in victory for the Party.[63] Most historians however went beyond this and treated these differences of opinion as though the discussion had been about rearmament in principle. By missing the point that the squabble between Schacht and the Party was over the scale and tempo of rearmament, historians have exaggerated the importance of 1936. In so doing they have gone on to insist that Hitler suddenly set the goal of autarky in order to pursue an expansionist policy in the near future.

Whilst accepting that rearmament was important in this context Barkai broadens the whole discussion by directing our attention to the fact that the Four Year Plan was quite consistent not only with National Socialist ideology but also with the movement towards a long-term crisis-free economic order.[64] The regime's decision in 1936 admittedly intensified rearmament but this was not the sole determinant. The existing arms programme had already worsened Germany's currency situation, as can be seen from the figures of German gold and currency reserves held by the Reichsbank. In 1936 these had slumped to 2.7 per cent of the 1930 total.[65] Faced with this problem the regime had three possible avenues of escape, one of which was to reduce the pace of rearmaments: this was clearly excluded on political grounds. Moreover as early as 1935 General Beck was demanding a quicker tempo of rearmament, citing the *external* situation as the reason. Similarly in the following year Keitel told the Reich Defence Council that the general European rearmament then taking place precluded any arms production standstill in Germany.[66] The second possibility, namely devaluation of the mark, also had its socio-political dangers and was accordingly rejected both by Schacht and Hitler as a swindle imposed on German savers.[67] The third route, an attempt to reduce Germany's dependence on outside sources, virtually chose itself and Meinck is surely correct in his asumption that Hitler's mind had already begun to move in this direction by the second half of 1936.[68] Consequently there is much in favour of Guillebaud's earlier description of the new programme of 1936 as the 'second' Four Year Plan. More recently Radkau formulated the same idea in a slightly different way by saying that 'The path (chosen by the NSDAP) of the Four Year Plan in autumn 1936 continued in principle the line of the New Plan even if it did lead to Schacht's downfall.' He goes on to make the important point that the bilateral trade agreements from 1933 onwards had already contrived to freeze the patterns of German trade and in this respect it was perfectly logical to take the process to its conclusion and to attempt to make Germany independent of foreign trade as far as possible.[69]

As long as the historical emphasis was on the Third Reich as a war economy it was inevitable that the Four Year Plan was seen largely in such terms. As Kroll argued within such a framework the plan ensured that self-generating growth of the German economy based mainly on consumer goods was largely pushed to one side in favour of rearmament.[70] Although Goering's slogan of 'guns before butter' was not literally implemented this does not of course mean that the ratio of consumer expenditure within the GNP remained constant after 1936. On the contrary, Guillebaud and Erbe both demonstrated that it fell quite sharply in the last peacetime years of the National Socialist regime. This suggested to some observers that it would have been *technically* feasible to have resolved the problem of an overheated economy by 1938 by switching resources from rearmament to domestic consumption. The fact that this was not done did not in itself resolve the question for historians as to whether the government continued with the hectic tempo of rearmament as a deliberate preparation for war or whether by now the National Socialists had to a very real extent lost control of the economy. To rephrase the fundamental issue: did Hitler set the goal of autarky in order to pursue an expansionist policy, if necessary through war, or alternatively was he forced into war in 1939 as a result of economic pressures generated by the simultaneous pursuit of self-sufficiency and continued rearmament? The current debate about the *effectiveness* of the Four Year Plan can obviously help here by examining quite simply how efficiently the programme of 1936 prepared Germany for war within the framework of its own self-imposed timetable.

The question conceals a difficulty of definition within it, namely as to what sort of war Germany was supposed to be preparing for. Until recently there was broad agreement that the Four Year Plan could not be seen as an instrument gearing Germany to a long war of attrition. Could it however be explained by reference to planning for *Blitzkrieg*, as Milward above all has argued? Both issues have to be considered in the light of the growing empirical evidence about the state of the German economy on the eve of the Second World War. Mason pointed out that the Four Year Plan only reached its targets in six sectors out of 26, principally due to labour shortages.[71] The more general question about how far the programme made Germany independent of outside sources was the chief preoccupation of Petzina's standard work on the Four Year Plan, *Autarkiepolitik im Dritten Reich.* His general conclusion was that in this respect the plan was not wholly successful. Other research on the steel sector for instance has proved particularly informative. Jäger has shown that Germany's surprisingly powerful war effort after the outbreak of hostilities owed less to the Four Year Plan than to the additional resources available to the Third Reich through external conquest after 1939.[72] What is true of steel can be shown to have applied also to the continuing problem over the fuel requirements of Hitler's Germany. So acute was this that by September 1933 I. G. Farben were demanding the installation of an energy commission together with a four year scheme for fuel needs. The request was not met but in the following December the firm actually got a ten year contract from the government assuring it of fixed prices from 1936 onwards in return for guaranteed deliveries of synthetic benzine. In this connection it is probably not without significance that one of its directors, Karl Krauch, apparently played a considerable part in the preparation of Hitler's memorandum accompanying the Four Year Plan.[73] Even so, despite the concentration on this sector Germany was still by 1938-9 suffering from severe shortages of fuel.[74] Similar considerations can be applied to ammunition, as the words of General Thomas of the Wehrmacht economic planning staff have confirmed. Whereas the Army had asked for four months' reserve as the minimum requirement at the outbreak of any future war, in 1938 only six weeks' supply was in fact available.[75]

Clearly then the Four Year Plan has to be questioned, even as an adequate instrument for *Blitzkrieg*, since there is at least a possibility that far from this type of war being fought because it had been planned, it was rather the case that Hitler was obliged to resort to lightning war simply because the level of German preparation in 1939 permitted no alternative. In the final analysis a value judgement is involved here. It may well be that there is an element of hindsight involved in any account of the German economy between 1936 and 1939 which sees in it evidence for a planned and coordinated advance towards the predetermined goal of *Blitzkrieg*. For Mason on the other hand *Blitzkrieg* was possibly the expression of a desperate bid to shake off economic disaster, an enforced leap forward which only looked 'planned' in retrospect.[76] He has developed this theme elsewhere in a more general way by suggesting that the limitations imposed on the arms programme meant that it was not even sufficient for *Blitzkrieg*.[77] Much of this debate centres around the actual state of the German economy in 1938-9, which Mason describes as a crisis, and moreover so severe that along with the other international factors which he takes into account it affected the actual timing of the war. Hostile reactions to this thesis strongly suggest that at the heart of the controversy lies the question of definition, as we have argued above. Taylor in his reply to Mason's analysis, possibly because he was chiefly concerned with diplomatic relations, found no particular evidence to suggest that there was a crisis.[78] Yet when do economic difficulties constitute a crisis, to the extent that the entire economy may reasonably be described as no longer under the full control of the government? Two contemporary observers of differing political persuasions, Guillebaud and Lederer, both discussed ways in which the regime could avoid future economic difficulties, which at least suggested that serious problems existed; equally they seemed to feel that the political control of the economy was still possible. Significantly, however, the sort of adjustment which Lederer felt was likely to avoid possible inflationary dangers entailed a 'massive limitation of armaments expenditure'.[79] On one level then, to talk of a 'crisis' is to confirm that possible economic decisions to slow down rearmament were ideologically unacceptable to the regime, particularly in view of its internal dynamic, which Mason has always been keen to stress.

His argument does of course go beyond this, and suggests that Guillebaud seriously underrated the actual economic problems which Germany was facing at the time.[80] A recent study supported Mason insofar as it stressed that it was the general tempo of rearmament and the unrestrained demands of the various sections of the Wehrmacht in contributing to this pace which brought Germany's economic problems to crisis level. It emphasized the lack of clear political aims and coordination in the rearmament programme and pointed out that only when the cracks began to appear in 1936-7 was a minimum of overall direction introduced.[81] Interservice rivalry as a factor worsening the economic situation has now been well documented by Dülffer. As early as 1938 the Navy was asking German shipyards in the North to try and obtain skilled labour from South Germany and in the following year was trying itself to entice specialized workers from factories already engaged on arms contracts for the Luftwaffe and the Army.[82] The competition between the Armed Forces had been made more acute by Hitler's decision to give priority to the German Navy in January 1939 (the 'Z' Plan—see p.119).[83] More localized evidence is also slowly accumulating about the way in which the requirements of the Armed Forces were impinging on the German civilian economy as a whole. In Würtemberg by the spring of 1939 civil construction was almost at a standstill due to shortage of labour and raw materials.[84] The acute deficiency of the former is well illustrated by the fact that whereas in 1914 the German construction industry had been able to release half of its labour for armaments purposes, by 1938 the building sector itself was already short of workers.[85] So acute was lack of labour in general that by late 1939 some firms were actually turning down armaments contracts.[86] Nor was shortage of workers confined to the industrial and commercial sectors. From 1933 800,000 people left the land in Germany, according to the Minister of Agriculture himself in his speech in autumn 1938. So serious had the situation become that the plans to maximize indigenous food production in order to save imports were being threatened.

This had obvious implications for the goal of self-sufficiency and underlines the fact that Germany cannot be looked at in isolation as though it was not still to a very real extent involved in international trade. Forstmeier and Volkmann have demonstrated how an unexpected recovery in world commerce in 1937 actually assisted Germany in trying to accommodate rearmament within a national economy desperately short of foreign currency, by increasing exports. The American recession at the end of that year, however, narrowed Germany's room for manoeuvre yet again and by the middle of 1938 her foreign trade position had once more become shaky.[87] By the spring of 1939 the situation was such that a member of the Four Year Plan staff produced an evaluation of Germany's immediate economic future which can only be described as gloomy. In particular the problem of exports and of foreign currency shortage was becoming ever more acute.[88]

These problems can be seen in two ways, to revert for a moment to the implications of our earlier question about the relationship between economic policy and expansionism. Firstly, they can be regarded simply as the product of a painful attempt to produce an economy which would make Germany proof against blockade in any future possible war. Here the nightmare of 1918-19 clearly played an important part as it did in other aspects of National Socialist foreign policy. Never again must Germany be defeated in a war as a result of a breakdown of civilian morale at a time when her front line troops are victorious, which is how the National Socialists interpreted the 'November Revolution'. In many respects, and particularly if due weight is given to the Party's economic theorizing prior to 1933, with its clearly expressed neo-mercantilism, this is a perfectly comprehensible interpretation of the regime's economic policy. A high degree of self-sufficiency would obviously permit an independent foreign policy. What complicates the issue is that neo-mercantilism could also serve the ends of expansionism, although it would be an oversimplification to regard it as having been designed solely for that purpose. Such complexities exacerbated the economic difficulties evident during 1938-9.

To what extent, however, were the National Socialists leaders themselves aware of the true significance of Germany's economic problems and what effect did these have on the formulation of their foreign policy decisions? From what has been said already the power of decision making was bound to be circumscribed and there is indeed some evidence to suggest that there was an increasing perception among the leaders that this was the case. For example, as early as 14 October 1938, Goering said in a speech to Wehrmacht leaders: 'Now is the time for the private economy to show whether its existence is justified or not. If it fails I shall go over ruthlessly to state control.'[89] His remark would make little sense if it had been made in the context of a smoothly functioning economy since it clearly implies the need for possible change. By the following May he actually told the British Ambassador that the German armaments industry was so overheated that only two escape routes were possible: either the German economy became completely reintegrated into international trade through agreements or it could right itself through a very short war.[90] Moreover Dülffer suggests that Hitler's speeches to his generals show that he was aware of current difficulties although it is not clear whether he comprehended the full extent of these.[91] On 22 August 1939 he told Wehrmacht leaders that economically Germany could only carry on for a few years, which Goering could confirm. It was therefore necessary to act. In other quarters the same feeling seemed to prevail: General Fromm of Army Headquarters had already concluded that the immediate situation for the Wehrmacht was threatening to become unbearable, especially from 1940 onwards. This led him to ask whether any definite timetable for the commitment of the Armed Forces had in fact been worked out. His general conclusion was that now the Wehrmacht had been brought to a certain pitch either it would have to be used fairly quickly or the rearmaments programe would have to be cut.[92]

As Herbst stresses in his critique of Mason's work the latter's contribution to mapping out the limits within which the National Socialist government had to operate has been invaluable.[93] Is his account adequate however to explain why Germany went to war in 1939? Of course Mason is not saying that without what he maintains was a crisis there would have been no war, but he does argue that the economic situation was an important determinant in the timing and direction of hostilities. His formulation of the economic situation in Germany prior to the outbreak of war as both a peacetime and a wartime economy running hand in hand—indeed that an important dimension to the crisis was the simultaneous provision of both guns and butter—is more convincing than Erbe's characterization of the National Socialist system as a war economy in peacetime. More than a mere play on words is at issue here. Erbe's explanation suggests yet again that the sole object of the National Socialist economy was to prepare the country for war. Like the earlier historiographical stress in general on the 'planning for war' in the Germany economy Erbe's account assumes a greater degree of control of economic management than was possible in the conditions of the 1930s. Mason's assumption that social demands in Germany limited a further rearmament programme and his thesis about the crisis of the late 1930s takes due account of the complex prevailing economic difficulties in the Third Reich.

Certainly, National Socialist economic policy never excluded conflict as an option, to the extent that the Party was determined to place Germany in a position where it would not lose any future war, but we have now also established that the National Socialists did formulate their own economic policies prior to 1933 and that nothing in their management of the German economy after that date ran contrary to their principles. Overy's recent important biography of Goering confirms this, and he stresses that the regime never lost sight of the prospect of having to fight 'a large war with a variety of strategies'. At the same time he wholly denies that the National Socialists were being impelled towards war by a domestic/economic crisis. 'Economic pressure was all for postponing war in 1939, not for for speeding it up'. Yet precisely by admitting that Hitler was not ready for the sort of war coming in 1939, Overy still leaves himself with the task of explaining *why* Hitler took such major foreign policy risks in 1939, even if he actually wanted a localized conflict with Poland. In that sense, Overy cannot wholly dispel our feeling that there *was* crisis in Germany by 1938-9 and that the failure of the regime adequately to manage its neo-mercantilist economy was due to a combination of various factors, of which the most important was the attempt to meet both social demands and armaments needs at a time when Germany's room for manoeuvre was seriously limited due to the exigencies of the world economic situation.

Ultimately this chapter is concerned with the connection between economic and foreign policy and from the foregoing there remains a sense in which the war and the New order can still be seen as the outcome of a 'flight forward' to escape the crisis of economic management. War did not, however, become a substitute for economic policy, as Bullock argued, but was a logical outcome of neo-mercantilism. Germany's occupation policies were also more than simply the expression of a long standing continuity in the German capitalist economy, as Kühnl suggested, with the implication that capitalism rather than National Socialism called the tune.[94] Admittedly the New Order furthered economic policy by other than normal peacetime means but it did not stop there. It included the practice of racial ideology and even in economic terms can be represented in many respects as a departure from the liberal-capitalist order. All that we wish to state here is that the New Order and German capitalism were not necessarily synonymous. Military domination of the continent can also be seen as an attempt to realize the ideas nurtured within the movement of a *Grossraumwirtschaft,* which might not in itself have been ultimately beneficial to capitalism. Moreover the whole New Order needs to be seen in conjunction with the *Stufenplan* (p. 116). Autarky achieved through conquest of the Soviet Union would put Germany in a position to fight an inter-continental war.[95] As the German Foreign Office cabled to its embassy in Tokyo on 25 August 1941, the subjection of the Ukraine would solve Germany's food problem for all time.[96] The defeat of the Soviet Union offered the additional advantage that it eliminated her as an economic rival in the Balkans.[97] There is no doubt either that on the other side of Europe the capture of the raw materials which the French had stockpiled for their own war effort substantially assisted Germany to overcome its own shortages.[98] German conquests therefore eased many of the problems of economic management and facilitated the prolongation of the conflict, thus making up for the shortcomings of the Four Year Plan.[99]

Short term problems undoubtedly arose—not least in actually feeding the populations now under German rule[100]—but as elsewhere it should not be forgotten that Germany did not plan for defeat. Research on the methods by which the National Socialists actually organized the European economy during the war has revealed in general a lack of coordination leading to an inability to exploit European resources efficiently. This is an interesting addition to our knowledge of National Socialist polyocracy (Chapter 3) and of the way in which racial ideology frequently collided with pragmatism.[101] It would however be dangerous to draw from this the facile conclusion that the regime's economic policy was merely a stumbling from one make-shift measure to another. The fact is that winning the war had to take priority over planning for the post war era.[102] The economic management of the New order was no more smooth running than it had been in the Third Reich but the prospect beckoned, following victory, of a high living standard for Germans at the expense above all of East Europeans. Therefore the absence of a unified apparatus for the exploitation of the New Order is not in itself particularly significant and cannot be taken as proof of economic illiteracy.[103]

Indeed the economic reorganization of Europe continued also to reflect the durability of National Socialist attempts to bring into being a viable alternative both to centralized state planning, as under Marxism, and to the liberal capitalist order which they had seen collapse in 1929; an order which they also disliked on racial grounds because it rested on unregulated international trade and therefore unregulated human contacts between racially different peoples. The New Order and National Socialist economic policy in general represented not merely a departure from but a positive threat to the bourgeois capitalist system, as Neumann observed long ago in *Behemoth.* Since the principles which governed the New Order, governmental, racial and economic, have been considered in the two previous chapters (3 and 5) and in the earlier part of the present one, there is little to add on its historiography as such. There is no doubt that the National Socialist restructuring of the European economy was consistent with the Party's racialist ideology and with its neo-mercantilist principles. What is also important moreover is that it provides further valuable evidence to help us understand more fully the general connection in the Third Reich between capitalism on the one hand and the political executive on the other. The question as to which of these had the last word will be taken up in the final chapter.

# 7 National Socialism: the problem of a general interpretation

> 'Twenty years after the Third Reich the essence of fascism is still elusive.' *(Journal of Contemporary History,* 1966)

> 'But as so often happens in a historical debate where ideological motivation figures prominently there has been an inclination to overreact and the fashion in recent years has all too often been to deny the existence of common features or to regard them as purely accidental and of no significance.' *(Journal of Contemporary History,* 1976)

Whether to discuss National Socialism as a general problem or to analyse its individual aspects continues to be a controversial question amongst historians. This is at least partly due to the methodological difficulties involved. To talk about 'National Socialism' is to imply that there existed a uniform, coherent body of doctrine to which all National Socialists simultaneously subscribed. Most writers seem to agree that there were certain basic components to 'National Socialism', although of course they are not always of the same mind as to what those components were. Clearly there was initially almost a compulsion for scholars to find some theoretical basis for a movement which was apparently so irrational. Equally, since the very earliest stages of the National Socialist phenomenon explanations have inevitably become differentiated according to the political standpoint of the observer. There has of course also been a dramatic accumulation of the fruits of empirical research over the past 50 years but the triviality of some of this detailed work has in itself tended to push people almost in despair back towards general theorizing.

We are not of course denying the value of trying to formulate a general theory in order to bring us to an understanding of National Socialism. There comes a point in research into any historical problem where some kind of explanatory framework has to be imposed on the mass of empirical detail. There are certain reasons why the first people seriously to attempt this task belonged to the political Left, and their theorizing began with Hitler's rise to power. It was noticeable that conservative writers did not take National Socialism seriously as an ideology until much later. Undoubtedly one of the reasons for this was the reluctance of conservatives and liberals to face up to the main thrust of left wing explanations, namely that Hitler's movement was the product of the crisis of capitalism then occurring. Whatever the defects of this approach it had the merit of directing attention towards the importance of the socio-economic context of National Socialism, and indeed of fascism generally. Apart from producing serious investigations into Hitler's actual system, which yielded a great deal of social and economic data on how the Third Reich was actually being run, it raised the more fundamental question of the precise nature of the relationship between capitalism on the one hand and National Socialism on the other. We ought first therefore to remind ourselves of the main views on this relationship. On one side there is a Marxist group which maintains that a structural identity of monopoly capitalism and National Socialism existed. Such historians include D. Eichholtz, Czichon and Gossweiler. Although such views are strongly represented in East Germany it does not follow that all its adherents belong to that country. A second major thesis is provided by those such as Hallgarten, Schweitzer, Sohn-Rethel and Petzina, who accept that a connection existed between big business and National Socialism but who nonetheless maintain that the Third Reich was increasingly characterized by the primacy of politics, in that the political executive, whatever its initial relationship to big business, gradually became independent of it. Finally, there is that school of thought, chiefly among American and West German historians, which sets out to deny any systematic connections between capitalism and National Socialism and therefore seeks explanations of the rise of the Hitler movement in other factors; to this belong Gustav Stolper, Louis Lochner, Wilhelm Treue, H. A. Turner and G. Schulz.[1]

A good early example of the left wing analysis was provided by Robert Brady.[2] In his view the regime which the National Socialists proceeded to establish was by the very nature of the major interests which sponsored it, '*a dictatorship of monopoly capitalism. Its fascism is that of business enterprise organized on a monopoly basis, and in full command of all the military, police, legal and propaganda power of the state.'* Brady does not mean by this merely a formal dictatorship over economic affairs, but a defence of 'all the theories and practices of a class-ordered capitalist society', which to him had been under attack from the left.[3] The beauty of the 'crisis of capitalism' theory is that it kills two birds with one stone, since it can be used to explain both Hitler's accession to power and his subsequent policies, including that of war. In other words, as Neumann put it, only a war of imperialist aggression could in the long run solve 'the discrepancy between the potentialities of Germany's industrial apparatus and the actuality that existed and continues to exist.'[4] For these theorists the object of German foreign policy was primarily to secure new markets for German goods, as the normal operations of the capitalist system had simply failed to do this. It would be a mistake, however, to assume that all early left wing writers produced identical explanations even within the framework of this general interpretation. Neumann recognized more clearly than Brady that the National Socialist dictatorship embraced at least four distinct ruling groups: 'Fascism is the dictatorship of the fascists (NSDAP), the bureaucracy, the army and big business, the dictatorship over the whole of the people for complete organization of the nation for imperialist war.'[5] Despite Neumann's recognition that these groups did not necessarily possess an absolute identity of interest many left wing contemporaries would not even concede that. For Horkheimer, for example, fascism was quite simply the most modern *form* of monopoly capitalism.[6]

Horkheimer's dictum, 'He who desires not to talk about capitalism should remain silent on fascism', has served as a starting point for the non-orthodox Marxist theories which began to appear in West Germany in the mid-1960s. These are descended from the early 1930s theorists, or it might be more accurate to say are an offshoot of these. The main stem continues to flourish in East Germany, where the attempt to explain National Socialism wholly in terms of the crisis of capitalism finds its purest form (Stamokap), as may be illustrated by the following comment on German capitalists in the Hitler era: 'Krauch, Krupp, Schmitz and Zaggen commanded no armies, planned no military operations, ran no concentration camps and murdered nobody, but they produced war, murder, violence and oppression.' It is possible to trace an almost continuous line here from Lenin's maxim that free competition in the business world produces bourgeois democracy, whereas the monopoly stage of capitalism leads to political reaction.[7] The argument was continued by the Comintern Congress resolution of 1928 and that of 1933, where fascism was represented as the most reactionary and chauvinistic element of monopoly capitalism; a theme which the future leader of the GDR, Ulbricht, took up in his book in 1945, where facism was still a mere manifestation of capitalism.[8]

The inevitable conflict about interpreting Germany's recent past which flows from the clash between the 'New Left' in West Germany and the DDR historians is further complicated by the fact that the orthodox Left in the Federal Republic necessarily had to come to terms after 1945 with its own part in the failure to prevent the rise of National Socialism. A classic example was afforded by Richard Loewenthal's 1946 work, *Jenseits des Kapitalismus,* written under the name of Paul Sering. No doubt such considerations give support to Kühnl's assertion that it is within the two Germanies above all that the theoretical discussions about National Socialism rage most vehemently today.[9] The fact that the dispute is not simply about the doctrinal purity of Marxist explication but reflects also the present day rivalry between the FDR and GDR is best illustrated by a quotation from a recent work on the *Reichsnährstand:* 'The agrarian policy of the present day government in Bonn is increasingly adopting the methods of the fascist *RNS*'. Whilst admitting that there were certain subtle differences the article goes on to assert that there is an essential similarity between the agricultural policies of the Third Reich and Bonn, in that both seek to subordinate the interests of agriculture and especially of the peasantry to the expansionist needs of armament monopolies.[10] This attitude is also exemplified in Lärmer's statement that West German historians are avoiding a real confrontation with the history of fascism in Germany because their own society has a similar foundation.[11]

Despite these examples and however blunt Stamokap theory sometimes seems to be as a conceptual instrument, there is no denying that its practitioners have significantly increased our stock of empirical information on the Third Reich. Nor is it accurate or fair to suggest that the analysis is always lacking in refinement; East German historians recognize very well, for example, the nature and significance of the differences of opinion inside the ruling cliques of the Third Reich, as witness the introduction to a recent collection of documents on German history published in East Berlin.[12] It remains true, however, to say that as an explanatory model for Hitler's Germany Stamopkap theories are too schematic and over-simplified. Their persistence in East Germany is almost certainly due to the intra-German rivalry on the ideological plane.

A rather more sophisticated approach to explaining National Socialism has become increasingly popular with western non-orthodox Marxists, and may be subsumed under the general heading of 'Bonapartism', a concept touched on earlier in this book.[13] Like so many theories of the Third Reich its origins predate Hitler's arrival in power. Indeed as early as 1871 Marx, in his *Civil War in France,* had written of Bonapartism, exemplified in the career of Napoleon III, as a necessary stage of historical development; according to him it was 'The only possible form of government at a time when the bourgeoisie had already lost its capacity to rule the nation and the working class had not yet acquired that capacity.'[14] In view of the source of this definition it is not surprising that after the First World War it should have come to serve the Left as a way of explaining fascism in general, or National Socialism in particular, as these phenomena became manifest. After all, in Germany after March 1930 bourgeois government did break down, partly at least owing to the withdrawal of the SPD from government, which made even less likely any satisfactory resolution of the political and economic crisis. In other words the first half of Marx's statement appeared literally to come true. As to the second part, the fratricidal strife between the SPD and the KPD meant that the working class could not govern either. In 1933 the latter day Louis Napoleon was therefore able to come to power in the kind of vacuum that Marx had predicted.

The Bonapartist model of explanation was further developed by August Thalheimer, who had been thrown out of the KPD in 1928 precisely because his views on the rise of fascism in Germany differed from those held in the then Stalinist KPD. At the beginning of 1930 in *Gegen den Strom,* a journal in opposition to the official communist line, he began to develop the idea of Bonapartism as a state of affairs where the political executive became autonomous within the existing capitalist order. In other words Thalheimer was dissatisfied with the Stalinist KPD view that there was an identity between capitalism and National Socialism. As he saw it the bourgeoisie at a time of crisis were prepared to forego their political power and their normal individual privileges in order to preserve the endangered social and economic order.[15] Trotsky did not agree with

Thalheimer's analysis. As Dülfer puts it: 'Bonapartism becomes in his (Trotsky's) interpretation a warning signal of the approach of fascism'.[16] According to Trotsky therefore the counterpart of Napoleon III was General von Schleicher and not Hitler himself.

After Hitler's accession to power the Bonapartist theory tended to get submerged beneath the weight of the official Stalinist line, as exemplified in the 1933 Comintern definition of fascism already cited. In retrospect, however, it is clear that Thalheimer's insights were never entirely lost and traces of them can clearly be seen in Franz Neumann's *Behemoth.* In particular he wished to stress that in the long run the new political order which Hitler had erected, far from being identical to the capitalist system, was actually developing in such a way that in the long run it would have endangered it. Although this is not an explicit reference to Thalheimer it suggests that Neumann was prepared to entertain the idea of an increasingly autonomous political executive. Since he effectively denies the complete identity of National Socialism and capitalism his work has not been accepted in the GDR. In West Germany by the middle of the 1960s, however, interest was reawakening in the original Thalheimer concept of Bonapartism. It is interesting to note that Thalheimer's original 1930 text was reprinted for the first time in 1967,[17] in connection with the revival of neo-Marxism among younger West German historians. In more recent years the Bonapartist thesis has come to be associated above all with T. W. Mason and with the West German historian, A. Kuhn. Mason's version of the autonomous political executive is encapsulated in his phrase 'the primacy of politics', that is to say, over economics. His work may be said to have been seminal in this respect and has certainly fuelled controversy over the validity of Bonapartism as an explanatory tool, which Stamokap historians naturally wish to deny.[18] Kuhn has taken the debate somewhat further in his thesis that foreign policy in the Third Reich was determined by an independent political executive.[19]

At first sight Saage's statement that the Bonapartist theory is the best instrument for understanding Hitler's Germany is plausible. Bonapartism seems to him the correct designation of what he considers the Third Reich actually to have been, namely 'The social expression of an alliance of two forces of society (capitalism and Party leadership) whose interests were by no means homogeneous but which came closer to one another in the context of total social development.'[20] An important dimension of the debate concerns the precise time at which the political executive made itself 'independent'. A strong case has now been built not only by Mason but by Petzina and Schweitzer, to show that the turning point in this respect was 1936 . It was Schweitzer's study of big business in the Third Reich which although not Marxist in tone nonetheless produced valuable evidence to underpin the Bonapartist theory, as understood and propagated by Mason.[21] In his appraisal of Mason's work Winkler is adamant that his concept of the primacy of politics after 1936 has never satisfactorily been rebutted.[22] The Bonapartist line of explanation is far more satisfactory than the Stamokap model in accounting for Hitler's 'Scorched earth' order of March 1945, the directive demanding the destruction of Germany's industrial infrastructure in order to prevent it falling into the hands of the oncoming allies. This was hardly in the interest of the industrialists round Speer who naturally wished to survive the fall of fascism in order to carry on with their business afterwards.[23] If Hitler really was nothing more than the agent of big business, as East German historians insist, then how could this conflict ever have arisen? Further proof of the greater explanatory power of Bonapartism as compared with the agent theory is provided by the attitude of the official German big business association (RGI) in their report on future political and economic collaboration with France, which they issued in May 1941. The RGI pointed out that it was difficult to know precisely what shape postwar cooperation would have, since it would be determined largely by a peace treaty between the two countries, the terms of which were of course at that time unknown to them.[24] This means quite simply that the leaders of German industry were waiting for a decision by the political executive before they could finalize their own plans.[25]

To summarize at this point, there are essentially two kinds of Marxist explanation of National Socialism. The first of these holds that political power in the Third Reich was the expression of, and inseparable from, monopoly capitalism, a view which prevails in the GDR. A development of this is the Bonapartist theory, which sees in Hitler's Germany a relative and growing independence of the political executive from the capitalist order. This latter theory covers a range of views from those concerned with the number and composition of ruling groups within the Third Reich to those preoccupied with the precise division of responsibility between the political and economic sectors and with emphasizing the primacy of politics. The implication here is that ultimately the political leadership could act against the interests of capitalism and the bourgeois order.[26] Useful as the latter model is for illuminating the mechanics of government and administration in the Third Reich—as are Marxist theories in general—there are certain flaws. Hanisch is probably correct in his statement that no-one has been able to compare with Marxists in the scope of their theories about National Socialism, but that there are nonetheless certain pertinent questions which still have to be put to them.[27] Included among his questions are: a need to explain why fascism did not break through in the most developed capitalist countries, what interest capital could have in a total war which destroyed its own means of production, why if the petit bourgeoisie was threatened by capitalism it associated itself with an ideology which was supposed to be produced by a Party which was the agent of capitalism. Finally, how do Marxists explain the total collapse of organized labour in Germany in 1933?

Although Hanisch here opens up an interesting field of discussion, Marxists might well succeed in providing a perfectly satisfactory answer to the last two of these questions. The petite bourgeoisie associated itself with National Socialism because it failed to understand that the apparently anti-capitalist ethos expressed in some Party circles prior to 1933 did not guarantee that the lower middle classes would be protected against big business once the Party came to power. As to the working class collapse in 1933, Marxists would easily explain this by reference to the regime's use of terror, coupled with nationalist propaganda for the masses aimed at secondary integration. This still leaves open the first two questions formulated by Hanisch but it seems self-evident, as regards the second, that no capitalist could conceivably have any interest in destroying his own means of production.

Another obvious question, which Hanisch for some reason does not raise, concerns the Party's ideology. Marxism fails to explain the origins and significance of the basic ideology of Social Darwinism and race, perhaps because this is a dimension of the human mind which Marxism is not equipped to elucidate, since no positivistic, quasi-scientific ideas system could possibly do so. A Marxist like Mason has in fact realised the force of such arguments by pointing to the economic irrationality of the Holocaust, which as we know diverted transport away from the front line during the military campaign against the Soviet Union, sent skilled metal workers to the gas chamber and annihilated the economically valuable artisan class in White Russia.[28] What serious studies we do have of National Socialist ideology confirm that its origins and development have to be set firmly in the context of German history since the nineteenth century, but however much it may be explained by a national sense of failure, a great deal of its ethos still defies rational explanation. The point has been made by W. Abel that German romanticism (of which National Socialism was a latter day example) has always preferred the organic to the rational. Since this is in itself an emotional commitment, particularly in the case of National Socialism which often functioned as a substitute religion, it falls almost by definition outside the bounds of logical analysis. Marxism remains unable to explain why large sectors of the population of any country, including the working classes, should place devotion to their country and a spirit of nationalism above their own apparent class interests.

In addition, as Grebing has argued, Marxists have developed what she feels to be two incompatible historiographical trends. On the one hand they have attempted to construct general theories about facism to which their explanations of National Socialism are assimilated, but which are felt to have a more universal application. On the other, they frequently write about Germany as a special case, in that the structure of her industry and the continuing political influence of the traditional alliance between landowners and heavy industrialists directly facilitated Hitler's rise to power. The latter is an obvious attempt to get round the central weakness of the Marxist historiography of fascism, namely why it failed to come to power in other advanced capitalist societies, particularly Britain and America.[29] As Kühnl himself is aware, capitalism can produce other forms of government, making it difficult to identify it with fascism.[30]

There are of course a number of historians who either deny that any systematic connection between National Socialism and capitalism existed, or who feel as in the case of Turner that there is not yet sufficient empirical knowledge available about a possible relationship between the two to enable us to formulate a general model which assumes such a link.[31] This is not to say that all such historians attempting to explain National Socialism have abandoned interest in the historical development of German capitalism. Indeed they are extremely concerned with how it evolved in the nineteenth century and above all with both the speed and lateness of Germany's transition from an agrarian to an urbanized-industrialized society.

Thus Germany forms an important element in Barrington Moore's general theory about the transition from feudalism to industrialization in differing societies, and in particular how this has determined their various routes to modernization.[32] Whereas Britain and France took the first route, namely through parliamentary democracy, and at the other extreme the Soviet Union and China followed the third path, Germany pursued the second way. It was more advanced than pre-communist Russia but at the same time failed to modify its authoritarian structure. The incomplete form of democracy represented by the Second Reich under the Bismarckian constitution and later during the period of the Weimar Republic failed to survive the acute economic socio-political crisis of the early twentieth century. The rise of National Socialism was thus not necessarily connected with the structure of capitalism as such, but rather with the strains produced by the uneasy balance between the forces of industrialization and the surviving remanants of pre-industrial society. As Winkler puts it in another context, National Socialism had at least as much to do with feudalism as it did with capitalism, at least in its origins if not in its effects, which as we suggested in Chapter 4 may ultimately have helped to modernize German society. Barrington Moore is not of course alone in having attempted to formulate a theory linking the social effects of industrialization to political extremism. Lipsett's work also argued that there are three forms of political extremism which arise as a result of the industrialization process; the third of these, right wing extremism, flourishes where the traditional right holds on to power in societies which are less politically developed than for example Britain or America.[33] Germany's problem of being a kind of halfway house in terms of political and economic development—that is more advanced than Eastern Europe but behind the West—was compounded by its similarly intermediate geographical position, in the middle of Europe. This combination of factors has been seen as a major source of German phobias about encirclement and long-term survival as a major power. Thus for Kühnl German imperialism, unlike the British and French varieties, eventually turned to fascism both because Germany was a late industrial developer and because the non-European world had already been divided up amongst the older imperial powers by the time it became united.[34]

The whole concept of Germany as a late developer, or to refer to the title of Plessner's book, *Die verspätete Nation*, is linked with the much canvassed idea that Germany's difficulties as a latecomer were a consequence of its failure to undergo the sort of revolution which preceded industrial development in Britain and France. This has become a central idea for many historians, including Marxists, who have coined the phrase the 'missing bourgeois revolution' to account for Germany's later problems. This is how Laski arrived at his idea of Germany as an eighteenth century state with modern technology. According to him 'The biggest event in its history during the nineteenth and twentieth centuries was the revolution which failed to occur.'[36] Meinck is one of the many who continue this tradition of historical explanation when he writes: 'The bourgeoisie disappeared from German history as a revolutionary force after the failed revolution of 1848 and abandoned its interest in the exercise of sole power in favour of an alliance with the aristocracy. From then on it just assured its own economic power.'[37] According to the late development school of explanation the fragility of German society, caused by its failure to absorb the spirit as well as the letter of liberalism, meant that a longstanding anti-Western tradition made it especially vulnerable to the kind of political instability which would have been engendered in any society by the Depression. This produced a new, emotionally laden anti-capitalism and anti-rationalism which materially assisted the rise of National Socialism.[38]

The anti-capitalist emphasis in this explanatory model tends to reinforce the criticism frequently made of Marxist explanations, that they have always been prone to underestimate the importance and significance of the support given to Hitler by the lower middle classes. Moreover, as Winkler has argued, big entrepreneurs in general tended to remain sceptical about the political aims of the National Socialists longer than did the master artisans.[39] The behaviour of these groups cannot be explained by any Marxist reference to a particular crisis of capitalism, but must be related to the process of industrialization over a much longer period. Such an approach sees the supporters of National Socialism, or indeed of fascism, as losers in the process of modernisation. This would seem to imply that the end of the *Kaiserreich* in October 1918, and simultaneously what was perceived as the end of the old order, was more significant for certain sections of the German community than was the Great Depression from 1929 onwards. It has been strongly urged that their original belief in the Empire was at least partly due to the direct protection which it had afforded them against a developing industrialization.[40] As Childers puts it, 'The consistency displayed by the (statistic) coefficients from 1924 to 1932 strongly suggests that Nazi support within the Old Middle Class was not the product of transient economic distress, but the result of congenital(sic) dissatisfaction with long-term trends of the German economy.'[41] As was suggested earlier, this explanation also throws light on the class basis of National Socialism in general.

Although the concept of the 'losers' forms part of the discussion of theories concerning economic forces, it also provides a bridge to explanations based on wider sociological and psychological factors. In this connection it is important to remember that it is not really 'classes' which lose so much as individuals. Merkl's investigation of Nazi supporters suggests that a large number of them were drawn from the ranks of the dissatisfied and disgruntled, which echoes S. Neumann's earlier contemporary analysis.[42] Adolf Hitler—a major non-achiever before 1926—provided a classic picture of frustration typical of so many Germans after defeat and revolution in 1918. A summary of losers would in fact suggest three broad groupings. Firstly, the old middle classes, who increasingly by about 1928 began to perceive in National Socialism an antidote to the long-term development of capitalism which threatened their own socio-economic base. Secondly, those members of the new middle classes, for example both white and blue collar workers, converted to the category of losers overnight during the economic crisis. Thirdly, there were the Merkl type of losers, those who failed to fit themselves into existing society, the permanently disgruntled and discontented. These three streams merged from about 1928 onwards to form a substantial part of the National Socialist flood. Alternatively, the losers have been seen in a wider framework than the merely socio-economic, in the sense that some theories of National Socialism have interpreted it as a flight from rationality in itself, a tendency which would be clearly accentuated by the presence within its ranks of those dissatisfied groups just described. Erich Fromm for example has posed the thesis that reversion to an authoritarian form of government, as exemplified by National Socialism, is the system of mass reluctance to assume political responsibility.[43] Many German historians since 1945 have been particularly interested in finding the origins of this tendency in the Bismarckian-Wilhelminian system of government, which simultaneously increased the number of middle class people in Germany through industrial development and impeded the development of parliamentary democracy. Such a theory, with the suggestion that Germany took a 'wrong turning' in 1871, reinforces the idea that the tame submission to Hitler in 1933 had definite historical roots.

This opens the door to explanations of National Socialism which are more purely psychological in nature. To what extent was the Hitler movement a reaction against the positivism of the nineteenth century, where science was always taken as the model for explication, sometimes to the point where other dimensions of the human spirit are ignored? Anyone analysing National Socialism has to take particular account of beliefs about the strength of the human will. After all, according to Maser, Schopenhauer's book *Die Welt als Wille und Vorstellung* was the only major philosophical work with which Hitler was apparently conversant, even to the extent that he claimed he had carried it with him in the trenches of the First World War.[44] As Trevor-Roper once wrote: 'To him (Hitler), reality, especially political reality, was not a fact but an artefact; it was made by the human mind, the human will.'[45] Goebbels apparently subscribed to similar beliefs, which suggests that this kind of approach was widespread enough to enable us to include it as one of the major aspects of the National Socialist approach to life. In his novel, *Michael,* published in 1929, he suggested that '*what* we believe is not as important as the fact that we *do* believe'.[46] This is not to say, as Mosse wishes to suggest, that fascism was an attitude rather than a theory.[47] The fact that National Socialism was frequently anti-rationalist and anti-positivist does not preclude the fact that in some respects it was governed by deliberate and reasoned choice. The fact that National Socialists were emotionally anti-capitalist and anti-liberal did not automatically preclude them from developing tenaciously held intellectual criticisms, not only of liberal capitalism but also of Marxism, as we have seen in Chapter 6.

The rational aspects of National Socialism do not of course provide an adequate explanation of the movement's internal dynamism. Might it be the case for instance, that to the countless ex-servicemen in the ranks of the Party National Socialism was essentially a chance to recreate under other conditions the wartime cameraderie of the trenches, a comradeship which both parliamentary democracy—with its party system—and the class struggle orientated ideology of Marxism had destroyed since 1918? Certainly, for whatever reason, the tasks which the government of the Third Reich set before the German people were very often framed in simplistic military language. Germany's jobless were the target for the 'battle for employment', its food problems were to be solved by the 'battle for production' on the land. No doubt this was partly due to the presence of so many ex-servicemen but it also reflected more generally an attitude towards life based on Social Darwinism and the strength of the human will. An interesting example of Hitler's application of the latter was the appointment of Goering as commissioner for the Four Year Plan, in spite of his publicly admitted ignorance of economic affairs. All technical obstacles could be overcome by the exercise of faith and determination.

However varied all these general explanations of National Socialism may have been they can still be classified according to distinct periods, as becomes apparent from a brief chronological survey. This is not to say that the explicatory models considered above have been mutually exclusive, nor is it necessarily the case that any one type has dominated to the exclusion of all others at any particular period of time. Nonetheless, broadly speaking the 1930s saw a strong emphasis on the 'German fascism' model of National Socialism. Due to the intellectual dominance of the Left at that time this interpretation was frequently linked to the 'crisis of capitalism' theory, where all emanations of fascism were seen as a political epiphenomenon developing from the structure of bourgeois society as such. The idea of a 'fascist era' is not, however, confined to left wing writers. There is now a school of thought which seeks to place National Socialism in a broad horizontal context by stressing the importance of the First World War and of the Russian Revolution in facilitating the downfall of parliamentary democracy in Europe as a whole between the wars.[48] Such historians are in effect attempting to preserve and refurbish the concept of 'fascism' as a general explanation, but without linking it exclusively to the crisis, although they recognize the great importance and political significance of economic depression in the interwar years. One major advantage of assimilating National Socialism to fascism in general, and of seeing it in terms of an 'epoch', is that it enable us to underline the similarities between Italian fascism and the Third Reich which remain important despite key differences. The many points of resemblance include the social composition of Mussolini's Party and the NSDAP, the charismatic leader, the popular base, the use of terror and the neo-imperialist expansionism.[49] Moreover such an explanatory framework gives due weight to the strength of the reaction in Europe unleashed by the Russian Revolution. In other words, as Goebbels recognized in the 1920s, the need for National Socialism was made more urgent by the arrival in power in Moscow of international Marxism, with its threat to property relations. As he said in an open letter at the time: 'Socialism is the ideology of the future. It can only be carried out inside the national state.'[50]

Another school of historical explanation refuses to recognize any significant distinctions between authoritarian regimes of the Left or of the Right. As early as November 1929 *The Times* in an article on non-parliamentary government was talking of a current reaction in favour of a totalitarian or unitary state, whether fascist or communist.[51] Even then the idea was not wholly new since in the early 1920s Francesco Nitti was comparing Bolshevism to fascism on the grounds that they were both opposed to freedom and the principles of liberalism.[52] In view of this evidence the onset of the Cold War has to be seen as reviving such an approach rather than initiating it, as conservatives and liberals began to equate National Socialist Germany with the Soviet Union under Stalin and to make much play with the concept of totalitarianism. In this period political scientists tended to make the running rather than historians and many superficial similarities between the methods of the Third Reich and Stalinist Russia were stressed, whilst the 'isms' in totalitarianism, as Groth puts it, were not sufficiently critically examined.[53]

A representative model for a comparative study was produced by Friedrich, based on what he assumed to be the fundamentals common to all totalitarian systems. These were: the use of ideology, the existence of a mass party, a system of terror, the manipulation of public opinion, control over military power, and central supervision and direction of the entire economy inside the framework of the primacy of politics.[54] In other words such explanations were dominated about all by a concentration on the purely political factors of National Socialism, to the neglect of economic and social aspects. How much this study came under the shadow of that particular phase of the ideological conflict between East and West can be illustrated from the words of an education ministers' conference in West Germany in 1962: 'The confrontation with totalitarianism is one of the essential tasks in the political education of our youth. All teachers are therefore obliged to familiarize children with the main features of Bolshevism and National Socialism as the most important totalitarian systems of the twentieth century.[55] The development of detente in the early 1960s helped to break down the rigidity of this approach, although judging from a 1973 entry in a popular West German encyclopedia the notion of explaining National Socialist Germany, at least to some extent, by comparing it with the Soviet Union, still lingered on.[56] Now that the model is, however, in general decline as historians continue to evaluate the economic and social structures of Germany under Hitler as it actually existed, we can see in retrospect how pertinent was Schoenbaum's description of the concept of 'totalitarianiasm' as a 'scholarly formulation of our ignorance.'[57]

Whether this is accepted or not, the fact remains that the past decade has witnessed a tremendous outpouring of research into the structure of National Socialist government and society, concerned with such issues as whether it was a centralised dictatorship or a polyocracy, which has gone a long way towards remedying the ignorance to which Schoenbaum referred. Implicit in much of this research is the attempt to explain National Socialism *sui generis* rather than to rely on any general theory which seeks to account for it through comparison with some other dictatorship. In this respect the purest form of latter day investigation is what the Germans themselves call *Alltagsgeschichte,* which broadly speaking means the history of everyday life. Again, as in other areas of research on the Third Reich, this 'new' approach has recognizeable antecedents, which go back at least as far as 1932 when Ernst Ottwald, a member of the Communist Party, produced the idea of the 'unknown National Socialist'. What he means by this was probably best summarized in his maxim that 'Wherever people cease openly to talk about National Socialism, there its real meaning and menace begins'.[58] His main concern was to uncover the connections between the local NSDAP and the local bourgeoisie, especially officials. It was its tacit acceptance by the latter which he saw as the true danger of National Socialism, since this threatened to colour and pervade every aspect of daily life and administration, without at the same time presenting any clearly visible target for its opponents.

The rediscovery of this type of investigation, concentrating on daily life at micro-level, was to a very considerable extent a result of West German teachers' need to explain to their pupils how the Third Reich had come about. This coincided with the attempt by practising historians to retreat somewhat from pervasive general theories, the formulation and discussion of which, especially in West Germany, was becoming a fascinating but sterile debate. Since this tendency was especially noticeable on the 'New Left' it is ironic that one of the progenitors of *Alltagsgeschichte* should himself have been a communist. A clear statement of what the new *Alltagsgeschichte* should be is contained in Broszat's introduction to the massive recent study of Bavaria under Hitler, the most significant so far of a series of investigations carried out and still being carried out in this line.[59] According to this, studies of daily life should avoid seeing socio-political phenomena solely in terms of theory, and should concentrate instead on actual concrete events and on relating these experiences to the individual in a flexible manner, but without degenerating to the level of a 'mere' accumulation of facts.

Regrettably, until now the results of such investigations tend to show how difficult it is to fulfil Broszat's own demanding criteria. As Hennig has pointed out, local and regional studies of this type have so far tended to be both eclectic in the accumulation of fact and descriptive rather than analytic in tone.[60] It is at least questionable whether the information that the chief concern of peasants in a rather poor rural area was the struggle for daily bread, and that this was what made them indifferent to politics, really explains anything new about National Socialism. In addition, there can be no guarantee that were such exhaustive research to be duplicated in every country district in Germany it would yield anything more than a mass of similar facts. Welcome as any attempt is to redress an undue concentration on abstract speculation, by the New Left in particular, it is difficult at the moment to see where *Alltagsgeschichte* is leading us. What was intended to some extent as a retreat from high theory seems somewhat predictably to be leading to an amassing of facts backed up by very little conceptualization.

If we now finally look back at the changing image of the Third Reich from its inception to the present day it is apparent that various explanatory models have always coexisted. Probably the most consistent of these has centred around the notion of the crisis of capitalism, which finds its most orthodox expression today in the Eastern block, with its assumption of an identity between monopoly capitalism and National Socialist dictatorship. The Bonapartist model, which stresses the growing autonomy of the political executive from 1936 onwards, offers a serious qualification of the orthodox Marxist model. On the whole it seems to us to have a great deal more value in explaining National Socialism, although like the crisis of capitalism theory in general, it does have two obvious weaknesses. It fails to explain why National Socialism or some similar system did not achieve power in countries such as Britain and France and secondly it totally neglects the racial ideology of the NSDAP. By contrast, the theory which develops the concept of Germany as a late developer does take these points into account. Above all it places Hitler and the NSDAP in the context of recent history as a whole. That is to say that it shows how the speed and lateness of German industrialization helped to determine both the structure of German capitalism and the development of political attitudes. This provided the crucial framework within which the movement grew, aided by the lost war and the Depression. At most, the immediate crisis of capitalism in the late 1920s accelerated the whole process. The late developer theory has the merit of demonstrating that there was little in National Socialist or economic ideology which was *wholly* original. In addition, unlike Germanophobe explanations particularly during the War and immediate postwar period, it makes Hitler perfectly comprehensible as a man of the twentieth century rather than a latter day Attila the Hun. It confines itself to the period of German industrialization, but by showing that we need to go back that far it also discredits attempts to demonize Hitler by presenting him out of context. As to the totalitarian theory which also overstresses the importance of Hitler as a charismatic leader—this really belongs to an earlier era, when the existing ideological conflicts between East and West heavily coloured historical investigation of the Third Reich, and to a very real extent distorted it.

These three explanatory models—fascism (whether Marxist or otherwise), totalitarianism, the late developer theory (that is, the view of National Socialism as *sui generis*)—which are by no means mutually exclusive, have been accompanied by a truly massive accumulation of empirical fact about the Third Reich. The effect of this has been to knock out the totalitarian theory without, apparently, significantly altering the balance between the other two. And yet it does seem to us that in the last decade, notwithstanding the general proliferation of studies in the mid-1970s, often produced by the New Left, the balance has begun to shift perceptibly towards the late developer model. The empirical findings themselves have put us in a better position to understand what actually happened inside the Third Reich, which can in turn be related more accurately to recent German history. It would be pleasant to assume that *Alltagsgeschichte* will reinforce this trend but there is always a danger that it might confuse the issue by its frequent concentration on trivial details of daily life—important though these may have been to the individuals they would in many cases not have been different under any other political system, and they cannot automatically tell us anything particular about National Socialism. We are certainly not denying the value of detailed micro-investigations as such, so much as presenting the case for a breathing space to absorb the mass of data which now exists. Here we have tried to further such an aim by critically assessing the main lines of explanation and investigation which have developed over the past 50 years, in the endeavour to make National Socialism comprehensible.

# Notes

**List of abbreviations used in Notes and Bibliography**

AHR American Historical Review
APSR Amercian Political Science Review
ASG Archiv für Sozialgeschichte
CEH Central European History
ESR European Studies Review
G&G Geschichte und Gesellschaft
GWU Geschichte in Wissenschaft und Unterricht
HJ Historical Journal
HZ Historische Zeitschrift
JBW Jahrbuch für Wirtschaftsgeschichte
JCH Journal of Contemporary History
JMH Journal of Modern History
NPL Neue Politische Literatur
PP Past and Present
PSQ Political Science Quarterly
PVS Politische Vierteljahrsschrift
RA Revue d'Allemagne
RGM Revue de la II Guerre Mondiale
SH Social History
SJP Sozialwissenschaftliches Jahrbuch für Politik.
VJH Vierteljahrssheft für Zeitgeschichte
VSW Vierteljahrasschrift für Sozial und Wirtschaftsgeschichte
ZAG Zeitschrift für Agrargeschichte und Agrarsoziologie
ZG Zeitgeschichte
ZGW Zeitschrift für Geschichtswissenschaft
ZP Zeitschrift für Politik

**Chapter 1**

1 K. Feiling, *The life of Neville Chamberlain,* Macmillan, 1946, p.366.
2 K. Heiden, *'Hitlers Kometenbahn; Vossische Zeitung,* 1932. Copy in regional archives Baden-Württemberg, E.131./148-9.

3 S. Roberts, *The house that Hitler built,* Methuen, 1937.
4 R. Brady, *The spirit and structure of German fascism,* Left Book Club, 1937.
5 H. Trevor-Roper, *The last days of Hitler,* Pan Books, 1968, p.54.
6 A. Bullock, *Hitler: A study in tyranny,* Odhams, 1960.
7 ibid., p.345.
8 Cf. R. Kühnl, 'Neuere Ergebnisse und Tendenzen in der Faschismusforschung', *PVS,* II, 1980, p.133.
9 P. W. Fabry, *Mutmassungen über Hitler. Urteile von Zeitgenossen,* Droste, Düsseldorf, 1969, p.9.
10 E. Calic, *Ohne Maske,* Societätsverlag, Frankfurt, 1968.
11 R. Kühnl, op.cit., p.134.
12 See ibid., pp.128, 134.
13 W, Horn, 'Zur Geschichte und Struktur des Nationalsozialismus und der NSDAP', *NPL,* 1973, pp.194-5.
14 K. Hildebrand, 'Nationalsozialismus ohne Hitler?', *GWU,* no.5, 1980, p.292.
15 K. D. Bracher, 'The role of Hitler', in W. Lacqueur (ed.), *Fascism, A Reader's Guide,* Pengiun Books, 1979, p.212.
16 J. C. Fest, *Hitler. Eine Biographie,* Propyläen Verlag, Frankfurt, 1973, p.143.
17 R. Kühnl, 'Der deutsche Faschismus', *NPL,* 1970, p.14.
18 W. Michalka, 'Das Geplante Utopie, Zur Ideologie des Nationalsozialismus,' *NPL,* 1973.
19 G. Schöllgen, 'Das Problem einer Hitler-Biographie', *NPL,* 1978, pp.433-4.
20 W. Maser, *Hitler,* Bechtle Verlag, Munich, 1974 and *Hitlers Mein Kampf,* Bechtle Verlag, Munich, 1966, and *Hitlers Briefe und Notizen,* Econ. Verlag, Düsseldorf, 1973. For a criticism of the factual accuracy of the latter work see H. Auerbach, 'Hitlers Handschrift und Masers Lesefehler', *VJH,* 1973, vol. 21, pp.334ff.
21 H. Turner, 'Hitlers Einstellung zur Wirtschaft', p.95.
22 G. Weinberg (ed.), *Hitlers Zweites Buch,* Stuttgart, 1961, p.53.
23 M. Steinert, *Hitlers Krieg und die Deutschen,* Econ. Verlag, Düsseldorf, 1970, p.95.
24 Cited in W. Michalka, op.cit., p.210.
25 P. Villard, 'Antiquité et Weltanschauung hitlérienne', *RGM,* no.88, 1972, pp.12-13.
26 P. Schramm, *Hitler: The man and military leader,* Allen Lane, 1972, p.77 and K. F. Werner, *Das nationalsozialistische Geschichtsbild und die deutsche Geschichtswissenschaft,* W. Kohlhammer, Stuttgart, 1967, p.25.
27 P. Villard, op.cit., p.5.
28 A. Hillgruber, 'Innen-und Aussenpolitik Deutschlands 1943-5', *GWU,* 4, 1974, p.229.
29 Turner, op.cit., pp.92-3.
30 See E. Nolte, *Der Faschismus in seiner Epoche,* R. Piper, Munich, 1963, p.505.
31 ibid., p.359.
32 Bullock, op.cit., p.362.

33 Nolte, op.cit., p.506.
34 E. Erikson, 'Hitler's imagery and German youth', *Psychiatry,* no.5, 1942, pp.475-93.
35 D. M. Kelley, *22 cells in Nuremberg: A psychiatrist examines the Nazi criminals,* N.Y., 1947, pp.201-236.
36 G. Schaltenbrand, 'War Hitler geisteskrank?', in *Ein Leben aus freier Mitte,* Göttingen, 1961, pp.331-4.
37 Bradley F. Smith, *Adolf Hitler, his family, childhood and youth,* Stanford U.P., 1967, p.167.
38 Bullock, op.cit., p.350.
39 K. Hildebrand, 'Hitlers Mein Kampf', *NPL,* p.72.
40 W. Maser, *Hitler,* op.cit., and *Hitlers Mein Kampf,* op.cit.
41 J. Thies, 'Hitlers Endziele: Zielloser Aktionismus, Kontinentalimperium, oder Weltherrschaft?' in W. Michalka, (ed.), *Nationalsozialistische Aussenpolitik,* Wissenschaftliche Buchgesellschaft, Darmstadt, 1978, p.82.
42 K. Lärmer, *Autobahnen in Deutschland 1933 bis 1945 -zu den Hintergründen,* Akademie Verlag, Berlin, 1975, p.50.
43 R. Loewenberg, 'Psychohistorical perspectives on modern German history', *JMH,* no.47., p.244.
44 ibid., p.244.
45 R. G. L. Waite, 'Adolf Hitler's guilt feelings', *Journal of Interdisciplinary History,* no. 1, 1971, pp.222-49.
46 Cited by J.P. Fox, 'Adolf Hitler: the continuing debate', *International Affairs,* vol.55, no.2, 1979, p.259.
47 ibid., p.257.
48 Cf. G. Schöllgen, op.cit., p.430.
49 Cited in Loewenberg, op.cit., p.245.
50 R. Kühnl, 'Neuere Ergebnisse', op.cit., p.135.
51 H. -U. Wehler, 'Zum Verhältnis von Geschichtswissenschaft und Psychoanalyse', *HZ,* no.208, p.1969.
52 Steinert, op.cit., p.600.
53 Nolte, op.cit., p.446.
54 W. Horn, 'Hitler und die NSDAP', *NPL,* 1968, p.471.
55 J. Leuschner, 'Der Nationalsozialismus, Hitler und das Dritte Reich', *NPL,* 1966, p.248.
56 For a criticism of this viewpoint see A. Hillgruber, 'Literaturbericht, Innen-und Aussenpolitik Deutschlands 1933-1945', *GWU,* no.8, 1976, p.510.
57 M. Broszat, *The Hitler State,* Longman, 1981, p.25.
58 J. Nyomarkay, cited in W. Horn, 'Hitler und die NSDAP', p.476.
59 B. Seidel, S. Jenkner, (eds.), *Wege der Totalitarismusforschung,* Wissenschaftliche Buchgesellschaft, Darmstadt, 1968, p.37.
60 H. Buchheim, *Totalitäre Herrschaft. Wesen und Merkmale,* Kösel Verlag, Munich, 1962, p.41.
61 W. Carr, *Hitler. A study in personality and politics,* Edward Arnold, 1978, p.144.
62 K. Hildebrand, 'Der Fall Hitler', *NPL,* 1969, p.378. For Hitler's health see

J. Recktenwald, *Woran hat Hitler gelitten?,* Munich, 1963.
63 H. Heiber, *Goebbels–Reden,* vol.II, Droste Verlag, Düsseldorf, 1972, p.256.
64 H. R. Trevor-Roper, (ed.), *The testament of Adolf Hitler,* Cassell, 1961, p.59.
65 Bullock, op.cit., p.345.
66 J. Freymond, *Le troisième Reich et la réorganisation de l'Europe 1940-42,* A. W. Sijhoff, Leyden, 1974, p.58.
67 H. R. Trevor-Roper, *Testament,* p.58.
68 K. Hildebrand, 'Hitlers Mein Kampf', p.81.
69 In E. M. Robertson, (ed.), *The origins of the Second World War,* Macmillan, 1969.
70 H. Turner, 'Hitlers Einstellung', op.cit., pp.102-3.
71 Bullock, op.cit., p.121.
72 J. Fest, *The face of the Third Reich,* Weidenfeld and Nicolson, 1970, p.41.
73 Cited in J. Hiden, *Germany and Europe 1919-1939,* Longman, 1977, p.142.
74 H. A. Winkler, *Revolution, Staat, Faschismus,* Vandenhoeck & Ruprecht, Göttingen, 1978, p.97.
75 P. Hüttenberger, 'Nationalsozialistische Polykratie', *G&G,* no.2, 1976, p.432.
76 M. Broszat, *Hitler State,* p.265.
77 Bullock, op.cit., p.349.
78 P. E. Schramm, *Hitler,* p.20.
79 R. J. Overy, 'Hitler and Air Strategy', *JCH,* no.15, 1980, p.405ff.
80 Schramm, op.cit., pp.21-2.
81 H. Backe, Grosser Bericht, Bundesarchiv. This impression is confirmed by H. Kehrl, *Krisenmanager im Dritten Reich,* Droste, Düsseldorf, 1973.
82 K Feiling, op.cit., p.367 and S. Roberts, op.cit., p.21.
83 W. Domarus, *Hitler: Reden und Proklamationen,* vol.I, Süddeutscher Verlag, Munich, 1965, p.8.
84 G. Meinck, *Hitler und die deutsche Aufrüstung 1933-7,* Franz Steiner, Wiesbaden, 1959, p.125.
85 ibid., p.126.
86 G. Thomas, *Geschichte der deutschen Wehr-und Rüstungswirtschaft 1918-1945,* Harold Boldt, Boppard, 1966, p.33. See also A. Milward, *The German economy at war,* Athlone Press, 1965.
87 See B. H. Liddell-Hart, *The other side of the hill,* Cassell, 1951.
88 M. van Creveld, 'War Lord Hitler: some points reconsidered', *ESR,* IV, no.1, 1974, p.57.
89 ibid., p.69.
90 Carr, op.cit., p.83.
91 H. R. Trevor-Roper, *Testament,* p.24.
92 Cited in Thomas, op.cit., p.19.
93 ibid., p.147.
94 R. J. Overy, op.cit., p.406, and W. Carr, op.cit., p.80.
95 Thomas, op.cit., p.233ff. and p.288.
96 H. Heiber, op.cit., vol.I, p.19, and p.278.
97 H. R. Trevor-Roper, *Testament,* p.2.

98 Cited in H. R. Trevor-Roper, *The last days of Hitler,* p.89.
99 K. Hildebrand, 'Der Fall Hitler', p.376.
100 J. Fest, 'Thinking about Hitler', *Encounter,* September 1975, p.81ff.
101 R. Kühnl, 'Neuere Ergebnisse', *PVS,* no.2, 1980, p.137.
102 N. Stone, *Hitler,* Hodder, 1980.
103 H. R. Trevor-Roper, *The last days of Hitler,* p.90.

**Chapter 2**

1 A. Hitler, *Mein Kampf,* Munich, 1928, p.506.
2 H. R. Trevor-Roper, *The last days of Hitler,* Pan Books, 1968, p.55.
3 Cf. the comments in W. Horn, 'Hitler und die NSDAP', op.cit., p.467.
4 R. Butler, *The roots of National Socialism 1789-1933,* 1942. Reprinted, Howard Fertig, N.Y., 1968.
5 W. Shirer, *The rise and fall of the Third Reich,* cited in J. Strawson, *Hitler as military commander,* Batsford, 1971, p.58.
6 H. Kohn, *The Mind of Modern Germany,* Scribner, N.Y., 1960.
7 E. K. Bramsted, *Germany,* Prentice Hall, New Jersey, 1972, p.113.
8 F. L. Carsten, 'The historical roots of National Socialism', in E. J. Feuchtwanger (ed.), *Upheaval and Continuity,* Oswald Wolff, 1973, p.116. Cf. G. L. Mosse, *The crisis of German ideology: intellectual origins of the Third Reich,* Weidenfeld and Nicolson, 1966; F. L. Stern, *The politics of cultural despair; a study in the rise of the German ideology,* Univ. of California Press, 1961.
9 See especially O. E. Schüddekopf, *Linke Leute von Rechts,* W. Kohlhammer, Stuttgart, 1960; K. Sontheimer, *Anti-demokratisches Denken in der Weimarer Republik,* Nymphenburger, Munich, 1968; A. Mohler, *Die Konservative Revolution in Deutschland 1918-1932,* Wissenschaftliche Buchgesellschaft, Darmstadt, 1972; P. H. Silfen, *The völkisch ideology and the roots of Nazism,* Exposition, N.Y., 1973.
10 H. Grebing, 'Erneuerung des Konservatismus?', *PVS,* 3, 1978, p.376ff; cf. A. Hillgruber, 'Literaturbericht', *GWU,* 4, 1974, p.244ff.
11 L. A. Bentin, *Johannes Popitz und Carl Schmitt. Zur wirtschaftlichen Theorie des totalen Staates in Deutschland,* C. H. Beck, Munich, 1972; I. Maus, *Bürgerliche Rechtstheorie und Faschismus. Zur sozialen Funktion und aktuellen Wirkung der Theorie Carl Schmitts,* Fink, Munich, 1976.
12 K.-J. Siegfried, *Universalismus und Faschismus. Das Gesellschaftsbild Othmar Spanns,* Europa, Vienna, 1974. See also M. Schneller, *Zwischen Romantik und Faschismus,* Klett, Stuttgart, 1976.
13 For example D. Schoenbaum, *Hitler's social revolution,* Weidenfeld and Nicolson, p.129, note 21.
14 For general reviews on Spann, Grebing, op.cit., and K. Fritzsche, 'Konservatismus im gesellschaftlich-geschichtlichen Prozess', *NPL,* 1979, p.304.
15 B. Jenschke, *Zur Kritik der konservative-revolutionären Ideologie in der Weimarer Republik,* Beck, Munich, 1971.
16 H. Grebing, op.cit., p.378.
17 Fritzsche, op.cit., p.306.
18 Moeller van den Bruck, *Germany's Third Empire,* Allen and Unwin, 1934.

19 ibid., p.241.
20 J. Petzold, *Konservative Theoretiker des deutschen Faschismus,* VEB Verlag, Berlin, 1978.
21 K. Fritzsche, *Politische Romantik und Gegenrevolution. Fluchtwege in der Krise der bürgerlichen Gesellschaft. Das Beispiel des Tat-Kreises,* Frankfurt, 1976.
22 Moeller van den Bruck, op.cit., p.153.
23 H. Holborn, 'Origins and political character of Nazi ideology', *Political Science Quarterly,* LXXIX, 1964, p.543.
24 For example, R. C. K. Ensor, *Herr Hitler's self-disclosure in Mein Kampf,* O.U.P., 1939.
25 E. Jäckel, *Hitler's Weltanschauung, A blueprint for power,* Wesleyan, U.P., Middletown, 1972.
26 B. M. Lane, 'Nazi ideology. Some unfinished business', *CEH,* 7, 1974, p.3. See also B. M. Lane and L. Rupp, *Nazi Ideology before 1933,* University of Texas Press, Austin, 1978.
For a selection on Hitler's ideas see W. A. Jenks, *Vienna and the young Hitler,* Columbia U.P., N.Y. 1960; R. H. Phelps, 'Hitler als Parteiredner im Jahre 1920', *VJH,* 11, 1963, p.274ff and 'Hitlers "grundlegende" Rede über den anti-Semitismus', *VJH,* 16, 1968, p.390ff: P. Villard, 'Antiquite et Weltanschauung hitlérienne', op.cit., p.1ff; E. Jaeckl and A. Kuhn, *Hitlers sämtliche Aufzeichnungen 1919-1924,* D. V. A., Stuttgart, 1980; F. Heer, *Der Glaube des Adolf Hitlers: Anatomie einer politischen Religiosität,* Bechtle Verlag, Munich, 1968; K. Barthel, *Friedrich der Grosse im Hitlers Weltanschauung,* Frankfurter Historische Vorträge, 1977; H. Auerbach, 'Hitlers politische Lehrjahre und die Münchener Gesellschaft 1919-1923', *VJH,* 25, 1977, p.1ff; A. Banus, 'Das Völkische Blatt "Der Scherer". Ein Beitrag zur Hitlers Schulzeit', *VJH,* 18, 1970, p.196ff; W. Daim, *Der Mann, der Hitler die Ideen gab,* Isar, Munich, 1958. (The title promises more than the book delivers).
27 The best works on Rosenberg are J. Billig, *Alfred Rosenberg dans l'action idéologique, politique et administratif du Reich hitlérien*, C.D.J.C. Paris, 1963 and more recently, R. Cecil, *The myth of the master race: Alfred Rosenberg and Nazi ideology*, Batsford, 1972; For Feder see O. J. Hale, 'Gottfied Feder calls Hitler to order', *JMH*, XXX, 1958, p.358ff; for the Strasser brothers, R. Kühnl,'Zur Programmatik der NS Linken: Das Strasser Programm von 1925/1926', *VJH*, 14, 1966, p.317ff, and *Die nationalsozialistische Linke 1925-1930,* Anton Haim, Meisenheim am Glan, 1966; for Himmler, J. Ackermann, *Heinrich Himmler als Ideologe*, Musterschmidt, Göttingen, 1970, B. F. Smith, *Heinrich Himmler. A Nazi in the making, 1900-1926*, Hoover Inst. Press, Stanford, 1971, and B. F. Smith and W. T. Angress, 'Diaries of Heinrich Himmler's early years', *JMH*, XXXI, 1959, p.206ff.
28 Bundesarchiv, Nachlass Backe, Mappe 5, nos.1 and 3.
29 For the Göttingen group in general see J. Noakes, 'Conflict and development in the NSDAP 1924-7', *JCH*, 1, no.4, 1966 and *The Nazi Party in Lower Saxony 1921-1933*, O.U.P., 1971.
30 For a further discussion of this point, B. Perz and H. Safrian, 'Wege und Irrwege der Faschismusforschung', *ZG*, 7, 1979-80, p.437ff.

31 A. Mohler, op.cit., p.193 for the 'five types' of National Socialist.
32 B. M. Lane, op.cit., p.3.
33 K. F. Werner, 'On some examples of the National Socialist view of history', *JCH*, vol.3, no.2, 1968, p.193ff. See also his *Das nationalsozialistische Geschichtsbild und die deutsche Geschichtswissenschaft*, W. Kohlhammer, Stuttgart, 1967.
34 E. Jaeckl, op.cit.
35 See L Gruchmann, 'Euthanasie und Justiz im Dritten Reich', *VJH*, 20, 1972, p.235ff. Cf. A. Hillgruber's comments on the gaps in our research into National Socialism in 'Tendenzen, Ergebnisse und Perspektiven der gegenwärtigen Hitler-Forschung', *HZ*, 226, 1978, p.619.
36 For the background to Nordic superiority as a concept see H. J. Lutzhöft, *Der nordische Gedanke in Deutschland 1920-1940*, Klett, Stuttgart, 1971, and M. H. Kater, *Das "Ahnenerbe" der SS 1935-1945*, D. V. A., Stuttgart, 1974.
37 For literature on the legal system see H. Boberach, (ed.), *Richterbriefe. Dokumente zur Beinflussung der deutschen Rechtssprechung 1942-1944*, Boldt, Boppard, 1975; W. Johe, *Die gleichgeschaltete Justiz*, Europäische Verlagsanstalt, Frankfurt, 1967.
38 J. W. Jones, *The Nazi conception of law*, O.U.P., 1939.
39 K. Anderbrügge, *Völkisches Rechtsdenken: Zur Rechtslehre in der Zeit des Nationalsozialismus*, Duncker and Humblot, Berlin, 1978, p.24; see also H. Robinsohn, *Justiz als politische Verfolgung. Die Rechtssprechung in 'Rassenschandefällen' beim Landesgericht Hamburg 1936-43*, D. V. A., Stuttgart, 1977.
40 Anderbrügge, op.cit., p.28.
41 Jones, op.cit., p.22.
42 Anderbrügge, op.cit., p.78.
43 J. Meinck, *Weimarer Staatslehre und Nationalsozialismus*, Campus, Frankfurt, 1978, p.189.
44 On pre-1933 thinking in the area of farm legislation see W. Willikens in NSDAP Year Book 1929 and 1930.
45 On this function of the Weltanschauung see T. W. Mason, *Sozialpolitik im Dritten Reich*, Westdeutscher Verlag, Opladen, 1977, especially Chapter 1.
46 For a full list of publications on National Socialist legal concepts especially on the relationship between the individual and the community see M. Stolleis, 'Gemeinschaft und Volksgemeinschaft', *VJH*, 22, 1972, p.16ff.
47 Cf. R. Kühnl's review of V. Losemann, *Nationalsozialismus und Antike*, Hoffman & Campe, Hamburg, 1977, in PVS, no.II, 1980, p.131.
48 U. Kiesenkoetter, *Gregor Strasser und die NSDAP,* Schriftenreihe der *VJH,* Stuttgart, 1978, p.30.
49 B. M. Lane, op.cit., p.12.
50 E. Nolte, *Der Faschismus in seiner Epoche*, op.cit., pp.502-3.
51 J. Ackermann, op.cit., p.25; see also W. T. Angress, B. F. Smith, 'The diaries of Heinrich Himmler's early years', *JMH*, XXI, 1959, pp.221-2.
52 I. Kershaw in M. Broszat et al (eds.), *Bayern in der NS-Zeit*, Oldenbourg, Vienna, 1977, pp.334-5.

53 W. Horn, 'Hitler und die NSDAP', op.cit., p.467.
54 M. Broszat, *The Hitler State*, op.cit., p.357. See also G. Schöllgen, 'Das Problem einer Hitler-Biographie', *NPL*, 1978, p.430 regarding the extent of anti-semitism and its implications.
55 M. G. Steinert, op.cit., pp.58ff, 76.
56 I. Kershaw, op.cit., p.346.
57 D. Irving, *Hitler's War*, Hodder and Stoughton, 1977.
58 For this view, U. D. Adam, *Judenpolitik im Dritten Reich*, Droste, Düsseldorf, 1972.
59 K. D. Erdmann, *Die Zeit der Weltkriege*, Klett, Stuttgart, 1976, p.337. (This is part of the series, *Handbuch der deutschen Geschichte*, edited by B. Gebhardt).
60 M. Broszat, 'Hitler und die Genesis der "Endlösung"', *VJH*, 25, 1977, p.739ff. Cf. Schöllgen, op.cit., p.422, (note 54).
61 For this letter see E. Deuerlein, 'Hitlers Eintritt in die Politik und die Reichswehr', *VJH*, 7, 1959, p.204.
62 See A. Hillgruber, 'Literaturbericht', GWU 4, 1974, p.242.
63 C. Browning, 'Zur Genesis der Endlösung; eine Antwort an Martin Broszat', *VJH*, 29, 1981, p.101. See also his *The 'final solution' and the German Foreign Office*, Holmes and Meier, N.Y., 1978..
64 E. Goldhagen, 'Weltanschauung und Endlösung', *VJH*, 24, 1976, p.384.
65 *Mein Kampf*, Munich, 1933, p.69.
66 Quoted in Schöllgen, op.cit., p.422.
67 T. W. Mason, 'Intention and Explanation. A current controversy about the interpretation of National Socialism.' in *Der Führerstaat: Mythos und Realität*, German Historical Institute, vol.8, 1981.
68 See. E. Goldhagen, op.cit., p.383 for Himmler's views in 1936 and on the use of the phrase 'the devilish agent of human decay' (coined by Richard Wagner) in National Socialist propaganda in general to describe the Jewish role in world affairs.
69 K. D. Erdmann, op.cit., p.347.
70 H. Heiber (ed.), *Goebbels-Reden*, vol.1, *1932-1939*, Droste, Düsseldorf, 1971, p.1.
71 M. Steinert, op.cit., p.26.
72 Heiber, op.cit., p.161, no.10.
73 W. Horn, 'Hitler und die NSDAP', op.cit., p.467.
74 M. Domarus, *Hitler. Reden und Proklamation,* vol.1, Messerschmidt, Würzburg, 1962, p.201.
75 T. W. Mason, 'The legacy of 1918 for National Socialism', in A. Nicholls and E. Matthias (eds.), *German democracy and the triumph of Hitler*, Allen and Unwin, 1971, p.215ff.
76 See in general the arguments developed in Mason, *Sozialpolitik*, Chapter 1.
77 See T. W. Mason on the legacy of 1918; A. J. Nicholls, E. Matthias, (eds.), *German democracy and the triumph of Hitler*, Allen and Unwin, 1971.
78 H. A. Turner, 'Hitlers Einstellung zur Wirschaft', *G&G*, 1976, p.100.
79 Mason, *Sozialpolitik*, Chapter 1.
80 F. Neumann, *Behemoth: The structure and practice of National Socialism*, Left Book Club, 1942, p.357.

81 Cf. A. Bullock, *Hitler, a study in tyranny*, Odhams, 1960, p.49.
82 M. Broszat, *Hitler State*, p.23.
83 Cited in C. R. Lovin, 'Die Erzeugungsschlacht 1934-1936', *ZAG*, 22, 1974, p.211. For a detailed description of National Socialist ceremonial see K. H. Schmeer, *Die Regie des öffentlichen Lebens im Dritten Reich*, Pöhl & Co., 1956.
84 Erdmann, op.cit., p.347.
85 G. L. Mosse, *The nationalization of the masses*, Howard Fertig, N.Y., 1975, p.1.
86 J. Dülffer, 'Der Beginn des Krieges 1939: Hitler, die innere Krise und das Mächtesystem', *G&G*, 4, 1976, p.458. See also J. Petsch, *Baukunst und Stadtplanung im Dritten Reich*, Carl Hanser, Munich, 1976.
87 R. Kühnl, 'Literaturbericht', *PVS*, II, 1980, p.131.
88 Mosse, op.cit., p.3.
89 ibid., p.4.
90 As Erdmann, op.cit., p.346 and Mosse, op.cit., p.6ff seem to suggest.
91 Erdmann, op.cit., p.340.
92 Cf. Steinert, op.cit., p.24.
93 ibid., p.17.
94 ibid., p.21.
95 T. W. Mason, 'Labour in the Third Reich 1933-1939', *P&P*, 33, 1966, p.113.
96 See J. Meinck, op.cit., pp.218-9.
97 F. Neumann, op.cit., p.356.
98 R. Kühnl, 'Literaturbericht', *PVS*, II, 1980, p.128.
99 See among others: E. Kogon, *The theory and practice of hell*, Secker and Warburg, 1950; S. Aronson, *Reinhard Heydrich und die frühgeschichte von Gestapo und SD*, D.V.A., Stuttgart, 1971; H. Buchheim, *SS und Polizei im NS-Staat,* Selbstverlag der Studiengesellschaft für Zeitprobleme, Bonn, 1964; J. Delarue, *The history of the Gestapo*, MacDonald, 1964; H. Höhne, *The Order of the Death's Head*, Secker and Warburg, 1969; H. Krausnick et al., *The anatomy of the SS State*, Collins, 1968; G. H. Stein, *The Waffen SS: Hitler's elite,* Cornell U.P., 1966; J. Billig, *L'hitlérisme et le système concentrationnaire,* Presse Universitaire, Paris, 1967.
100 E. Lederer, *Kapitalismus, Klassenstruktur und probleme der Demokratie in Deutschland 1910-1940*, edited by J. V. Kocka, Vandenhoeck and Ruprecht, 1979, p.246.
101 S. Rauschenbusch, *The march of fascism*, Yale U.P., 1939, p.358.
102 See T. W. Mason, *Sozialpolitik im Dritten Reich*, Chapter 1 for this passage.
103 M. Broszat, *The Hitler State*, pp.340-1.
104 Steinert, op.cit., p.20ff.
105 K. I. Flessau, *Schule der Diktatur: Lehrpläne und Schulbücher des Nationalsozialismus*, Fischer Taschenbuch Verlag, Frankfurt, 1979, pp.9-20.
106 P. D. Stachura, 'The ideology of the Hitler Youth in the Kampfzeit', *JCH*, 8, no.3, p.155ff; *Nazi Youth in the Weimar Republic*, Clio Press, Santa Barbara, 1975.

107 R. Eilers, *Die nationalsozialistische Schulpolitik*, cited Flessau, op.cit., p.74.
108 Flessau, op.cit., pp.21-2.
109 ibid., pp.75-88.
110 ibid., pp.25-27.
111 ibid., p.118.
112 ibid., p.195ff.
113 ibid., pp.26-27. For educational studies in general, U. D. Adam, *Hochschule und Nationalsozialismus*, Mohr, Tübingen, 1977; E. Y. Hartshorne, *The German universities and National Socialism*, Allen and Unwin, 1937; H. Hauschild, *Erzieher im Dritten Reich*, Rütten, Münchengladbach, 1976; K. Lingelbach, *Erziehung und Erziehungstheorien im NS Deutschland*, Beltz, Weinheim, 1970; E. Mann, *School for barbarians*, Drummond Ltd, 1939; E. Nyssen, *Schule im Nationalsozialismus*, Quelle und Meyer, Heidelberg, 1979; K. F. Werner, *Das nationalsozialistische Geschichtsbild und die deutsche Geschichtswissenschaft*, W. Kohlhammer, Stuttgart, 1967; P. F. Wiener, *German with tears*, Cresset Press, 1942; G. Zeimar, *Education for death*, O.U.P., 1941; D. Orlow, 'Die Adolf Hitler Schulen', *VJH*, 13, 1965, p.272ff; J. Stephenson, 'Girls' Higher Education in Germany in the 1930s', *JCH*, 10, 1, 1975, p.41ff.
114 F. L. Carsten, 'The historical roots of National Socialism', in E. J. Feuchtwanger, op.cit., p.116.
115 Cf. N. H. Baynes, *Hitler's speeches 1922-1939*, vol.1, O.U.P., 1941, p.337.
116 The most recent discussion of the controversy over the suggestions of Nolte and Hillgruber can be found in *German History*, 6, no.1, 1988.

**Chapter 3**

1 N. H. Baynes, *Hitler's speeches*, vol.I, O.U.P., 1941, p.209.
2 K. Pinsdorf, 'Nature and aims of the National Socialist German Labour Party', *American Political Science Review*, vol.25, no.2, pp.377-9.
3 E. N. Peterson, *The limits of Hitler's power*, Princeton U.P., 1969.
4 D. Schoenbaum, op.cit.
5 P. Diehl-Thiele, *Partei und Staat im Dritten Reich*, Beck, Munich, 1969, p.202.
6 ibid., p.241.
7 M. Broszat, *Hitler State*, p.358.
8 G. Meinck, *Weimarer Staatslehre und Nationalsozialismus*, op.cit., pp.140-1.
9 Steinert, op.cit., p.26.
10 Diehl-Thiele, op.cit., p.200.
11 W. Horn, 'Zur Geschichte und Struktur des Nationalsozialismus und der NSDAP', *NPL*, 1973, p.208.
12 Broszat, op.cit., p.43.
13 R. Janssen, 'Todt et Speer', *Revue de la Duexième Guerre Mondiale*, no.84, 1971.
14 S. Haffner, *Anmerkungen zu Hitler*, Kindler, Munich, 1978, p.14.
15 W. Michalka, 'Geplante Utopie', op.cit., p.215.
16 P. Hüttenberger, 'Nationalsozialistische Polykratie', op.cit., p.421.

17 R. Kühnl, 'Neuere Ergebnisse', *PVS*, 2, 1980, p.137.
18 F. Neumann, *Behemoth*, op.cit., pp.297ff.
19 Horn, op.cit., p.224.
20 Hüttenberger, op.cit., p.427.
21 R. Saage, 'Zum Verhältnis von Nationalsozialismus und Industrie', *Das Parlament,* 1975, Beilage 9, p.35; A. Schweitzer, *Big business in the Third Reich*, Indiana U.P., Bloomington, 1964.
22 Broszat, op.cit., pp.194-5.
23 E. Fraenkel, *The dual state*, O.U.P., 1941.
24 Broszat, op.cit., p.358.
25 R. Bollmus, *Das Amt Rosenberg und Seine Gegner,* DVA, Stuttgart, 1970, p.245.
26 Saage, op.cit., p.36.
27 Horn, op.cit., p.224.
28 For a critique of New Left theories, see H. A. Winkler, *Revolution, Staat Faschismus. Zur Revision des historischen Materialismus*, Vandenhoeck & Ruprecht, Göttingen, 1978, p.70ff.
29 T. W. Mason, *Arbeiterklasse und Volksgemeinschaft*, Westdeutscher Verlag, Opladen, 1975.
30 E. Nolte, *Theorien über den Faschismus*, Kiepenheuer & Witsch, Cologne-Berlin, 1967, p.37.
31 Cf. Saage, *'Konservatismus, Faschismus'*, *PVS*, 2, 1978, p.261.
32 U. D. Adam, *Judenpolitik im Dritten Reich*, Droste, Düsseldorf, 1972, p.360.
33 O. Dietrich, *The Hitler I knew*, Methuen, 1955.
34 H. Rauschning, *Germany's Revolution of Destruction*, Heinemann, 1939.
35 Dietrich, op.cit.
36 Diehl-Thiele, op.cit., p.252.
37 T. W. Mason, *Sozialpolitik*, p.266.
38 Cited in Diehl-Thiele, op.cit., p.119.
39 Bollmus, op.cit.
40 U. Kiesenkoetter, op.cit., pp.66-7.
41 H. Mommsen, *Beamtentum im Dritten Reich*, DVA, Stuttgart, 1966, p.10.
42 H. Mommsen, 'National Socialism. Continuity and change', in W. Lacqueur (ed.), op.cit., p.196.
43 Petersen, op.cit., p.4ff, p.15ff.
44 N. Rich, *Hitler's War Aims*, vol.I, Deutsch, 1973.
45 Broszat, op.cit., p.318.
46 K. Hildebrand, 'Nationalsozialismus ohne Hitler?', *GWU*, 5, 1980, p.289; J. Dülffer, 'Der Beginn des Krieges 1939', *G&G*, 4, 1976, p.450.
47 Cited in Hildebrand, op.cit.
48 Cited in U. Kiesenkoetter, op.cit., p.52.
49 Diehl-Thiele, op.cit., pp.174-5.
50 E. Fröhlich, M. Broszat, 'Politische und soziale Macht auf dem Lande. Die Durchsetzung der NSDAP im Kreis Memmingen', *VJH*, 25, 1977, p.563.
51 Diehl-Thiele, op.cit., p.175.
52 ibid., p.6.
53 ibid., p.29.

54 Broszat, *Hitler State*, p.112; Diehl-Thiele, op.cit., p.68.
55 Diehl-Thiele, op.cit., p.191.
56 Mommsen, *Beamtentum*, p.62.
57 Diehl-Thiele, op.cit., pp.8-9.
58 ibid., p.40ff.
59 ibid., p.68.
60 ibid., p.191.
61 ibid., p.66.
62 Mommsen, *Beamtentum*, p.21.
63 ibid., pp.13-15.
64 ibid., p.39.
65 Tape discussion between T. W. Mason and J. Noakes, 'The Nazi seizure of power', Audio Learning Ltd.
66 Broszat, *Hitler State*, p.242ff.
67 Hüttenberger, op.cit., p.430.
68 Diehl-Thiele, op.cit., p.178.
69 Kühnl, 'Neuere Ergebnisse', *PVS*, 2, 1980, p.129.
70 F. Kübler, 'Die nationalsozialistische Rechtsordnung', *NPL*, 1970, p.296; Broszat, *Hitler State*, p.335.
71 ibid., p.328.
72 See H. Höhne, *The Order of the Death's Head*, Secker and Warburg, 1969.
73 M. Broszat, *Hitler State*, p.328ff.
74 Hüttenberger, op.cit.
75 Broszat, *Hitler State*, p.335.
76 Meincke, op.cit., p.219.
77 J. L. Heinemann, *Hitler's First Foreign Minister*, University of California Press, 1979, p.117.
78 Broszat, *Hitler State*, p.236.
79 J. Klenner, *Das Verhältnis von Partei und Staat dargestellt am Beispiel Bayerns*, Neue Schriftenreihe des Stadtarchivs, Munich, 1974, p.217.
80 Diehl-Thiele, op.cit., p.113; Broszat, *Hitler State*, p.105.
81 P. Hüttenberger, *Die Gauleiter, DVA,* Stuttgart, 1969.
82 Diehl-Thiele, op.cit., p.115.
83 ibid., p.94.
84 ibid., p.94.
85 In F. Forstmaier, H. E. Volkmann, *Wirtschaft und Rüstung am Vorabend des Zweiten Weltrieges*, Droste, Düsseldorf, 1975, p.87.
86 J. Caplan, 'The politics of administration. The Reich Interior Ministry and the German Civil Service', *Historical Journal*, 20, 3, 1977, p.707.
87 A. von Boerner, 'The NSDAP in the German constitutional order', *American Political Science Review*, XXXII, 6, 1938, p.1061.
88 See E. Hennig, 'Regionale Unterschiede bei der Entstehung des deutschen Faschismus', *PVS*, 2, 1980, pp.152-68.
89 Cited in Flessau, op.cit., p.147.
90 Meincke, op.cit., p.192.
91 Hüttenberger, 'Nationalsozialistische Polykratie', pp.429.30.
92 Cf. H. Heiber, *Goebbels*, vol.I, p.91: 'He (Goebbels) sold National Socialism like others sold washing powder.'

93 Bollmus, op.cit., p.242.
94 H. Mommsen, 'Entteuffelung des Dritten Reiches?', *Der Spiegel*, no.II, 1967.
95 R. Vogelsang, *Der Freundekreis Himmler*, Musterschmidt, Göttingen, 1972, p.138.
96 Erdmann, op.cit., p.540.
97 Heinemann, op.cit., pp.107-8.
98 ibid., p.193.
99 ibid., pp.193-4.
100 ibid., pp.197-8.
101 K. Drechsler, et al, 'Politik und Strategie des faschistischen Deutschlands im zweiten Weltkrieg, *ZGW*, 1, 1966, p.7.
102 ibid., p.10.
103 D. Eichholtz, 'Expansionsrichtung Nordeuropa', *ZGW*, 1979, 1, p.18.
104 Erdmann, op.cit., p.542.
105 See D. Dallin's account, *German rule in Russia 1941-1945*, London, 1957.
106 In general, see W. Dlugoborski, C. Madajczyk, 'Ausbeutungssysteme in den besetzten Gebieten Polens und der USSR', in Forstmeier and Volkmann, op.cit.
107 For correspondence see Bundesarchiv Koblenz, R.26/IV, no.33.
108 Fest, *Gesicht des Dritten Reichs*, p.160.
109 H. Heiber, quoted in K. F. Werner, 'Some examples of National Socialist views of history', *JCH*, 1968.
110 W. Michalka, *Deutsche Aussenpolitik*, is an exception here.
111 Hüttenberger, 'Nationalsozialistische Polykratie', p.417.
112 Diehl-Thiele, op.cit., p.83.
113 Bollmus, op.cit., pp.245, pp.247-9.

**Chapter 4**

1 Goebbels, 23 July 1928. Cited in Schoenbaum, op.cit., p.246.
2 J. Farquharson, *The Plough and the Swastika*, Sage Publications, 1976, p.63.
3 R. Koehl, 'The Feudal aspects of National Socialism', *American Political Science Review*, Dec. 1960. 1960, p.921.
4 F. Neumann, op.cit., p.123.
5 Koehl, op.cit., p.92.
6 Schoenbaum, op.cit., p.287.
7 R. Dahrendorf, *Society and Democracy in Germany*, Doubleday, N.Y., 1967.
8 G. L. Mosse, 'Genesis of fascism', *JCH*, 1, no.1, 1966, p.22.
9 K. D. Bracher, 'The role of Hitler' in W. Laqueur (ed.), op.cit., p.220.
10 In A. Nicholls, E. Matthias (eds.), *German democracy and the triumph of Hitler*, Allen and Unwin, 1971.
11 See, for example, H. Winkler, 'Hitler, German society and the illusion of restoration', *JCH*, no.11, 1976, p.1ff.
12 H. R. Trevor-Roper, *Hitler's table talk*, Weidenfeld and Nicolson, 1953, p.xxvi.
13 ibid., p.268ff.

14 Schoenbaum, op.cit.
15 Domarus, op.cit., vol.I, p.68ff.
16 J. W. Falter, 'Wer verhalf der NSDAP zum Sieg?', *Das Parlament*, 1979, Beilage 28, pp.9-10.
17 T. Childers, 'The social bases of the National Socialist vote', *JCH*, 11, no.4, 1976, p.18ff.
18 See E. Hanisch, 'Neuere Faschismus Theorien', *ZG*, 1973-4, no.1, p.21 for the critique of Kühnl. For Geiger see B. Perz, H. Safrian, 'Wege und Irrwege der Faschismusforschung, *ZG*, 1979-80, no.7, p.443ff. See also L. Zumpe, *Wirtschaft und Staat in Deutschland 1933 bis 1945*, Akademie, Berlin, 1980.
19 Perz, Safrian, op.cit., pp.452-3.
20 W. Sauer, 'National Socialism: Totalitarianism or Fascism?', *AMH*, 1967, p.417.
21 H. A. Winkler, *Mittelstand, Demokratie und Nationalsozialismus*, Kiepenheuer & Witsch, Cologne, 1972, pp.35, 178.
22 K. D. Bracher, *Die Auflösung der Weimarer Republik*, Ring Verlag, Villingen, Schwarzwald, 1960.
23 Childers, op.cit., p.29.
24 L. K. Waldmann, *Strain producing situations and support for social movements: the case of the Nazis*, Ohio State University, 1975, p.32; E. Hennig, 'Regionale Unterschiede bei der Entstehung des deutschen Faschismus', *PVS*, no.2, 1980, p.161ff. Cf. D. Orlow, *History of the Nazi Party*, vol.I, p.90.
25 E. Lederer, 'Ende der Klassengesellschaft' in H. Speier, (ed.), *Kapitalismus, Klassenstruktur und Probleme der Demokratie in Deutschland 1910-1940*, Göttingen, Vandenhoeck & Ruprecht, 1979, p.239ff.
26 H. Lasswell, cited in E. Nolte, *Theorien ueber den Faschismus*, Kiepenheuer & Witsch, Berlin-Cologne, 1967, p.444.
27 Kiesenkoetter, op.cit., p.14.
28 J. Lutzhöft, op.cit., pp.70-1.
29 H. Heiber, op.cit., vol.I, p.110.
30 A. Barkai, *Das Wirtschaftssystem des Nationalsozialismus. Der historische und ideologische Hintergrund 1933-36*, Verlag Wissenschaft und Politik, Berendt & Nottbeck, Cologne, 1977, p.10.
31 M. Müller, 'Die Stellung des Arbeiters im nationalsozialistischen Staat', *GWU*, 1975, no.1, p.5.
32 W. Böhnke, *Die NSDAP im Ruhrgebiet 1920-1933*, Verlag Neuer Gesellschaft, Bonn, 1974, p.225.
33 E. Calic, op.cit., p.127.
34 H. Neisser, 'Sozialstatistische Analyse der Wahlergebnisse', *Die Arbeit*, 1931, pp.654-9.
35 G. Schulz, *Aufstieg des Nationalsozialismus*, Propyläen, Frankfurt, 1975, pp.471ff, 631ff.
36 Falter, op.cit., p.12. See also P. Manstein, *Die Mitglieder und Wähler der NSDAP*, Lang, Frankfurt, 1988, pp.11 ff.
37 Erdmann, 'Die Zeit der Weltkriege', p.354.
38 For example, M. Ohlsen, 'Ständischer Aufbau und Monopole 1933/34',

*ZGW*, no.1, 1974, pp.28ff.
39 Cf. Falter, op.cit., p.19.
40 D. Mühlberger, 'The sociology of the NSDAP: the question of working class membership', *JCH*, July 1980, pp.493ff.
41 R. Saage, 'Zum Verhältnis von Nationalsozialismus', *Das Parlament*, 1975, Beilage 9, p.18.
42 Falter, op.cit., p.16.
43 ibid., p.19.
44 Cf. the votes cast for the winning party in British general elections in recent years, which amounted in 1979 to fewer than 14 million from a total electorate numbering just over 40 millions.
45 K. D. Erdmann, 'Nationalsozialismus', *GWU*, no.8, 1976, p.462 agrees with Bracher that the NSDAP has to be seen primarily not as a class party but rather as a unification movement which pulled together antagonistic groupings, Hüttenberger, 'Nationalsozialistische Polykratie', op.cit., p.425 accepts this point.
46 Sauer, op.cit., p.417.
47 Saage, 'Zum Verhältnis', op.cit., p.9.
48 J. Radkau, 'Nationalsozialismus und Wirtschaft', *NPL*, no.15, 1970.
49 See Broszat, *Hitler State*, p.20 for dislike of NS 'proletarianism' in Nationalist circles.
50 See, for example, Schoenbaum, op.cit., p.179.
51 H. A. Winkler, *Revolution, Staat und Faschismus*, op.cit., p.74ff.
52 R. Kühnl, 'Probleme einer Theorie über den internationalen Faschismus', *PVS*, no.1, 1975, pp.110-111.
53 H. A. Turner, 'Big business and the rise of Hitler', *AMH*, 1969-70, p.59.
54 Schulz, *Aufstieg*, p.635; M. Vogt, 'Zur Finanzierung der NSDAP zwischen 1924-1928', *GWU*, no.4, 1970, p.234ff.
55 See also Saage, op.cit.
56 For the allegation that Henry Ford sent money to Hitler in the 1920s see J. and S. Pool, *Who financed Hitler?* Macdonald and Jane's, 1979, Chapter 3.
57 G. W. Hallgarten, 'Adolf Hitler and German heavy industry', *CEH*, 1968, p.239.
58 E. Nolte, *Der Faschismus in seiner Epoche*, op.cit., p.413.
59 Erdmann, 'Die Zeit der Weltkriege', p.356.
60 A. Barkai, op.cit., p.16.
61 H. A. Turner, 'Big business', p.64.
62 H. A. Turner, 'Hitler's secret pamphlet for industrialists, 1927', *JMH*, 1968.
63 Erdmann, op.cit., p.356.
64 Cf. A. Hillgruber, 'Innen-und Aussenpolitik Deutschlands 1933-1945', *GWU*, no.4, 1974, p.240.
65 See E. Nolte, *Theorien*, p.413.
66 G. W. Hallgarten, *Hitler, Reichswehr und Industrie*, Frankfurt, 1955, p.116.
67 C. Bloch, *Die SA*, pp.144-5; see also his point, p.147, that big business really wanted to see who would win until the Röhm affair.
68 L. Zumpe, *Wirtschaft und Staat in Deutschland 1933-1945*, op.cit., p.434.

69 A. Sohn-Rethel, *Ökonomie und Klassenstruktur des deutschen Faschismus. Aufzeichnungen und Analysen*, Ed. J. Agnoli et al., Suhrkamp, Frankfurt, 1973, p.173.
70 T. W. Mason, 'Der Primat der Politik-Politik und Wirtschaft in Nationalsozialismus', *Das Argument*, no.4, 1966, p.475.
71 L. Lochner, *Die Mächtigen und der Tyran,* Darmstadt, 1955, p.144. D. Abraham, *The Collapse of the Weimar Republic*, Princeton U.P. 1981, 2nd ed., 1986. For an idea of the virulence of the controversy over Abraham's book, see J. Caplan, J. Wiener, 'Drama in the history department', *New Statesman*, 3 May 1985, pp.25-7.
72 F. Fischer, *Bündnis der Eliten: Zur Kontinuität der Machtstrukturen in Deutschland 1871-1945*, Droste, Düsseldorf, 1979, p.43.
73 Bloch, op.cit., pp.144-5.
74 Erdmann, op.cit., p.396.
75 M. Ohlsen, op.cit., pp.28ff. See also Zumpe, op.cit., p.45 for agreement with this point.
76 Ohlsen, op.cit.
77 H. Lebovics, *Social conservatism and the middle classes in Germany 1914-33*, Princeton U.P., 1969.
78 Meinck, op.cit., p.85.
79 Ohlsen, op.cit., p.29. Zumpe, op.cit., p.45.
80 J. John, 'Rüstungsindustrie und NSDAP Organisation in Thüringen 1933 bis 1939', *ZGW*, no.4, 1974, pp.414-5.
81 See A. von Saldern, *Mittelstand im Dritten Reich*, Campus, Frankfurt, 1979, p.238ff. for this thesis.
82 M. Wolffsohn, *Industrie und Handwerk in Konflikt mit staatlicher Wirtschafts politik?*, Duncker & Humblot, Berlin, 1977, p.120ff.
83 M. Müller, 'Die Stellung des Arbeiters', p.11.
84 See H. Gies, 'Der Reichsnährstand—Organ berufsständischer Selbstverwaltung oder Instrument staatlicher Wirtschaftslenkung?', ZAG, 1973, p.227.
85 W. Schieder, op.cit., p.109ff.
86 W. Bauer, P. Dehen, 'Landwirtschaft und Volkseinkommen', *Vierteljahrsheft zur Wirtschaftsforschung*, 1938-9, no.4, p.427.
87 Hüttenberger, op.cit., p.439.
88 Cited in Broszat, *Hitler State*, p.68.
89 Mason, *Sozialpolitik*, p.118.
90 ibid., Chapter I for these views.
91 Müller, op.cit., p.11.
92 Cited in Erdmann, 'Nationalsozialismus, Faschismus', p.455.
93 Müller, op.cit., p.8.
94 Kiesenkoetter, op.cit., p.80.
95 H. G. Schumann, *Nationalsozialismus und Gewerkschaftsbewegung*, Hannover-Frankfurt, 1958, p.89ff.
96 H. Roth, 'Die nationalsozialistische Betriebszellen Organisation von der Gründung bis zur Röhm-Affäre', *JBW*, 1978, no.1, pp.49ff.
97 H. A. Turner, 'Hitlers Einstellung', pp.106-7.
98 Mason, *Sozialpolitik*, p.115.

99 J. Aretz, *Katholische Arbeiterbewegung und Nationalsozialismus*, Matthias Grünfeld, Mainz, 1978.
100 Domarus, *Hitler Reden*, I, p.349.
101 G. Mosse, *Nationalisation of the masses*, pp.208-9.
102 Mason, *Sozialpolitik*, Chapter I.
103 K. Lärmer, *Autobahnen in Deutschland*, p.2.
104 R. Mann, 'Widerstand gegen den Nationalsozialismus', *NPL*, 1977, vol.22, p.429.
105 Mason, *Sozialpolitik*, Chapter I.
106 M. Müller, op.cit., pp.9-10.
107 *Völkischer Beobachter*, 30 Jan 1939, cited ibid.
108 M. Müller, op.cit., pp.6-7.
109 Cited in H. Heiber, vol.I, pp.206ff.
110 C. W. Guillebaud, *The economic recovery of Nazi Germany 1933-1938*, C.U.P., 1941, p.20ff. Contrast, however, O. Nathan, *The Nazi economic system*, Durham, N.C., 1944, p.197ff.
111 Sohn-Rethel, op.cit., p.175, and Mason, op.cit., p.157.
112 J. Dülffer, 'Der Beginn des Krieges', *G&G*, vol.4, 1976, p.447.
113 Steinert, op.cit., pp.588ff.
114 Schoenbaum, op.cit., p.245ff.
115 Meinck, op.cit., p.169.
116 Kühnl, 'Der deutsche Faschismus', *NPL*, 1970, p.39.
117 Hüttenberger, op.cit., p.426.
118 Broszat, *Hitler State*, pp.190-1.
119 W. Goerlitz, *Die Junker. Adel und Bauer im deutschen Osten,* C. A. Starke Verlag, Limburg, 1964.
120 Cf. Zumpe, op.cit., p.110.
121 Radkau, 'Entscheidungsprozesse und Entscheidungsdefizite', *G&G*, no.1, 1976, p.50.
122 Steinert, op.cit., p.601.
123 L. Kettenacker, in *Der Führer Staat. Mythos und Realität*, German Historical Institute, 1981, pp.98-131.

**Chapter 5**

1 A. Hitler, *Mein Kampf*, J. Murphy, Hurst and Blackett, 1939, p.523.
2 H. R. Trevor-Roper, 'Hitlers Kriegsziele', *VJH*, April 1960, p.125.
3 ibid., p.125.
4 F. H. Hinsley, *Hitler's Strategy*, C.U.P., 1951.
5 Cf. A. J. P. Taylor, *The course of German history*, Hamish Hamilton, 1945.
6 A. J. P. Taylor, *The origins of the Second World War*, Hamish Hamilton, 1961.
7 A. S. Milward, *The German economy at war*, Athlone Press, 1965.
8 B. H. Klein, *Germany's economic preparations for war*, Harvard U.P., 1959.
9 F. Fischer, *Griff nach der Weltmacht*, Droste, Düsseldorf, 1967.
10 H. W. Gatzke, *Germany's drive to the west*, O.U.P., 1966.
11 E. Jaeckl, *Hitlers Weltanschauung*, Wesleyan U.P., 1969; R. K. Ensor, *Who Hitler is*, O.U.P., 1939.
12 Cf. J. Dülffer, 'Der Beginn des Krieges', *G&G*, 1976, p.444.

13 See J. Hiden, 'National Socialism and Foreign Policy 1919-1933', in P. Stachura (ed.), *Hitlers Machtergreifung 1933*, Allen and Unwin, 1983.
14 See K. Lange, *Hitlers unbeachtete Maximen*, Kohlhammer, Stuttgart, 1968; W. Maser, *Hitlers Mein Kampf*, Bechtle, Munich, 1966; K. Hildebrand, 'Hitlers Mein Kampf. Propaganda oder Programm?', *NPL*, 1969, p.73ff.
15 G. Stoakes, 'The evolution of Hitler's idea on foreign policy 1919-1925', in P. Stachura (ed.), *The shaping of the Nazi State*, Croom Helm, 1978, p.23; G. Schubert, *Anfänge nationalsozialistischer Aussenpolitik*, Cologne, 1963; A. Kuhn, *Hitlers Aussenpolitisches Programm*, Stuttgart, 1970.
16 J. Dülffer, 'Beginn des Krieges', p.465.
17 J. Ackermann, op.cit., p.194.
18 Cf. R. Breitling, *Die nationalsozialistische Rassenlehre*, Anton Hain, Meisenheim am Glan, 1971.
19 See H. A. Turner, 'Faschismus und anti-Modernismus', in W. Michalka, op.cit., p.156.
20 H. A. Turner, 'Hitlers Einstellung', p.94.
21 D. Eichholtz, 'Grossgermanisches Reich und Generalplan Ost', *ZGW*, 11, 1980, p.835ff.
22 Erdmann, op.cit., p.347.
23 Cf. his remark in July 1920 to the effect that an alliance between Germany and Russia would only be possible if the Jewish elements were removed from the latter country.
24 See A. Kuhn, op.cit.
25 A. V. N. Woerden, 'Hitlers Verhältnis zu England', in W. Michalka (ed.), *Nationalsozialistische Aussenpolitik*, Wissenschaftliche Buchgesellschaft, Darmstadt, 1978, p.220ff.
26 O. E. Schüddekopf, *Linke Leute vom Rechts*, op.cit., pp.196ff.
27 Stoakes, op.cit.
28 K. Hildebrand, 'Innenpolitische Antriebskräfte der National-sozialistischen Aussenpolitik', in Michalka, op.cit., p.179.
29 F. Fischer, *Bündnis der Eliten*, pp.93-4.
30 ibid., p.77.
31 K. Lange, 'Der Terminus "Lebensraum" in Hitlers Mein Kampf', *VJH*, 1959.
32 Aigner, in Michalka, op.cit., p.68.
33 Woerden, op.cit., p.236; G. Niedhart, 'Deutsche Aussenpolitik und internationales System im Krisenjahr 1937', in Michalka, op.cit., p.365. See also, E. H. Haraszti, *Treaty breakers or Realpolitiker?*, Boldt, Boppard, 1974.
34 J. Henke, *England im Hitlers politischen Kalkül 1935-9*, Boppard, 1973, p.38.
35 J. Dülffer, 'Der Beginn des Krieges', p.464.
36 A. Kuhn, op.cit., p.209.
37 Niehardt, op.cit., p.361.
38 Dülffer, op.cit., p.465.
39 K. Hildebrand, 'Der zweite Weltkrieg: Probleme und Methoden seiner Darstellung', *NPL*, 1968, p.492.
40 Dülffer, 'Der Beginn des Krieges', p.465.

41 J. Dülffer, 'Politik zum Kriege. Das Deutsche Krieg und die Mächte auf dem Weg in den Zweiten Weltkrieg', *NPL*, 1981, p.50.
42 Dülffer, 'Der Beginn des Krieges', p.466.
43 In E. Robertson (ed.), *The Origins of the Second World War*, Macmillan, 1971.
44 See B. Martin, *Friedensinitiativen und Machtpolitik im Zweiten Weltkrieg, 1939-1942*, Droste, Düsseldorf, 1974.
45 D. Eichholtz, 'Expansionsrichtung Nord Europa', *ZGW*, 1979, 1, p.17.
46 J. Dülffer, *Weimar, Hitler und die Marine: Reichspolitik und Flottenbau 1920-1939*, Droste, Düsseldorf, 1973.
47 C. J. Burckhardt, *Meine Danziger Mission*, Munich, 1960, p.348.
48 Haushofer, cited in *VJH*.
49 K. Hildebrand, 'Der Zweite Weltkrieg', p.488.
50 Trevor-Roper, *The Testament of Adolf Hitler*, Cassell, 1951, p.17.
51 H. Abendroth, *Hitler in der spanischen Arena*, Ferdinand Schoeningh, 1973, p.323.
52 G. Meinck, *Hitler und die deutsche Aufrüstung, 1933-1937*, Franz Steiner, Wiesbaden, 1959, pp.157-8.
53 See G. Wagner (ed.), *Lagevorträge des Oberbefehlshabers der Kriegsmarine vor Hitler, 1939-1945*, Lehmann, Munich, 1972.
54 Zumpe, op.cit., p.402.
55 R. Cecil, *Hitler's decision to invade Russia 1941*, Davis-Poynter, 1975.
56 As shown in G. Wagner, op.cit.
57 A. Hillgruber, *Deutschlands Rolle in der Vorgeschichte der beiden Weltkriege*, Göttingen, 1967.
58 Radkau, op.cit., p.57.
59 Ministerialdirigent von Jagdwitz memo, 31 March 1939, Bundesarchiv R.26/IV, no.51.
60 Freymond, op.cit., pp.128-9.
61 Erdmann, op.cit., p.540.
62 K. Mielcke, *Deutsche Aussenpolitik 1933-1945*, Albert Linbach, Brunswick, 1960, pp.63-4.
63 Cited in J. Hiden, *Germany and Europe 1919-1939*, Longman, 1977, p.168. Cf. K. Hildebrand, *Das Dritte Reich*, Oldenbourg, Munich, 1979, p.55.
64 Freymond, op.cit., p.198. Cf. Ackermann, op.cit., p.178ff.
65 W. Präg and W. Jacobmeyer (eds.), *Das Diensttages Buch des Generalgouverneurs im Polen 1939-1945*, Deutsche Verlags-Anstalt, Stuttgart, 1975.
66 For Bohemia and Moravia see Ackermann, op.cit., p.208ff. In the case of the Soviet Union, D. Dallin, *German Rule in Russia 1941-1945*, Macmillan, 1957.
67 C. Streit, *Keine Kameraden: Die Wehrmacht und die sowjetischen Kriegsgefangenen 1941-5*, DTV, Stuttgart, 1978. Cf. H. Krausnick and H. H. Wilhelm, *Die Truppe des Weltanschauungskrieges. Die Einsatzgruppen der Sicherheitspolizei und des SD, 1938-1942*, Stuttgart, DVA, 1981. W. Dlugoborski and C. Madajczyk, 'Ausbeutungssysteme in den besetzten Gebiete', in F, Forstmeier, H. E. Volkmann (eds.), *Kriegswirtschaft und Rüstung 1939-1945*, Droste, Düsseldorf, 1977, p.394

suggest that Wehrmacht protests against ruthless exploitation were often prompted merely by tactical considerations, since an unsettled population could have caused trouble.

68 For the Netherlands, Freymond, op.cit., p.168ff and Akermann, op.cit., p.208ff. On Norway, H. D. Loock, *Quisling, Rosenberg und Terboven. Zur Vorgeschichte und Geschichte der nationalsozialistischen Revolution in Norwegen*, DVA, Stuttgart, 1970. See also M. Menger, F. Petrick and W. Wilhelmus, 'Nordeuropa unter der Vorherrschaft des faschistischen deutschen Imperialismus, 1940-1945', *ZGW*, no.5, 1976.

69 H. Mommsen, in M. Funke (ed.), op.cit., p.45.

70 Broszat, *Hitler State*, p.359.

71 H. Mommsen, 'National Socialism: Continuity and change', in W. Laqueur (ed.), op.cit., pp.198-9.

72 ibid., p.199.

73 Broszat, *Hitler State*, p.xiv.

74 Mommsen, op.cit., p.199.

75 Broszat, *Hitler State*, p.359.

76 H. A. Jacobsen, *Von der Strategie der Gewalt zur Politik der Friedenssicherung*, Droste, Düsseldorf, 1977.

77 P. Seabury, 'Ribbentrop and the German Foreign Office', *Political Science Quarterly*, 66, 1951, p.553.

78 See, for example, R. Bollmus, *Das Amt Rosenberg und seine Gegner*, DVA, Stuttgart, 1970.

79 J. Fest, *The face of the Third Reich*, Weidenfeld and Nicolson, 1970, p.177; W. Michalka, *Ribbentrop und die deutsche Weltpolitik 1933-40,* Wilhelm Fink, Munich, 1980.

80 K. Drechsler et al., 'Politik und Strategie des faschistischen Deutschlands im zweiten Weltkrieg', *ZGW*, 1, 1976, p.5ff.

81 Cited by Aigner in Michalka, op.cit., p.55.

82 See, for example, K. Drechsler et al, op.cit., p.1ff.

83 As a classic example, W. Schumann (ed.), *Griff nach Südosteuropa*, VEB, Berlin, 1973.

84 For example, D. Eichholtz, 'Grossgermanisches Reich', pp.835-6, where the tendency to see the New Order as an overall system of exploitation plays down the regional variations between East and West.

85 D. Eichholtz, K. Gossweiler, 'Noch einmal: Politik und Wirtschaft 1933-1945', *Das Argument*, 47, 1968, p.221.

86 Niedhart, in Michalka, op.cit., pp.367-8.

87 K. Lärmer, op.cit., p.115, p.143ff.

88 For the debate between them and Mason see T. W. Mason, 'Der Primat der Politik—Politik und Wirtschaft im Nationalsozialismus', *Das Argument*, 41, p.474ff; E. Czichon, 'Der Primat der Industrie im Kartell der nationalsozialistischen Macht', ibid., no.47, p.168ff; T. W. Mason, 'Primat der Industrie? Eine Erwiderung', ibid., no.47, p.192ff; D. Eichholtz and K. Gossweiler, 'Noch einmal; Politik und Wirtschaft, 1933-1945', ibid., 47, p.210ff.

89 T. W. Mason, *Sozialpolitik*, p.286.

90 Mason, 'Primat der Industrie', p.197.

91 G. Niedhart, 'Weltherrschaft versus World Appeasement?', *NPL*, 23, 1978, p.283.
92 Aigner in Michalka, op.cit., p.53.
93 K. Hildebrand, 'Hitlers Ort in der Geschichte des preussisch-deutschen Nationalstaats', *HZ*, 1973, p.584ff.
94 W. Hammer, *Adolf Hitler. Ein deutscher Messias*, Delp Verlag, Munich, 1972.
95 H. R. Trevor-Roper, *The Testament of Adolf Hitler*, p.15.

**Chapter 6**

1 Speech to building workers at Berchtesgaden 20 May 1937, cited P. Krüger, 'Zu Hitlers "nationalsozialistischen Wirtschaftserkenntnissen"' *G&G*, no.2, 1980, p.265.
2 J. Heyl, 'Hitler's economic thought. A reappraisal', *CEH*, no.6, 1973, p.83. See also G. Kroll, *Von der Weltwirtschaftskrise zur Staatskonjunktur*, Duncker and Humblot, Berlin 1958.
3 A. Barkai, 'Die Wirtschaftsauffassung der NSDAP', *Das Parlament*, no.9, 1975, p.3ff; *Das Wirtschaftssystem des Nationalsozialismus*, Verlag Wissenschaft und Politik, Berendt and Nottbeck, Cologne, 1977. See also his 'Sozialdarwinismus, Antiliberalismus im Hitlers Wirtschaftkonzept', *G&G*, 1977, p.406ff.
4 H. A. Turner, 'Hitlers Einstellung', p.89ff.
5 Cf. Kroll, op.cit., p.421; Barkai, *Wirtschaftssystem*, p.9.
6 ibid., p.20.
7 Kroll, op.cit., p.456.
8 Barkai, *Wirtschaftssystem*, pp.27-8.
9 U. Kiesenkoetter, *Gregor Strasser und die NSDAP*, Schriftenreihe der *VJH*, Stuttgart, 1978, p.26.
10 Cited in Turner, 'Hitlers Einstellung', p.112.
11 H. A. Turner Jr (ed.), *Hitler: Memoirs of a Confidant*, Yale U.P., New Haven-London, 1985.
12 ibid., p.114.
13 ibid., p.114.
14 Barkai, *Wirtschaftssystem*, pp.33-7.
15 Kroll, op.cit., p.426.
16 Kiesenkoetter, op.cit., p.119ff.
17 Kroll, op.cit., p.433.
18 Barkai, *Wirtschaftssystem*, p.39.
19 ibid., p.33.
20 For a detailed discussion see P. Krüger, 'Zu Hitlers "National-sozialistischen Wirtschaftserkenntnissen"', p.263ff.
21 H. Backe
22 Kroll, op.cit., p.435.
23 See E. Czichon, *Wer verhalf Hitler zur Macht?*, Cologne, Pahl Rugenstein, 1972, 3rd edition.
24 Barkai, *Wirtschaftssysteme*, p.17.

25 Turner, 'Faschismus und Antimodernismus' in Michalka, op.cit., p.153.
26 See W. Deist, M. Messerschmidt et al., *Ursachen und Voraussetzungen der deutschen Kriegspolitik*, DVA, Stuttgart, 1979, p.185 for this trend.
27 D. Gessner 'Agrarprotektionismus und Welthandelskrise 1929-1932', *ZAG*, no.26, 1978, pp.166-7.
28 E. Lederer, 'Gegen Autarkie und Nationalismus' in J. Kocka (ed.), *Kapitalismus, Klassenstruktur und Probleme der Demokratie in Deutschland 1910-1940*, Göttingen, Vandenhoeck & Ruprecht, 1979, p.199ff.
29 J. Radkau, 'Entscheidungsprobleme', p.64.
30 Bloch, op.cit., p.28.
31 Krüger, op.cit., p.268.
32 W. Fischer, *Deutsche Wirtschaftspolitik 1918-1945*, Leske, Opladen, 1978, p.62.
33 Zumpe, op.cit., pp.150ff.
34 Kroll, op.cit., p.471. But see Zumpe, op.cit., p.65 and Barkai, *Wirtschaftssysteme*, p.15, who insist that work creation and rearmament cannot really be separated in practice.
35 R. J. Overy, 'Cars, roads and economic recovery in Germany 1932-9', *EHR*, XXVIII, 1975, p.466ff, 'Transport and rearmament in the Third Reich', *HJ*, XVI, 1973, p.389ff.
36 See K. Lärmer, op.cit., p.30ff. for the point about propaganda value. The question of modernization and the Four Year Plan is raised by B. Martin, 'Friedensinitiativen', pp.74-5.
37 Radkau, op.cit., p.48.
38 Cf. Zumpe, 'Weltwirtschaftslage und faschistische Aussenwirtschafts-regulierung', *JBW*, no.4, 1978, p.203ff. See also her 'Stand und Probleme der wirtschaftshistorischen Imperialismusforschung', *ZGW*, no.5, 1975, p.498.
39 P. Krüger, op.cit., p.274.
40 A. S. Milward, 'The Reichsmark Bloc and the international economy', in *Der Führer Staat*, p.377.
41 C. W. Guillebaud, *The economic recovery of Germany*, p.158.
42 R. Frommelt, *Paneuropa oder Mitteleuropa. Einigungsbestrebungen im Kalkül deutscher Wirtschaft und Politik 1925-1933*, DVA, Stuttgart, 1977.
43 B. Puchert, 'Einige Überlegungen zum deutschen Kapitalexport 1933 bis 1939', *JBW*, no.3, 1976, p.87. See also *Griff nach dem Südosten*, op.cit., for an overall background to German penetration in the Balkans from the Stamokap viewpoint.
44 Milward, op.cit., p.401. See also B. J. Wendt, 'Südost Europa in der nationalsozialistischen Grossraumwirtschaft', in *Der Führer Staat*, op.cit., p.414ff. He agrees with Milward at least that 'exploitation' is probably too strong a term for German-Balkan economic relations 1033-9.
45 H. J. Schroeder, 'Deutsche Südosteuropapolitik 1929-1936', *G&G*, no.1, 1976, p.32.
46 W. Deist et al., op.cit.
47 Milward, op.cit., p.295.
48 ibid., p.396.
49 Radkau 'Entscheidigunsprozesse', pp.46-7.

50 Kroll, op.cit., p.456.
51 P. Krüger. op.cit., pp.270-1.
52 O. Nathan, *The Nazi economic system; Germany's mobilization for war*, Durham, N. C., 1944. Cf. C. Bettelheim, *L'économie allemande sous le nazisme*, Bibliothèque générale d'économie politique, Paris, 1946.
53 R. Erbe, op.cit., p.4.
54 Kroll, op.cit., p.639.
55 See for example Barkai, *Wirtschaftssysteme*, p.13.
56 B. H. Klein, *Germany's economic preparations for war*, Harvard U.P., 1959.
57 A. S. Milward, *The German economy at war*, Athlone Press, 1965.
58 B. Carroll, *Design for total war*, Mouton, The Hague, 1968.
59 See A. Milward, 'Arbeitspolitik und Produktivität', in F. Forstmeier, H. E. Volkmann, (eds.), *Kriegswirtschaft und Rüstung*, p.86.
60 Cf. Freymond, op.cit., p.73.
61 A. Simpson, 'The struggle for control of the German economy 1936-7', *JMH*, XXXI, 1957, p.37.
62 Meinck, *Hitler und die deutsche Aufrüstung 1933-7*, Franz Steiner, Wiesbaden, 1959, pp.159-61.
63 For the differences within the NSDAP and German industry over the general policy to be followed see R. Saage, 'Zum Verhältnis', p.28.
64 Barkai, *Wirtschaftssystem*, pp.170-1.
65 Radkau, op.cit., p.55.
66 Deist, Messerschmidt, op.cit., p.708ff.
67 Radkau, op.cit., p.55.
68 Meinck, op.cit., pp.159-161.
69 Radkau, op.cit., p.55.
70 Kroll, op.cit., p.474.
71 Mason, *Sozialpolitik*, p.216ff.
72 J. J. Jaeger, *Die wirtschaftliche Unabhängigkeit des Dritten Reichs vom Ausland dargestellt am Beispiel der Stahlindustrie*, Berlin, 1969, p.305ff.
73 Eichholtz, 'Alte und Neue Konzeptionen', *JBW*, no.3, 1971, p.235ff.
74 H. H. Casper, 'Das Erdöl in den Raubplänen des deutschen Faschismus', *JBW*, no.3, 1976, pp.55ff.
75 Thomas, op.cit., p.147ff.
76 T. W. Mason, 'Innere Krise und Angriffskrieg 1938-9', F. Forstmeier, H. E. Volkmann, *Wirtschaft und Rüstung*, pp.158-88.
77 Mason, *Sozialpolitik*, op.cit., p.299ff.
78 A. J. P. Taylor in E. M. Robertson (ed.), *The origins of the Second World War*, Macmillan, 1971.
79 C. W. Guillebaud, '*Germany's economic recovery*', and E. Lederer, in J. Kocka (ed.), *Kapitalismus*, p.248.
80 Mason, *Sozialpolitik*, p.216ff.
81 Deist et al., *Ursachen*, pp.710-711.
82 J. Dülffer, 'Der Beginn des Krieges', p.455.
83 ibid., p.456.
84 P. Sauer, *Wuerttemberg in der NS Zeit*, p.272ff.
85 Thomas, op.cit., p.147ff.
86 Mason, *Sozialpolitik*, p.216ff.

87 Forstmeier and Volkmann, op.cit., p.164.
88 V. Jagdwitz report, 31 March 1939, Bundesarchiv-R26/IV 51.
89 Quoted in Dülffer, op.cit., p.454.
90 B. Martin, 'Friedensplannungen', p.76.
91 Dülffer, op.cit., pp.449-450.
92 ibid., pp.452-3.
93 L. Herbst, for a short account of the debate.
94 Kühnl, 'Probleme einer Theorie', p.110.
95 Cf. W. Dlugoborski and C. Madaczyk, 'Ausbeutungssysteme', p.393.
96 D. Eichholtz, 'Expansionsrichtung Nordeuropa', p.19.
97 Dlugoborski, Madaczyk, op.cit., p.386ff.
98 H. Winkel, 'Die Ausbeutung des besetzten Frankreich', in F. Forstmeier, H. E. Volkmann (eds.), *Kriegswirtschaft und Rüstung*, p.340.
99 J. Jaeger, op.cit., p.310.
100 See Darré to Hitler's staff, 25 April 1940, pointing out how German occupation of Poland and Norway had worsened the food situation. Bundesarchiv-NS10/107.
101 F. Kübler, 'Die Nationalsozialistische Rechtsordnung', *NPL*, 1970, p.443ff.
102 In February 1942 Speer got Hitler to ban planning for a peacetime European economic order as it interfered with the war effort—Freymond, op.cit., p.142.
103 Cf. Dlugoborski and Madaczyk, op.cit., p.376ff with Goering's directive of 17 August 1940, that the wartime economy should take precedence. As this document stated, after the war the economy should be so ordered as to ensure the German people the highest possible standard of living.

**Chapter 7**

1 R. Saage, 'Zum Verhältnis', p.17.
2 R. Brady, op.cit.
3 C. Schmidt, *The Plough and the Sword*, 1938.
4 Neumann, *Behemoth*, p.
5 ibid., p.
6 M. Horkheimer, 'Die Juden und Europa', *Zeitschrift für Sozialforschung*, VIII, 1939.
7 Cited in Zumpe, *Wirtschaft und Staat*, p.3. For the reference to Flick etc. see Drechsler et al., 'Politik und Strategie', *ZGW*, no.1, 1976, p.8.
8 E. W. Ulbricht, *Die Legende vom deutschen Sozialismus*, 1945.
9 Kühnl, 'Neuere Ergebnisse', Part 2, p.140.
10 W. Herferth, 'Der Reichsnährstand—ein Instrument der Kriegspolitik des faschistischen deutschen Imperialismus', *Wissenschaftliche Zeitschrift der Universität Rostock*, no.17, 1968, p.225.
11 Lärmer, op.cit., p.11.
12 W. Ruge and W. Schumann (eds.), *Dokumente zur deutschen Geschichte 1933-1935*, VEB Deutscher Verlag, Berlin, 1977, p.16.
13 For a general discussion on this theme see J. Dülffer, 'Bonapartism,

Fascism and National Socialism', *JCH*, 11, 1976, p.109-28.
14 ibid., p.111.
15 Nolte, *Theorien*, p.37.
16 Dülffer, 'Bonapartism', pp.113-14.
17 ibid., p.119.
18 See for example D. Eichholtz's review of D. Petzina's original dissertation on the Four Year Plan 1936, where Eichholtz attacks Petzina for assuming Bonapartism to be a valid model. *JBW*, no.3, 1971, p.239.
19 A. Kuhn, *Das faschistische Herrschaftssystem und die moderne Gesellschaft*, Hoffmann & Campe, Hamburg, 1973.
20 R. Saage, *Faschismus Theorien. Eine Einführung*, C. H. Beck, Munich, 1976, p.150.
21 See F. Kübler, 'Die nationalsozialistische Rechtsordnung', *NPL*, 1970, p.447.
22 H. A. Winkler, *Revolution, Staat, Faschismus*, p.94.
23 For their plans to survive the conflict see W. Schumann, 'Nachkriegsplanungen der Reichsgruppeindustrie in Herbst 1944', *JBW*, no.3, 1972, p.259ff.
24 See F. Kübler, op.cit., p.443.
25 Freymond, op.cit., p.158ff.
26 Winkler, *Revolution, Staat, Faschismus*, p.83 and Saage, 'Zum Verhältnis', p.38.
27 E. Hanisch, 'Neuere Faschismustheorien', *ZG*, no.1, 1973-4, pp.22-3.
28 Mason, 'Primat der Politik', *Das Argument*, 1966, p.473ff.
29 H. Grebing, *Aktuelle Theorien*, p.77.
30 Kühnl, 'Neuere Ergebnisse', Part 2, pp.138-9.
31 Turner, *Faschismus und Kapitalismus in Deutschland*, p.30.
32 Barrington Moore, *Social origins of dictatorship and democracy*, Penguin, 1977. For an application of a similar idea to pre-1945 Japan, see Y. Yamaguchi, 'Faschismus als Herrschaftssystem in Japan und Deutschland', *GWU*, no.2, 1976, p.89ff.
33 S. M. Lipsett, cited in Nolte, *Theorien*, p.390ff.
34 Kühnl, 'Probleme einer Theorie', Part 2, op.cit., p.110.
35 H. Plessner, *Die verspätete Nation—über die politische Verführbarkeit bürgerlichen Geistes*, Stuttgart—Cologne—Mainz, 1959 (Ist edition, 1935).
36 Cited in Nolte, *Theorien*, p.379.
37 Meinck, op.cit., pp.164-5. Cf. Grebing, *Aktuelle Theorien*, pp.50ff. In general see M. Klemenz, *Gesellschaftliche Ursprünge des Faschismus*, Suhrkamp, Frankfurt, 1972.
38 See W. Hock, *Deutscher Antikapitalismus. Der ideologische Kampf gegen die freie Wirtschaft im Zeichen der grossen Krise*, Frankfurt, 1960, for this thesis.
39 H. Winkler, *Mittelstand und Demokratie.*
40 H. Winkler, 'German Society, Hitler and the illusion of restoration 1930-33', *JCH*, 11, 1976, pp.1-16.
41 Childers, op.cit.
42 P. Merkl, *Political violence under the Swastika*, Princeton U.P., 1975; S. Neumann, *Die Parteien der Weimarer Republik*, Kohlhammer, Stuttgart (Ist

edition 1932), p.73ff.
43 E. Fromm, *The fear of freedom,*
44 W. Maser, *Hitler*, p.124.
45 H. R. Trevor-Roper, *Hitler's secret conversations*, Signet Books, 1953, p.25ff.
46 H. Heiber, *Josef Goebbels*, Colloquium, 1962, p.25ff.
47 G. Mosse, *Nationalisation of the masses*, pp.10-11.
48 K. D. Erdmann, 'Nationalsozialismus', p.457ff.
49 Winkler, *Revolution, Staat, Faschismus*, p.65.
50 Cited in Schüddekopf, op.cit., p.195.
51 H. Buchheim, *Totalitäre Herrschaft*, p.ii.
52 Cited Erdmann, op.cit., p.463.
53 A. J. Groth, 'The isms in totalitarianism', *American Political Science Review*, LVIII, Dec. 1964, p.888ff.
54 B. Seidel, S. Jenker (eds.), *Wege der Totalitärismus Forschung*, pp.2-3.
55 Cited in D. Albrecht, 'Zum Begriff des Totalitärismus', *GWU*, no.3, 1975, p.135.
56 K. D. Bracher, 'Der Faschismus', Sonderbeitrag aus Meyers *Enzyklopädisches Lexikon*, no.8, 1973, p.551. See also A. L. Unger, *The totalitarian Party. Party and people in Nazi Germany and the Soviet Union*, C.U.P., 1974.
57 See for this point, B. Perz, H. Safrian, op.cit., p.441 and E. Hennig, 'Industrie und Faschismus', *NPL*, 1970, p.434. For criticisms of historical comparisons between National Socialist Germany and Stalinist Russia see P. Dukes, J. W. Hiden, 'Towards an historical comparison of Nazi Germany and Soviet Russia in the 1930s', *New Zealand Slavonic Journal*, 1, 1979, pp.68-9.
58 Quoted in E. Hennig, 'Regionale Unterschiede', p.161.
59 M. Broszat et al. (ed.), *Bayern in der NS Zeit*, Oldenbourg, Vienna, 1977. Cf. P. Sauer, *Wurttemberg in der Zeit des Nationalsozialismus*, Süddeutsche Verlagsgesellschaft, Ulm, 1975. M. Domarus, *Nationalsozialismus. Krieg und Bevölkerung im Augsburg*, Neue Schriftenreihe des Stadtarchivs Munich, 1977, vol.91.
60 Hennig, 'Regionale Unterschiede', p.155.

# Bibliography

## 1 The personality of Adolf Hitler


ALEXANDER, E., *Der Mythos Hitler*, Europa Verlag, Zurich, 1937.

AUERBACH, H., 'Hitlers politische Lehrjahre und die Münchener Gesellschaft 1919-1923', *VJH*, 25, 1977, pp.1ff.

BANUS, A., 'Das völkische Blatt "Der Scherer". Ein Beitrag zur Hitlers Schulzeit', *VJH*, 18, 1970, pp.196ff.

BARTHEL, K., *Friedrich der Grosse in Hitlers Weltanschauung*, Frankfurter Historische Vorträge, 1977.

BAYNES, N. H. (ed.), *The speeches of Adolf Hitler*, O.U.P., 1942.

BERLIN, J., JOACHIM, D, *Was verschweigt Fest? Analyse und Dokumente zum Hitler Film*, Kleine Bibliothek Politik und Wissenschaft, Cologne, 1978.

BINION, R., *Hitler among the Germans*, N.Y., Oxford, 1976.

BRACHER, K. D., 'Das Phänomen Adolf Hitler', *Politische Literatur* 1, 1952, pp.207ff.

BULLOCK, A., *Hitler. A study in tyranny*, Odhams Press, 1952.

CARR, W., *Hitler. A study in personality and politics*, Edward Arnold, 1978.

CREVELD, M. VAN., 'War lord Hitler. Some points reconsidered', *ESR*, 4, no.1, 1974, pp.57ff.

DAVIDSON, E., *The making of Hitler*, Macmillan, 1977.

DEUERLEIN, E., *Hitler. Eine politische Biographie*, List, Munich, 1969.

—'Hitlers Eintritt in die Politik und die Reichswehr', *VJH*, 1959, pp.177ff.

DOMARUS, M., *Hitler: Reden und Proklamationen*. 2 vols, Messerschmidt, Würzburg, 1962, 1963.

FABRY, P. W., *Mutmassungen über Hitler. Urteile von Zeitgenossen*, Droste, Düsseldorf, 1969.

FEST, J., *Hitler*, Propyläen Verlag, Frankfurt, 1973.

FOX, J. P., 'Adolf Hitler. The continuing debate', *International Affairs*, 1979, pp.252ff.

GATZKE, H. W., 'Hitler and psychohistory', *AHR*, 78, no.2, 1973, pp.394ff.

GÖRLITZ, W., QUINT, H. A. *Adolf Hitler. Eine Biographie*, Steingrüben Verlag, Stuttgart, 1952.

GOSSET, P., GOSSET, R., *Adolf Hitler* (3 vols), R. Julliard, Paris, 1961-5.

GRAML, H., 'Problem einer Hitler-Biographie', *VJH*, 22, 1974, pp.76ff.

GRAML, H., 'Ein überflüssiger Film', *GWU*, 11, 1977, pp.669ff.
HAMMER, H., 'Die deutschen Ausgaben von Hitlers Mein Kampf', *VJH*, 4, 1956, pp.161ff.
HAMMER, W., *Adolf Hitler—ein deutscher Messias? Dialog mit dem 'Führer'*, I, Delp Verlag, Munich, 1970.
—*Adolf Hitler—der Tyrann und die Völker. Dialog mit dem 'Führer'* II, Delp Verlag, Munich, 1972.
HEER, F., *Der Glaube des Adolf Hitler. Anatomie einer politischen Religiosität*, Bechtle Verlag, Munich-Esslingen, 1968.
HEIBER, H., *Adolf Hitler. A short biography*, Oswald Wolff, 1961.
HEIDEN, K., *One man against Europe*, Penguin, 1939.
HILDEBRAND, K., 'Nationalsozialismus ohne Hitler?', *GWU*, 5, 1980, pp.289ff.
—'"Der Fall Hitler": Bilanz und Wege der Hitlerforschung', *NPL*, XIV, 1969, pp.375ff.
HILLGRUBER, A., 'Tendenzen, Ergebnisse und Perspektiven der gegenwärtigen Hitler-Forschung', *HZ*, 226, 1978, pp.600ff.
HITLER, A., *Hitler's Table Talk*, Weidenfeld and Nicholson, 1953.
—*Mein Kampf*, Franz Eher Verlag, Munich, 1933.
HOFFMANN, P., 'Hitler's personal security', *JCH*, 8, no.2, 1973, pp.25ff.
—*Die Sicherheit des Diktators. Hitlers Leibwachen, Schutzmassnahmen*, R. Piper, Munich, 1975.
HORN, W., 'Ein unbekannter Aufsatz Hitlers aus dem Frühjahr 1924', *VJH*, 16, 1968, pp.280ff.
JÄCKEL, E., *Hitler in History*, Brandeis U.P., Hanover and London, 1984.
JÄCKL, E., KUHN, A., *Hitlers sämtliche Aufzeichnungen 1919-1924*, DVA, Stuttgart, 1980.
JENKS, W. A., *Vienna and the young Hitler*, Columbia U.P., N.Y., 1960.
KALOW, G., *The shadow of Hitler. A critique of political consciousness*, Ropp and Whiting, 1968.
KOTZE, H. von, KRAUSNICK, H. (eds.), *Es spricht der Führer. Sieben examplarische Hitler Reden*, Gütersloh, 1966.
LANGE, K., *Hitlers unbeachtete Maximen 'Mein Kampf' und die Öffentlichkeit*, Kohlhammer, Stuttgart, 1968.
MANZMANN, A., *Hitlerwelle und historische Fakten*, Scriptor Verlag, Königstein, 1979.
MASER, W., *Hitler. Legende, Mythos, Wirklichkeit*, Bechtle, Munich, 1971.
—*Hitlers Mein Kampf*, Bechtle Verlag, Munich, 1966.
—*Hitlers Briefe und Notizen. Sein Weltbild in handschriftlichen Dokumenten*, Econ. Verlag, Vienna, Düsseldorf, 1973.
NIEKISCH, E., *Hitler. Ein deutsches Verhängnis*, Widerstands Verlag, Berlin, 1932.
PHELPS, R. H., 'Hitler als Parteiredner im Jahre 1920', *VJH*, 11, 1963, pp.274ff.
—'Hitlers "grundlegende" Rede über den Antisemitismus', *VJH*, 16, 1968, pp.390ff.
PICKER, H., *The Hitler Phenomenon. An intimate portrait of Hitler and his entourage*, David and Charles, 1974.
RAUSCHNING, H., *Hitler speaks*, Thornton Butterworth, 1939.
SCHIEDER, T. H., *Rauschnings 'Gespräche mit Hitler' als geschichtliche Quelle*, Westdeutscher Verlag, Opladen, 1972.

SCHÖLLGEN, G., 'Das Problem einer Hitler-Biographie', *NPL*, 1978, pp.421-34.
SCHRAMM, P. E., *Hitler. The man and military leader*, Penguin Press, 1972.
SHORT, K. R. M., *Hitler's fall: the newsreel witness*, Croom Helm, London, 1986.
SMITH, B. F., *Adolf Hitler. His family, childhood and youth*, Standford U.P., 1967.
STERN, J. P., *Hitler. The Führer and the people*, Fontana, 1974.
SYNDOR, C., 'The selling of Adolf Hitler. David Irving's Hitler's War', *CEH*, 12, 1979, pp.182ff.
TAYLOR, TELFORD, *Hitler's secret book*, Grove Press, N.Y., 1961.
TOLAND, J., *Adolf Hitler*, Garden City, N.Y., 1976.
TREVOR-ROPER, H. R., *The last days of Hitler*, Macmillan, 1947.
VILLARD, P., 'Antiquité et Weltanschauung hitlérienne', *RGM*, 88, 1972, pp.1ff.
WAGENER, O., in H. A. TURNER (ed.), *Hitler aus nächster Nahe. Aufzeichnungen eines Vertrauten (1929-1932)*, Ullstein, Frankfurt, 1978.
—*Hitler. Memoirs of a confidant*, ed. H. A. Turner Jr., Yale U.P., New Haven-London, 1985.
TYRELL, A., *Vom Trommler zum Führer*, Wilhelm Fink, Munich, 1975.
WAITE, R. G. L., *'The psychopathic God! Adolf Hitler'*, Basic Books, N.Y., 1977.
WIEDEMANN, F., *Der Mann, der Feldherr werden wollte*, Velbert, Kettwig, 1964.
ZITELMANN, R., *Hitler, Selbstverständnis eines Revolutionärs*, Berg, Londons, 1986.
ZOLLER, A., *Hitler privat*, Droste, Düsseldorf, 1949.

## 2 Ideology and the nationalization of the masses

ACKERMANN, J., *Heinrich Himmler als Ideologe*, Musterschmidt, Göttingen, 1970.
ADAM, U. D., *Hochschule und Nationalsozialismus. Die Universität Tübingen im Dritten Reich*, Mohr, Tübingen, 1977.
—*Judenpolitik im Dritten Reich*, Droste, Düsseldorf, 1972.
ADLER, H. G., *Der verwaltete Mensch. Studien zur Deportation der Juden aus Deutschland*, Mohr, Tübingen, 1974.
ALBRECHT, G., *Nationalsozialistische Filmpolitik*, Ferdinand Enke, Stuttgart, 1969.
ALY, G. et al., *Sozialpolitik und Jundenvernichtung. Gibt es eine ökonomie der Endlösung?*, Rotbuch Verlag, Berlin, 1987.
ANDERBRÜGGE, J., *Völkisches Rechtsdenken: Zur Rechtslehre in der Zeit des Nationalsozialismus*, Duncker and Humblot, Berlin, 1978.
ANGRESS, W. T., *Generation zwischen Furcht und Hoffnung, Jüdische Jugend im Dritten Reich*, Christians, Hamburg, 1985.
BAADER, G., SCHULTZ, U. (eds.), *Medizin und Nationalsozialismus*, Mabuse, Berlin, 1980.
BAIRD, J. W., *The mythical world of Nazi propaganda*, O.U.P., 1975.
BALFOUR, J. W., *Propaganda in war, 1939-1945. Organization, policies and publics in Britain and Germany*, Routledge and Kegan Paul, 1979.
BARKAI, A., *Vom Boykott zur 'Entjudung'. Der wirtschaftliche Existenzkampf der Juden im Dritten Reich*, Fischer Taschenbuch Verlag, Frankfurt, 1987.
BARTOV, O., The *Eastern Front, 1941-1945. German troops and the barbarisation of warfare*, Macmillan, 1986.
BAUMGÄRTNER, R., *Weltanschauungskampf im Dritten Reich. Auseinander-*

*setzungen der Kirchen mit Alfred Rosenberg*, Matthias Grunewald, Mainz, 1977.
BEER, M., 'Die Entwicklung der Gaswagen beim Mord an den Juden', *VJH*, 35, no.3, 1987, pp.403-17.
BENDERSKY, J. W., *Carl Schmitt, Theorist for the Reich*, Princeton U. P., 1983.
BENZ, W., DIESTEL, B. (eds.), *Dachauer Hefte, Studien und Dokumentation zur Geschichte der nationalsozialistischen Konzentrationslager*, Dachauer Hefte, Dachau, 1985.
BILLIG, J., *Alfred Rosenberg dans l'action idéologique politique et administrative du Reich hitlérien*, C.D.J.C., Paris, 1963.
—*L'hitlérisme et le système concentrationnaire*, Presses universitaire de France, Paris, 1967.
BOBERACH, H., *Meldungen aus dem Reich*, Luchterhand, Neuwied-Berlin, 1965.
BOECKENFOERDE, E.-W., (ed.), *Staatsrecht und Staatsrechtslehre im Dritten Reich*, Recht, Justiz, Zeitgeschehen, 41, C. F. Mueller, Heidelberg, 1985.
BOELCKE, W. A., *Die Macht des Radios. Weltpolitik und Auslandsrundfunk*, Ullstein, 1977.
BRAATZ, W. E., 'Two neo-conservative myths in Germany 1919-1932', *Journal of the History of Ideas*, 1971, pp.569ff.
BRAMSTED, E. J., *Goebbels and National Socialist propaganda 1925-1945*, East Lansing State U.P., Michigan, 1965.
BRANDENBURG, H-C., *Die Geschichte der Hitler Jugend. Wege und Irrwege einer Generation*, Verlag Wissenschaft und Politik, Cologne, 1968.
BRENNER, H., *Die Kunstpolitik im Dritten Reich*, Rororo, Reinbek, 1963.
BROSZAT, M., 'Soziale Motivation und Führerbindung des Nationalsozialismus', *VJH*, 18, 1970, pp.392ff.
—'Hitler und die Genesis der "Endlösung". Aus Anlass der Thesen von David Irving', *VJH*, 25, 1977, pp.739ff.
BROWNING, C., 'Zur Genesis der "Endlösung". Eine Antwort an Martin Broszat', *VJH*, 29, 1981, pp.97ff.
BRUSS, R., *Die Bremer Juden unter dem Nationalsozialismus,* Selbstverlag des Staatsarchivs der Freien Hansestadt Bremen, Bremen, 1983.
BUCHBENDER, O. (ed.), *Heil Beil! Flugblattpropaganda im Zweiten Weltkrieg*, Seewald Verlag, Stuttgart, 1974.
BURDEN, H. J., *The Nuremburg Party rallies*, Pall Mall Press, 1968.
BUTLER, R., *The roots of National Socialism 1783-1933*, 1942. Reprinted Howard Fertig, N.Y., 1968.
CARSTEN, F. L., 'The historical roots of National Socialism', in E. J. Feuchtwanger (ed.), *Upheaval and continuity. A century of German history*, Wolff, London, 1973.
CECIL, R., *The myth of the master race. Alfred Rosenberg and Nazi ideology*, Batsford, 1972.
COCKS, G., *Psychotherapy in the Third Reich. The Goering Institute,* O.U.P., N.Y.-Oxford, 1985.
COHN, N., *Warrant for genocide*, Penguin, 1970.
DAIM, W., *Der Mann, der Hitler die Ideen gab*, Isar, Munich, 1958.
DAMBERG, W., *Der Kampf um die Schulen in Westfalen, 1933-1945,* Matthias Gruenewald, Mainz, 1986.
DAWIDOWICZ, L. S., *The war against the Jews 1933-1945*, Holt, Rinehart and

Winston, N.Y., 1975.

DENKLER, H., PRUMM, K. (eds.), *Die deutsche Literatur im Dritten Reich*, Reclam, Stuttgart, 1976.

DOMARUS, W., *Nationalsozialismus, Krieg und Bevölkerung*, Neue Schriftenreihe des Stadtarchivs Munich, vol.91, 1977.

DÖRNER, K., 'Nationalsozialismus und Lebensvernichtung', *VJH*, 15, 1967, pp.121ff.

DROBITSCH, R., GOGUEL, MÜLLER, W., *Juden unter dem Hakenkreuz*, Deutsche Verlag der Wissenschaft, East Berlin, 1973.

DÜLFFER, J., THIES, J., HENKE, J., *Baupolitik im Dritten Reich*, Böhlau, Vienna-Cologne, 1977.

EHRHARDT, H., *Euthanasie und Vernichtung 'lebensunwerten Lebens'*, Stuttgart, 1965.

EILERS, R., *Die nationalsozialistische Schulpolitik. Eine Studie zur Tradition, Erziehung im totalitären Staat*, Westdeutscher Verlag, Cologne, 1963.

ERDMANN, K. D., "Lebensunwertes Leben". Totalitäre Lebensvernichtung und das Problem der Euthanasie', *GWU*, 26, 1975, pp.213ff.

FLEMING, G., *Hitler and the Final Solution*, O.U.P., 1986.

FLESSAU, K.-I., *Schule der Diktatur: Lehrpläne—Schulbücher des Nationalsozialismus*, Fischer Taschenbuch, Frankfurt, 1979.

FOCKE, H., STROCKA, M. (eds.), *Alltag der Gleichgeschalteten. Wie die Nazis Kultur, Justiz und Presse braun färbten,* Reinbek, Hamburg, 1985.

FOX, J. P., *Adolf Hitler and the Jewish question. A study in ideology and policy*, Macmillan, 1986.

FREI, N., *Nationalsozialistische Eroberung der Provinzpresse. Gleichschaltung, Selbstanpassung und Resistenz in Bayern*, DVA, Stuttgart, 1980.

—"'Wir waren blind, unglaübig und langsam', Buchenwald, Dachau, und die amerikanische Medien im Früjahr 1945", *VJH,* 35, no.3, 1987, pp.385-401.

FRÖHLICH, E., 'Die Kulturpolitische Pressekonferenz des Reichspropaganda-ministeriums', *VJH*, 22, 1974, pp.347ff.

GAMM, H.-J., *Der braune Kult. Das Dritte Reich und seine Ersatzreligion*, Rütten and Loening, Hamburg, 1962.

GANSSMÜLLER, C., *Die Erbgesundheitspolitik des Dritten Reiches*, Böhlau, Cologne-Vienna, 1987.

GASMAN, D., *The Scientific Origins of National Socialism. Social Darwinism in E. Haeckl and the German Monist League*, Macdonald, 1971.

GENSCHEL, H., *Die Verdrängung der Juden aus der Wirtschaft im Dritten Reich,* Musterschmidt, Göttingen, 1966.

GILES, G., *Students and National Socialism in Germany*, Princeton U.P., 1985.

GOLDHAGEN, E., 'Weltanschauung und Endlösung. Zum Antisemitismus der nationalsozialistischen Führungsschicht', *VJH*, 24, 1976, pp.379ff.

GORDON, S., *Hitler, Germans and the 'Jewish question',* Princeton U.P., 1984.

GRODE, W., *Die 'Sonderbehandlung 14 f 13' in den Konzentrationslagern des Dritten Reiches. Ein Beitrag zur Dynamik faschistischen Vernichtungspolitik*, Lang, Frankfurt, 1987.

GRUCHMANN, L., 'Euthanasie und Justiz im Dritten Reich', *VJH*, 20, 1972, pp.235ff.

HAGEMANN, W., *Publizistik im Dritten Reich. Ein Beitrag zur Methodik der Massenführung*, Hansischer-Gilden Verlag, Hamburg, 1948.

—*Die Pressenlenkung im Dritten Reich*, Bouvier, Bonn, 1970.

HALE, O. J., *Captive press in the Third Reich*, Princeton, U.P., N.J., 1964.

—'Gottfried Feder calls Hitler to order', *JMH*, XXX, 1958, pp.358ff.

HARTSHORNE, E. Y., *The German Universities and National Socialism*, Allen and Unwin, 1937.

HAUSCHILD, H., *Erzieher im Dritten Reich*, Rütten, Munchengladbach, 1976.

HEIBER, H. (ed.), *Goebbels—Reden*, 2 vols, Droste, Düsseldorf, 1971 and 1972.

HELLFELD, M., KLOENNE, A., *Die betrogene Generation. Jugend in Deutschland unter dem Faschismus. Quellen und Dokumente*, Pahl-Rugenstein, Cologne, 1985.

HERF, J., *Reactionary Modernism, Technology, culture and politics and the Third Reich*, C.U.P., 1986.

HILBERG, R., *The destruction of the European Jews*, Quadrangle Books, Chicago, 1960 and Leicester U.P., 1986.

HILLER, M., HENRY, C., *Lebensborne Vernichtung. Im Namen der Rasse*, Paul Zsolnay Verlag, Vienna, 1975.

HIRSCHFELD, G. (ed.), *The policies of genocide. Jews and Soviet prisoners of war in Nazi Germany*, Allen and Unwin, 1986.

HOLBORN, H., 'Origins and political character of Nazi ideology', *Political Science Quarterly*, LXXIX, 1964, pp.542ff.

HORN, W., *Fuehrerideologie und Parteiorganisation in der NSDAP*, Droste, Düsseldorf, 1971.

INSTITUTE FOR CONTEMPORARY HISTORY, MUNICH, *Medizin im Nationalsozialismus*, Munich, 1988.

JÄCKEL, E., *Hitler's Weltanschauung. A blueprint for power*, Wesleyan U.P., Middletown, Connecticut, 1972.

JAECKEL, E., *Hitlers Herrschaft. Vollzug einer Weltanschauung*, DVA, Stuttgart, 1986.

JAECKEL, E., ROHWER, J. (eds.), *Der Mord an den Juden im Zweiten Weltkrieg. Entschlussbildung und Verwirklichung*, DVA, Stuttgart, 1985.

JOHN, H., 'Nationalsozialismus und Christentum', *ZG*, 7, 1979-80, pp.427ff.

KATER, M. H., *Das 'Ahnenerbe' der SS. 1935-1945*, DVA, Stuttgart, 1974.

KERSHAW, I., *Der Hitler Mythos. Volksmeinung und Propaganda im Dritten Reich*, DVA, Stuttgart, 1980.

—*Popular opinion and political dissent in the Third Reich*, Clarendon Press, Oxford, 1984.

KIRCHNER, K., *Flugblätter. Psychologische Kriegsführung im Zweiten Weltkrieg in Europa.* Carl Hanser, Munich, 1976.

KLEE, E., *'Euthanasie' im NS-Staat. Die 'Vernichtung lebensunwerten Lebens'*, Fischer Taschenbuch, Frankfurt, 1985.

KOCH, H. W., *The Hitler Youth. Origins and development*, Macdonald and Janes, 1975.

KOEHL, R., *RKFDV: German resettlement and population policy 1939-1945*, Harvard U.P., 1957.

KOGON, E., *The theory and practice of Hell. The German concentration camps and the system behind them*, Farrah, Strauss, N.Y., 1950.

KOGON, E. et al., *Nationalsozialistische Massentoetungen durch Giftgas*, Fischer

Taschenbuch, Frankfurt, 1983.
KOLB, E., *Bergen-Belsen. Vom 'Aufenthaltslager' zum Konzentrationslager, 1943-45* (2nd revised edition), Vandenhoeck and Ruprecht, Göttingen, 1986.
KÜBLER, F., 'Die nationalsozialistiche "Rechtsordung" im Spiegel neuer juristischer Literatur', *NPL*, 1970, pp.291ff.
KUDLIEN, F. (ed.), *Ärzte im Nationalsozialismus,* Cologne, 1985.
KÜHNL, R., 'Zur Programmatik der NS Linken: Das Strasser Programm von 1925-6' *VJH*, XIV, 1966, pp.317ff.
—*Die nationalsozialistische Linke 1925-1930*, Anton Hain, Meisenheim am Glan, 1966.
LANE, B., 'Nazi Ideology. Some unfinished business', *CEH*, 7, 1974, pp.3ff.
LANE, B., RUPP, L., *Nazi ideology before 1933. A documentation*, Univ. of Texas Press, Austin, 1978.
LEISER, E., *Nazi Cinema*, Macmillan, 1975.
LILIENTHAL, G., *Der 'Lebensborn e.V'. Ein Instrument nationalsozialistischer Rassenpolitik*, Fischer, N.Y.-Stuttgart, 1985.
LINDER, M., *The Supreme Labour Court in Nazi Germany. A jurisprudential analysis*, Klostermann, Frankfurt, 1987.
LINGELBACH, K., *Erziehung und Erziehungstheorien im NS Deutschland*, Beltz, Weinheim, 1970.
LUTZHÖFT, H. J., *Der nordische Gedanke in Deutschland 1920-1940*, Klett, Stuttgart, 1971.
MANN, E., *Schools for barbarians,* Drummond, London, 1939.
MARTENS, E., *Zum Beispiel Das Reich*, Verlag Wissenschaft und Politik, Cologne, 1972.
MEINCK, J., *Weimarer Staatslehre und Nationalsozialismus*, Campus, Frankfurt, 1978.
MEYERS, P., RIESENBERGER, D. (eds.), *Der Nationalsozialismus in der historisch-politischen Bildung*, Vandenhoeck & Ruprecht, Göttingen, 1979.
MICHALKA, W., 'Geplante Utopie? Zur Ideologie des Nationalsozialismus', *NPL*, 1977, pp.211-24.
MILLER LANE, B., *Architecture and politics in Germany, 1918-1945*, Harvard U.P., Chicago, 1985.
MOSSE, G. L., *Nazi culture. Intellectual, cultural and social life in the Third Reich*, W. H. Allen, 1966.
—*The crisis of German ideology: intellectual origins of the Third Reich*, Weidenfeld and Nicolson, 1966.
—*The nationalisation of the masses,* Howard Fertig, N.Y., 1975.
MOSSE, W. E., *Jews in the German economy. The German Jewish elite 1820-1923*, O.U.P., Oxford-London, 1987.
MUELLER-HILL, B., *Tödliche Wissenschaft. Die Aussonderung von Juden, Zigeuner und Geisteskraenken 1933-45,* Rohwolt, Hamburg, 1984.
NAAKE, E., 'Die Herausbildung des Führernachwuchs etc', *ZG*, 1973.
NOWAK, K., *'Euthanasie' und Sterilisation im 'Dritten Reich'*, Vandenhoeck and Ruprecht, Göttingen, 1984.
NYSSEN, E., *Schule im Nationalsozialismus*, Quelle & Meyer, Heidelberg, 1979.
ORLOW, D., 'Die Adolf Hitler Schulen', *VJH*, 13, 1965, pp.272ff.
PÄTZOLD, K., *Faschismus, Rassenwahn, Judenverfolgung*, Deutscher Verlag der

Wissenschaft, Berlin, 1975.

PEHLE, W. H. (ed.), *Der Judenpogrom 1938,* Fischer Taschenbuch Verlag, Frankfurt, 1988.

PEUKERT, D., *'Volksgenossen und Gemeinschaftsfremde,* Bund Verlag, Cologne, 1982.

POIS, R. A., *National Socialism and the religion of nature,* Croom Helm, 1986.

RICHARD, L., *Le nazisme et la culture,* Maspéro, Paris, 1978.

RICHARZ, B., *Heilen, Pflegen Toeten. Zur Alltagsgeschichte* einer Heil- und Pflegeanstalt bis zum Ende des *Nationalsozialismus,* Göttingen, 1987.

RITCHIE, J. M., *German literature under National Socialism. 1933-45,* Croom Helm, 1983.

ROSENBERG, A., *Der Mythus des 20 Jahrhundert: eine Wertung der seelischgeistigen gestalten Kämpfe unserer Zeit,* Hoheneichen, Munich, 1930.

ROTH, K. H. (ed.), *Erfassung zur Vernichtung. Von der Sozialhygiene zum Gesetz ueber 'Sterbehilfe',* Mabuse, Berlin, 1984.

RUEPING, H., *Bibliographie zum Strafrecht im Nationalsozialismus. Literatur zum Straf-Strafverfahrens- und Strafvollzugsrecht mit ihre Grundlagen und einem Anhang: Verzeichnis der Öffentlichen Entscheidungen der Sondergerichte,* Oldenbourg, Munich, 1985.

SÄNGER, F., *Politik der Tauschungen. Missbrauch der Presse im Dritten Reich,* Europa Verlag, Vienna, 1975.

SAUDER, G. (ed.), *Die Bücherverbrennung. 10 Mai 1933,* Ullstein, Berlin-Vienna, 1985.

SAUER, P., *Die Schicksale der jüdischen Bürger Baden Württembergs während der nationalsozialistischen Verfolgungszeit 1933-45,* Kohlhammer, Stuttgart, 1969.

SCHACHNE, L., *Erziehung zum geistigen Widerstand. Das jüdische Landschulheim Herrlingen 1933 bis 1939,* Dipa Verlag, Frankfurt, 1986.

SCHEFFLER, W., *Judenverfolgung im Dritten Reich 1933-1945,* Colloquium, Berlin, 1964.

SCHMEER, K. H., *Die Regie des öffentlichen Lebens im Dritten Reich,* Pöhl & Co., Munich, 1956.

SCHMUHL, H.-W., *Rassenhygiene, Nationalsozialismus, Euthanasie, Von der Verhütung zur Vernichtung 'lebensunwerten Leben', 1890-1945,* Vandenhoeck and Ruprecht, Göttingen, 1987.

SCHNITZ, P., *Die Artamanen. Landarbeit und Siedlung bündischer Jugend in Deutschland 1924-35,* Pfaehler, Bad Neustadt, 1985.

SCHOLTZ, H., 'Die "NS-Ordensburgen"', *VJH,* 15, 1967, p.269.

—*NS-Ausleseschulen* etc, Vandenhoeck and Ruprecht, Göttingen, 1973.

—*Erziehung und Unterricht unterm Hakenkreuz,* Vandenhoeck and Ruprecht, Göttingen, 1985.

SILFEN, P. H., *The völkisch ideology and the roots of Nazism,* Exposition, N.Y., 1973.

SMITH, B., 'Two alibis for the inhumanities, A. R. Butz, The hoax of the twentieth century and D. Irving's Hitler's War', *German Studies Review,* 1, 1978, pp.333ff.

STEINERT, M. G., *Hitlers Krieg und die Deutschen,* Econ., Verlag, Düsseldorf, 1970.

STEPHENSON, J., 'Girls' higher education in Germany in the 1930s', *JCH,* 10, no.1, 1975, pp.41ff.

STERN, F. R., *The politics of cultural despair. A study in the rise of the German ideology*, Univ. of California Press, Berkeley, 1961.
STOKES, L. D., 'The German people and the destruction of the European Jews', *CEH*, 6, 1973, pp.161ff.
STOLLEIS, M., 'Gemeinschaft und Volksgemeinschaft—Zur juristischen Terminologie im Nationalsozialismus', *VJH*, 22, 1972, pp.16ff.
STROHTMANN, D., *Nationalsozialistische Literaturpolitik*, H. Bouvier, Bonn, 1964, 2nd edition.
SYWOTTEK, J., *Mobilmachung für den totalen Krieg*, Westdeutscher Verlag, Opladen, 1976.
THOMPSON, L. V., 'Lebensborn and the eugenics policy of the Reichsführer SS', *CEH*, 4, 1971, pp.54ff.
UEBERHORST, H. (ed.), *Elite für die Diktatur. Die nationalsozialistischen Erziehungsanstalten 1933-45. Ein Dokumentebericht*, Droste, Düsseldorf, 1969.
VAYDAT, P., *L'Utopie de la Nation Soldatique en Allmagne de 1900 à 1942*, Univ. de Paris, 1975.
VONDUNG, K., *Magie und Manipulation, Ideologischer Kult und politische Religion des Nationalsozialismus,* Vandenhoeck & Ruprecht, Göttingen, 1971.
WEINGARTNER, J. J., 'The SS Race and Settlement Main Office', *The Historian*, 1971, pp.62ff.
WERNER, K. F., 'On some examples of National Socialist views of history', *JCH*, 3, no.2, 1968, pp.193ff.
—*Das nationalsozialistische Geschichtsbild und die deutsche Geschichtswissenschaft*, Kohlhammer, Stuttgart, 1967.
WIENER, P. F., *German with tears*, Cresset Press, 1942.
ZEMAN, Z. A. B., *Nazi propaganda*, O.U.P., 1964.
ZIEMER, G., *Education for death. The making of the Nazi*, O.U.P., 1941.
ZISCHKA, J., Die NS-Rassenideologie. *Machttaktisches Instrument oder handlungsbestimmendes Ideal?,* Eur.Hochschulschriften, Bern-N.Y.-Frankfurt, 1986.

## 3 Centralized or polycentric dictatorship?

ARONSON, S., *Reinhard Heydrich und die Frühgeschichte von Gestapo und SD*, DVA, Stuttgart, 1971.
BAUM, W., 'Reichsreform im Dritten Reich', *VJH*, 3, 1955.
BENNECKE, H., *Hitler und die SA*, Günter Olzog Verlag, Munich-Vienna, 1962.
BIRN, R. B., *Die Hoeheren SS- und Polizeiführer Himmlers Verkehr im Reich und in den besetzten Gebieten,* Droste, Düsseldorf, 1986.
BLACK, P. R., *Ernst Kaltenbrunner. Ideological soldier of the Third Reich*, Princeton U.P., 1984.
BLOCH, C., *Die SA und die Krise des nationalsozialistischen Regimes 1934*, Suhrkamp Verlag, Frankfurt, 1970.
BOBERACH, H. (ed.), *Richterbriefe. Dokumente zur Beeinflüssung der deutschen Rechtssprechung 1942-1944*, Harold Boldt, Boppard, 1975.
BOERNER, A., 'The position of the NSDAP in the German constitutional order', *American Political Science Review*, 32, 1938, pp.1059ff.

BOLLMUS, R., *Das Amt Rosenberg und seine Gegner. Zum Machtkampf im nationalsozialistischen Herschaftssystem*, DVA, Stuttgart, 1970.
BRAMWELL, A., *Blood and soil. Richard Walther Darré and Hitler's 'Green Party'*, Kensal, Bourne End, Bucks, 1985.
BROWNING, C. R., *The final solution and the German Foreign Office*, Holmes and Meier, N.Y., 1978.
BUCHHEIM, H., *SS und Polizei im NS-Staat*, Selbstverlag der Studiengesellschaft für Zeitprobleme, Bonn, 1964.
CAPLAN, J., 'The politics of administration. The Reich Interior Ministry and the German Civil Service', *Historical Journal*, 20, 3, 1977, pp.707ff.
DELARUE, J., *The history of the Gestapo*, Macdonald, 1964.
DESCHNER, G., *Heydrich, Statthalter der totalen Macht*, Bechtle, Esslingen am Neckar, 1977.
DIEHL-THIELE, P., *Partie und Staat im Dritten Reich*, C. H. Beck, Munich, 1969.
DIELS, R., *Lucifer ante Portas. Es spricht der erste Chef der Gestapo*, DVA, Stuttgart, 1950.
DOESCHER, H.-J., *Das Auswärtige Amt im Dritten Reich. Diplomatie im Schatten der 'Endlösung'*, Siedler, Berlin, 1987.
DOMRÖSE, O., *Der NS-Staat in Bayern vor der Machtergreifung bis zum Röhm-Putsch*, Wölfle, Munich, 1974.
FEST, J., *The face of the Third Reich*, Penguin, 1972.
FRAENKEL, E., *The dual state*, O.U.P., 1941.
FREND, W. H. C., 'Hitler and his Foreign Ministry', *History*, 42, 1957, pp.118ff.
FRIEDRICH, C., 'Political leadership—charismatic power', *Journal of Politics*, 23, 1961, pp.3-24.
FRÖHLICH, E., 'Joseph Goebbels und sein Tagebuch', *VJH*, 35, no.4, 1987, pp.489-522.
FUNKE, M., 'Führer-Prinzip und Kompetenz-Anarchie im nationalsozialistischen Herrschaftssystem', *NPL*, 1975, pp.60ff.
GEORG, E., *Die wirtschaftlichen Unternehmungen der SS*, DVA, Stuttgart, 1963.
GERTH, H., 'The Nazi Party—its leadership and composition', *American Journal of Sociology*, XLV, 1940, pp.517ff.
GOEBBELS, J., *Die Tagebuecher. Sämtliche Fragmente von Joseph Goebbels* (ed. E. Froehlich), Teil I, *Aufzeichnung 1924-41*, Vols. 1-4, Sauer, Munich, 1987.
HANISCH, E., *Nationalsozialistische Herrschaft in der Provinz Salzburg im Dritten Reich*, Landespressebuero, Salzburg, 1983.
HEIBER, H. *Goebbels, A biography*, Robert Hale, 1973.
HEIBER, H. (ed.), *Reichsführer. Briefe an und von Himmler*, DVA, Stuttgart, 1968.
HERRNLEBEN, H. G., *Totalitäre Herrschaft. Faschismus, Nationalsozialismus, Stalinismus*, Ploetz, Freiburg-Würzburg, 1978.
HILL, L., 'The Wilhelmstrasse in the Nazi era', *Political Science Quarterly*, 82, 1967, pp.546ff.
HÖHNE, H., *The order of the 'Death's Head'. The story of Hitler's SS*, Secker and Warburg, 1969.
HÜTTENBERGER, P., *Die Gauleiter. Studie zum Wandel des Machtgefüges in der NSDAP*, DVA, Stuttgart, 1969.
—'Nationalsozialistische Polykratie', *Geschichte und Gesellschaft*, 2, 1976, pp.417ff.

IRVING, D., *The rise and fall of the Luftwaffe*, Weidenfeld and Nicolson, 1973.

JÄGER, H., *Verbrechen unter totalitärer Herrschaft*, Olten, Freiburg i. Breisgau, 1967.

JAMES, H., 'Schacht's attempted defection from Hitler's Germany', *HJ*, 30, no.3, 1987, pp.329-33.

JANSSEN, G., *Das Ministerium Speer. Deutschlands Rüstung im Krieg*, Ullstein, Berlin, 1968.

—'Todt et Speer', *RGM*, 84, 1971, pp.37ff.

JOHE, W., *Die gleichgeschaltete Justiz*, Europäische Verlagsanstalt, Frankfurt, 1967.

KEHRL, H., *Krisenmanager im Dritten Reich*, Droste, Düsseldorf, 1973.

KLEIN, T., *Die Lageberichte der Geheimen Staatspolizei über die Provinz Hessen-Nassau 1933-36*, Boehlau, Cologne-Vienna, 1986.

KLENNER, J., *Verhältnis von Partei und Staat 1933-45, dargestellt am Beispiel Bayerns*, Neue Schriftenreihe des Stadtarchivs Munich, Wölfle, Munich, 1974.

KOEHL, R., 'Feudal aspects of National Socialism', *American Science Review*, LIV, 1960, pp.921ff.

KRAUSNICK, HELMUT, et al., *The anatomy of the SS State*, Collins, 1968.

KRUEDENER, J. von., 'Zielkonflikte in der nationalsozialistischen Agrarpolitik', *Zeitschrift für Wirtschaft und Sozialwissenschaften*, 1974, pp.335ff.

KRÜGER, P., JAHN, E. J., Der Loyalitäts konflikt des Staatssekretärs Wilhelm von Bülow im Frühjahr 1933', *VJH*, 20, 1972, pp.376ff.

KUBE, A., *Pour le mérite und Hakenkreuz. Hermann Goering im Dritten Reich*, Oldenbourg, Munich, 1986.

KUEHNEL, F., *Hans Schemm. Gauleiter und Kultusminister (1891-1935)*, Selbstverlag des Stadtarchiv, Nuremberg, 1985.

KUHN, A., 'Herrschaftsstruktur und Ideologie des Nationalsozialismus', *NPL*, 1971, pp.395ff.

KUUSISTO, S., *Alfred Rosenberg in der nationalsozialistischen Aussenpolitik 1933-1939*, Suomen Studia Historica, Helsinki, 1984.

LANG, J. von., *Der Sekretär. Martin Bormann. Der Mann der Hitler beherrschte*, DVA, Stuttgart, 1977.

*—Der Adjutant Karl Wolff, der Mann zwischen Hitler und Himmler*, Herbig, Munich-Berlin, 1985.

LERNER, D., 'The Nazi elite', in H. D. Lasswell, D. Lerner (eds.), *World Revolutionary elites*, Cambridge, 1965.

LOCKNER, L. P. (ed.), *The Goebbels Diaries 1942-3*, Hamish Hamilton, 1948.

LOEWENBERG, P., 'The unsuccessful adolescence of Heinrich Himmler', *AHR*, 76, 1974, pp.612ff.

MAI, G., 'Warum steht der deutsche Arbeiter zu Hitler? Zur Rolle der DAF im Herrschaftssystem des Dritten Reiches', *G & G*, 12, no.2, 1986, pp.212-34.

MAIER, H., 'Die SS und der 20 Juli 1944', *VJH*, 14, 1966, pp.299ff.

MARTENS, S., *Hermann Goering. 'Erster Paladin des Führers' und 'Zweiter Mann im Reich'*, Schöningh, Paderborn, 1985.

MATZERATH, H., *Nationalsozialismus und kommunale Selbstverwaltung*, Kohlhammer, Stuttgart, 1970.

McKALE, D. M., *The Nazi Party courts*, Univ. Press of Kansas, Lawrence, 1974.

MILWARD, A. S., 'Fritz Todt als Minister für Bewaffnung und Munition', *VJH*, 14, pp.40ff.
MOMMSEN, H., 'Ein Erlass Himmlers zur Bekämpfung der Korruption in der inneren Verwaltung vom Dez. 1944', *VJH*, 16, 1968, p295.
—*Beamtentum im Dritten Reich*, DVA, Stuttgart, 1966.
MORSTEIN, F. M., *Government in the Third Reich*, McGraw Hill, N.Y., 1936.
NYOMARKAY, J., *Charisma and factionalism in the Nazi Party*, Univ. of Minnesota Press, Minneapolis, 1967.
OVERY, R. J., *Goering. The iron man,* Routledge, 1984.
PETERSEN, E. N., 'The bureaucracy and the Nazi Party, *Review of Politics*, 28, 1966, pp.184ff.
—*The limits of Hitler's power*, Princeton U.P., 1969.
PETWAIDIC, W., *Die autoritäre Anarchie*, Hoffmann & Campe, Hamburg, 1946.
PLUM, G., 'Staatspolizei und innere Verwaltung 1934-1936', *VJH*, 13, 1965, pp.191ff.
REIMANN, V., *Joseph Goebbels*, Molden, Vienna-Munich-Zurich, 1971.
ROBINSON, H., *Justiz als politische Verfolgung. Die Rechtssprechung in 'Rassenschandefällen' beim Landgericht Hamburg, 1936-43*, DVA, Stuttgart, 1977.
RUNGE, W., *Politik und Beamtentum im Parteienstaat. Die Demokratisierung der politischen Beamten in Preussen 1918-33*, E. Klett, Stuttgart, 1965.
SCHACHT, H., *My first seventy-six years*, Allen Wingate, London, 1955.
—*Abrechnung mit Hitler*, Rowohlt, Hamburg, 1949.
SCHÄFER, W., *NSDAP. Entwicklung und Struktur der Staatspartei des Dritten Reiches*, Schriftenreihe des Instituts für wissenschaftliche Politik in Marburg/Lahn, Nr 3, Hannover-Frankfurt, 1956.
SCHORN, H., *Der Richter im Dritten Reich,* Klostermann, Frankfurt, 1959.
SCHWABE, K. (ed.), *Die preussische Oberpräsidenten 1815-1945. Deutsche Führungsschichten in der Neuzeit,* Boldt, Boppard, 1985.
SCHWARZWÄLDER, W., *Der Stellvertreter des Führers-Rudolf Hess. Der Mann in Spandau*, Molden, Vienna-Munich-Zurich, 1974.
SEABURY, P., *The Wilhelmstrasse. A study of German diplomacy under the Nazi Regime*, Berkeley, Los Angeles, 1954.
—'Ribbentrop and the German Foreign Office', *Political Science Quarterly*, 66, 1951, pp.532ff.
SERAPHIM, H.-J. (ed.), *Das politische Tagebuch Alfred Rosenberg 1934/35 und 1939/40*, Deutscher Taschenbuch Verlag, 1956.
SIMPSON, A.E., *Hjalmar Schacht in perspective*, Mouton, The Hague, 1969.
—'The struggle for control of the German economy 1936-1937', *JMH*, 31, 1959, pp.37ff.
SMITH, B. F., ANGRESS, W. T., 'Diaries of Heinrich Himmler's early years', *JMH*, 31, 1955, pp.206ff.
—*Heinrich Himmler. A Nazi in the making 1900-1926*, Stanford U.P., 1971.
SMITH, F., PETERSON, A. E. (eds.), *Himmlers Geheimreden 1933 bis 1945 und andere Ansprachen*, Propyläen, Berlin, 1974.
SPEER, A., *The secret diaries*, Macmillan, 1976.
—*Inside the Third Reich*, Weidenfeld and Nicholson, 1970.
STAFF, I., *Justiz im Dritten Reich*, Frankfurt, 1964; 2nd edition, Fischer

Taschenbuch Verlag, Frankfurt, 1978.
STEIN, G. H., *The Waffen SS. Hitler's elite*, Cornell U.P., 1966.
STEINER, J. M., *Power, politics and social change in National Socialist Germany. A process of escalation into mass destruction*, Mouton, The Hague, 1976.
SWEET, W., 'The Volksgerichtshof 1934-1945', *JMH*, 46, 1974, pp.314ff.
SYNDOR, C. W., *Soldiers of destruction. The SS Death's Head Division*, Princeton U.P., 1978.
VOGELSANG, R., *Der Freundeskreis Himmlers.* Musterschmidt, Göttingen-Zurich-Frankfurt/M, 1972.
WAGNER, W., *Der Volksgerichtshof im nationalsozialistischen Staat*, DVA, Stuttgart, 1974.
WATT, D. C., 'The German diplomats and the Nazi leaders', *Journal of Central European Affairs*, 15, 1955, pp.148ff.
WEINKAUFF, H. (ed.), *Die deutsche Justiz und der Nationalsozialismus*, DVA, Stuttgart, 1968.
WIESEMANN, F., 'Arbeitskonflikte in der Landwirtschaft während der nationalsozialistischen Zeit', *VJH*, 25, 1977, pp.573ff.
WULF, J., *Martin Bormann—Hitler's Schatten*, Sigbert Mohn, Güttersloh, 1962.

## 4 Hitler's 'social revolution'?

ADOLPH, W., *Die katholische Kirche im Deutschland Adolf Hitlers*, Morus, 1974, Berlin.
ALBRECHT, D., *Katholische Kirche im Dritten Reich*, Grünewald, Mainz, 1976.
ALBRECHT, R. et al. (eds.), *Widerstand und Exil 1933-1945*, Campus, N.Y.-Frankfurt, 1986.
ANGRESS, W. T., 'The political role of the peasantry in the Weimar Republic', *Review of Politics*, 21, 1959.
ARETZ, J., *Katholische Arbeiterbewegung und Nationalsozialismus*, Matthias Grünewald, Mainz, 1978.
BAJOHR, S., *Die Hälfte der Fabrik. Geschichte der Frauenarbeit in Deutschland 1914-1945*, Verlag Arbeiterbewegung und Gesellschaftswissenschaft, Marburg, 1979.
—'Weiblicher Arbeitsdienst im "Dritten Reich"', *VJH*, 28, 1980, pp.331 ff.
BENDIX, R., 'Social stratification and political power', *American Political Science Review*, 46, 1952, pp.357ff.
BENNECKE, H., *Die Reichswehr und der Röhmputsch*, Munich, 1964.
BERGHAHN, V. R., 'NSDAP und "Geistige Führung" der Wehrmacht 1939-1943', *VJH*, 17, 1969, pp.17ff.
—'Wehrmacht und Nationalsozialismus', *NPL*, 1970, p.45ff.
BERND, M., 'Friedensplanungen der multinationalen Grossindustrie (1932-40) als politische Krisenstrategie', *G&G*, 1976, pp.66ff.
BESSEL, R. (ed.), *Life in the Third Reich*, O.U.P., Oxford-London, 1987.
BESSEL, R., JAMIN, M., 'Nazis, workers and the uses of quantitative evidence', *Social History*, 4, 1979, pp.111ff.
BETHGE, E., *Dietrich Bonhoeffer*, Collins, London, 1970.

## Bibliography (Chapter 4)


BLAICH, F., *Staat und Verbände im Deutschland zwischen 1871 und 1945*, Franz Steiner, Wiesbaden, 1979.

BOBERACH, H. (ed.), *Berichte des SD und der Gestapo über Kirchen und Kirchenvolk 1934-1944*, Grünewald, Mainz, 1971.

BOBERACH, H. (ed.), *Meldungen aus dem Reich 1938-1945. Die geheimen Lageberichte des Sicherheitsdienstes der SS*, 18 vols., Bundesarchiv, Herrsching, 1984.

BOEHNERT, G. C., 'The Third Reich and the problem of "Social revolution"? German Officers and the SS', in V. Berghahn, M. Kitchen (eds.), *Germany in the age of total war*, Croom Helm, 1981.

BOYENS, A., *Kirchenkampf und ökumene 1939-1945*, Christian Kaiser, Munich, 1973.

BREIT, G., *Das Staats-und Gesellschaftsbild deutscher Generäle beider Weltkriege im Spiegel ihrer Memoiren*, Boppard, 1973.

BREUNING, K., *Die Vision des Reiches. Deutscher Katholizismus zwischen Demokratie und Diktatur, 1929-1934*, Hueber, Munich, 1969.

BRY, G., *Wages in Germany 1871-1945*, O.U.P., 1960.

BUCHSTAB, G., KAFF, B., KLEINMANN, H.-O., *Verfolgung und Widerstand 1933-1945. Christliche Demokraten gegen Hitler*, Droste, Düsseldorf, 1986.

BÜCHEL, R., *Der deutsche Widerstand im Spiegel von Fachliteratur. Bericht und Bibliographie*, Bernard and Graefe, Stuttgart, 1975.

CARSTEN, F. L., *Reichswehr and politics*, O.U.P., 1966.

CHILDERS, T., 'The social bases of the National Socialist vote', *JCH*, 11, 1976, pp.17ff.

COLE, T., 'Corporate organization in the Third Reich', *Review of Politics*, 2, 1940.

CONWAY, J. S., *The Nazi persecution of the Churches 1933-45*, Weidenfeld and Nicolson, 1968.

—'Der deutsche Kirchenkampf', *VJH*, 17, 1969, pp.423ff.

COOPER, M., *The Germany Army 1933-1945*, London, 1978.

CRAIG, G. A., 'Reichswehr and National Socialism. The policy of Wilhelm Groener 1928-32', *Political Science Quarterly*, 63, 1948, pp.194ff.

CZICHON, E., 'Der Primat der Industrie im Kartell', *Das Argument*, 1968, pp.168ff.

—*Wer verhalf Hitler zur Macht. Zum Anteil der deutschen Industrie an der Zerstörung der Weimarer Republik*, Pahl-Rugenstein, Cologne.

DEIST, W., *The Wehrmacht and German rearmament*, Macmillan, 1986.

DEIST, W. (ed.), *The German military in the age of total war*, Berg, Leamington Spa, 1985.

DEMETER, K., *The German officer corps in society and state, 1650-1945*, Weidenfeld and Nicolson, 1965.

DENZLER, G., FABRICIUS, V., *Die Kirchen im Dritten Reich. Christen und Nazis Hand in Hand?* 2 vols, Fischer Taschenbuch Verlag, Frankfurt, 1984.

DEUEL, W. *People under Hitler*, Lindsay Drummond, 1942.

DEUTSCH, H. C., *The conspiracy against Hitler in the twilight war*, Univ. of Minnesota Press, 1968.

—*Hitler and his generals*, Univ. of Minnesota Press, 1974.

DIEHL, J. M., Victors or victims? 'Disabled veterans in the 3rd Reich', *JMH*, 59, no.4, 1987, pp.705-36.

DIMITROV, G., *The Working class against Fascism*, Studies in Fascism. Ideology and Practice, A. M. S. Press, N.Y. (reprint of 1935 edition).

DITTMANN, W., *Das politische Deutschland vor Hitler*, Zurich, 1945.

DÜLFFER, J., 'David Irving, Der Widerstand und die Historiker', *GWU*, 11, 1979, pp.686ff.

EAGLE, W., 'The progress of mass production and the German small-scale industries', *Journal of Political Economy*, 46, 1938, pp.376ff.

EICHHOLTZ, D., 'Manager des Staatsmonopolistischen Kapitalismus', *JBW*, 1974, III, pp.217ff.

EICHHOLTZ, D., GOSSWEILER, K., 'Noch einmal: Politik und Wirtschaft 1933 bis 1945', *Das Argument*, 1968, pp.210ff.

ELSNER, R., *Zur Osthilfepolitik des faschistischen deutschen Imperialismus,* Wissenschaftliche Zeitschrift, E. Berlin, 1964.

ERIKSON, R. P., 'Theologians in the Third Reich', *JCH*, 12, 1977, pp.595ff.

— *Theologians under Hitler*, Yale U.P., New Haven, Conn., 1985.

FALTER, J. W., 'Wer verhalf der NSDAP zum Sieg?', *Das Parlament*, Beilage 28/9, 1979, pp.3ff.

FARQUHARSON, J., 'The Agrarian Policy of National Socialist Germany' in MOELLER, R. G. (ed.), *Peasants and Lords in Modern Germany*, Allen and Unwin, 1986.

FARQUHARSON, J. E., *The plough and the swastika*, Sage, 1976.

FINKER, K., *Graf Moltke und der Kreisauer Kreis*, Union Verlag, Berlin, 1978.

FISCHER, F., *Bündis der Eliten: zur Kontinuität der Machtstrukturen in Deutschland 1871-1945*, Droste, Düsseldorf, 1979.

FLEMMING, J., 'Mittelstand und Faschismus', *Archiv für Sozialgeschichte*, 13, 1963, pp.641ff.

FORD, F. L., 'The 20th July in the history of German resistance', *AHR*, 51, 1945-6, pp.609ff.

FRAUENDORFER, M., 'Deutsche Arbeitsfront und ständischer Aufbau', NS Monatsheft, no.54, September 1934.

FRITZSCHE, K., 'Konservatismus im Gesellschaftlich-geschichtlichen Prozess', *NPL,* 1979, pp.295ff.

FRÖHLICH, E., BROSZAT, M., 'Politische und soziale Macht auf dem Lande. Die Durchsetzung der NSDAP im Kreis Memmingen', *VJH*, 25, 1977, pp.546ff.

GERHARD, D., *Antifaschisten, Proletarier Widerstand, 1933-45,* Klaus Wagenbach, Berlin, 1976.

GERSHENKRON, A., *Bread and democracy in Germany*, Howard Fertig, N.Y., 1966.

GERSDORFF, U. von, *Frauen im Kriegsdienst 1914-1945,* Schriftenreihe des Militärrgeschichtlichen Forschungsamtes, Stuttgart, 1969.

GERSTENMAIER, E., 'Der Kreisauer Kreis', *VJH*, 15, 1967, pp.221ff.

GESSNER, O., 'Agrarprotektionismus und Welthandelkrise 1929-32. Zum Verhältnis von Agrarpolitik und Handelspolitik in der Endphase der Weimarer Republik', *ZAG*, 26, 1978, pp.161.

— 'Agrarian protectionism in the Weimar Republic', *JCH*, 12, 1977, pp.759ff.

— *Agrarverbände in der Weimarer Republik,* Droste, Düsseldorf, 1976.

GIES, H. 'Der Reichsnährstand-Organ berufsständischer Selbstverwaltung oder Instrument staatlicher Wirtschaftslenkung', *ZAG,* 1973, pp.216ff.

— 'NSDAP und landwirtschaftliche Organisationen in der Endphase der Weimarer Republik', *VJH,* 1967, pp.341ff.

GILLESSEN, G., *Auf verlorenem Posten. Die Frankfurter Zeitung im Dritten Reich*, Siedler, Berlin, 1986.

GRAML, H. et al, *The German resistance to Hitler,* Berkeley, Univ. of California Press, 1970.

GREBING, H. von, 'Erneurung des Konservatismus', *PVS*, 1978, no.3, pp.372ff.

GREBING, H., *History of the German labour movement. A survey*, Berg, Leamington Spa, 1985.

GRUCHMANN, L., 'Ein unbequemer Amtsrichter im Dritten Reich. Aus den Personalakten des Dr. L. Kreyssig', *VJH*, 32, 1984, pp.463-88.

GRUNFELD, F. V., *The Hitler file. A social history of Germany and the Nazis 1918-1945,* Weidenfeld and Nicolson, 1974.

GUILLEBAUD, C. W., *The social policy of Nazi Germany,* C.U.P., 1941.

GURLAND, A., *The fate of small businessmen in Nazi Germany*, Washington, US Government Print Office, 1943.

HAHN, F., *Lieber Stürmer. Leserbriefe an das NS Kampfblatt 1924 bis 1945*, Leo Baeck Institute, N.Y., 1978.

HALLGARTEN, G. W., 'Adolf Hitler and German heavy industry 1931-1933', *Journal of Economic History,* 12, 1952, pp.222ff.

— *Reichswehr und Industrie. Zur Geschichte der Jahre 1918-1933,* Europäische Verlagsanstalt, Frankfurt, 1955.

HALLGARTEN, G., RADKAU, J., *Deutsche Industrie und Politik von Bismarck bis Heute*, Econ. Verlag, Düsseldorf, 1974.

HAM, W. J., 'The organization of farm labour in Germany', *Journal of Political Economy,* 44, 1936, pp.374.

HAMBURGER, L., *How Nazi Germany has mobilized and controlled labour*, Washington D.C., 1940.

HAMILTON, R., *Who voted for Hitler?*, Princeton, 1982.

HEBERLE, R., *Landbevölkerung und Nationalsozialismus,* DVA, Stuggart, 1963.

HELMRICH, E. C., *The German churches under Hitler,* Wayne State U.P., Detroit, 1979.

HENTIG, H. W. von, 'Beiträge zu einer Sozialgeschichte des Dritten Reiches', *VJH*, 16, 1968, pp.48ff.

HERBERT, U., *Fremdarbeiter. Politik und Praxis des 'Auslaendereinsatzes' in der Kriegswirtschaft des Dritten Reiches*, Dietz, Bonn-Berlin 1985.

HERLEMANN, B., *Auf verlorenem Posten. Kommunistischer Widerstand im Zweiten Weltkrieg. Die Knoechel-Organisation*, Verlag Neue Gesellschaft, Bonn, 1986.

HILLGRUBER, A., 'Hitler, ein Knecht der Monopole? Eine Ostberliner Dokumentation fordert die westdeutschen Historiker heraus', *Die Zeit*, 44, 1969, pp.19ff.

HISASHI, Y., *Huettenarbeiter im Dritten Reich. Die Betriebsverhaeltnisse und soziale Lage bei dr Gutehoffnungshuette etc. 1936-9*, Steiner, Stuttgart, 1986.

HOFFMANN, P., *Widerstand, Staatsstreich, Attentat. Der Kampf der Opposition gegen Hitler,* Piper, Munich, 1969.

HORN, D., 'Youth resistance in the Third Reich. A social portrait', *Journal of Social History,* 1973, pp.26ff.

— Zur Geschichte und Struktur des Nationalsozialismus und der NSDAP',

*NPL,* 1973, pp.194ff.

JACOBSEN, H.-A. (ed.), *Spiegelbild einer Verschwoerung. Die Opposition gegen, Hitler und der Staatsstreich vom 20 Juli 1944*, Seewald, Stuttgart, 1984.

JAMIN, M., 'Zur Sozialstruktur des Nationalsozialismus', PVS, 1, 1978.

JOHN, H., 'Nationalsozialismus und Christentum', *Zeitgeschichte,* 7, 1979-1980, pp.427ff.

KATER, M., *The Nazi Party. A Social Profile of Members and Leaders*, Cambridge, Mass., 1983.

KATER, M. H., 'Zur Soziographie der frühen NSDAP', *VJH,* 19, 1971, pp.124ff.

KELE, M. H., *Nazis and workers. National Socialist appeals to German Labour 1919-1933,*Univ. of N. Carolina Press, Chapel Hill, 1972.

KLAUS, M., *Maedchen im Dritten Reich. Der Bund Deutscher Maedel*, Pahl-Rugenstein, Cologne, 1985.

KLEINE, G. H., 'Adelsgenossenschaft und Nationalsozialismus', *VJH*, 26, 1978, pp.100ff.

KLEMPERER, K. von, *Konservative Bewegungen zwischen Kaiserreich und Nationalsozialismus,* Oldenbourg, Munich-Vienna, 1962.

— 'Glaube, Religion, Kirche und der deutsche Widerstand gegen den Nationalsozialismus', *VJH*, 28, 1980, pp.293ff.

KLÖNNE, A., *Gegen den Strom. Bericht über den Widerstand im Dritten Reich*, Nordt. Verl. Anstalt, Hannover-Frankfurt, 1957.

KLOTZBACH, K., *Gegen den Nationalsozialismus. Widerstand und Verfolgung in Dortmund*, Friedrich Ebert Stiftung, Hannover, 1969.

KOCKA, J., *Angestellte zwischen Faschismus und Demokratie. Zur politischen Sozialgeschichte der Angestellten USA/Deutschland 1890-1940 im internationalen Vergleich*, Vandenhoeck and Ruprecht, Göttingen, 1977.

KOEHLER, M., *Die Volksschule Harsum im Dritten Reich. Widerstand und Anpassung einer katholischen Dorfschule*, August Lax, Hildesheim, 1985.

KROHN, C.-D., STEGMANN, D., 'Kleingewerbe und Nationalsozialismus in einer agrarischmittelständischen Region', *Archiv für Sozialgeschichte*, 17, 1967, pp.41ff.

KUCZYNSKI, J., *Studien zur Geschichte des staatsmonopolistischen Kapitalismus in Deutschland 1918-1945*, Akademie Verlag, Berlin, 1963.

— *Germany, economic and labour conditions under Fascism*, International Publishers, N.Y., 1945

LEBER, A. et al, *Conscience in revolt. Sixty four studies of resistance in Germany 1933-1945*, Vallentine Mitchell, 1957.

LEBOVICS, H., *Social conservatism and the middle class in Germany 1914-1933*, Princeton U.P., N.J., 1969.

LEWY, G., 'The Catholic Church and Nazi Germany', *Political Science Quarterly*, 79, 1964, pp.184ff.

LIGGERHAUS, R., *Frauen untern Nationalsozialismus,* Hammer, Wuppertal, 1984.

LOOMIS, C. P., BEEGLE, J. A., 'The spread of German Nazism in rural areas', *American Sociological Review*, 11, 1946, pp.724ff.

LOVIN, C. R. 'Agricultural reorganisation in the Third Reich. The Reich Food Corporation 1933-1936', *Agricultural History*, 43, 1969, pp.447ff.

LOZEK, G., SCHMIDT, W., 'Die "Integrations" Konzeption-Grundlage bürgerlicher Verfälschung der Geschichte der Arbeiterbewegung', *Einheit*, 10, 1968.

LUDWIG, K. H., *Technik und Ingenieure im Dritten Reich*, Droste, Düsseldorf, 1974.

MALONE, H. O., *Adam von Trott zu Solz. Werdegang eines Verschwoerers 1909-1938*, Siedler, Berlin, 1986.

MAMMACH, K., *Die deutsche antifaschistische Widerstandsbewegung 1933-1939'*, Dietz Verlag, Berlin, 1974.

— *Widerstand 1933-Geschichte der deutschen antifaschistischen, Widerstandsbewegung im Inland und in der Emigration*, Pahl-Rugenstein, Cologne, 1984.

MANN, G., 'Helmuth James von Moltke', *Journal of European Studies*, 4, 1974, pp.368ff.

— 'Widerstand gegen den Nationalsozialismus', *NPL*, 1977, pp.425ff.

MASON, T. W., *Arbeiterklasse und Volksgemeinschaft*, Opladen, Westdeutscher Verlag, 1975.

— 'Der antifaschistische Widerstand der Arbeiterbewegung im Spiegel der SED-Historiographie', *Das Argument*, 9, 1967, pp.144ff.

— 'Labour in the Third Reich', *Past and Present*, 33, 1966, pp.112ff.

— *Sozialpolitik im Dritten Reich*, Westdeutscher Verlag, Opladen, 1977.

MATTHIAS, E., 'Resistance to National Socialism: The example of Mannheim', *Past and Present*, 45, 1969, pp.117ff.

MAYER-ZOLLITSCH, A., *Nationalsozialismus und Evangelische Kirche in Bremen*, Selbstverlag des Staatsarchiv, Bremen, 1985.

MEGERLE, K. (ed.), *Warum gerade die Nationalsozialisten?*, Wissenschaftlicher Autorenverlag, Berlin, 1983.

MESSERSCHMIDT, M., *Die Wehrmacht im NS-Staat. Zeit der Indoktrination*, Von Decker, Hamburg, 1969.

MOOSER, J., *Arbeiterleben in Deutschland 1900-1970. Klassenlagen, Kultur und Politik*, Suhrkamp, Frankfurt, 1984.

MÜHLBERGER, D., 'The sociology of the NSDAP. The question of working class membership', *JCH*, July 1980, pp.493ff.

MÜLLER, H., *Katholische Kirche und Nationalsozialismus. Dokumente 1930-1935*, Nymphenburger Verlagshandlung, Munich, 1963.

MÜLLER, K.-J., *Das Heer und Hitler. Armee und Nationalsozialistisches Regime 1933-1940*, DVA, Stuttgart, 1969.

— *Der deutsche Widerstand 1933-1945*, Schöningh, Paderborn-Munich, 1986.

— *The army, politics and society in Germany 1933-1945. Studies in the army's relations to Nazism*, Manchester U.P., 1987.

MÜLLER, M., 'Die Stellung des Arbeiters im nationalsozialistischen Staat', *GWU*, 1975, 1, pp.1ff.

MUELLER-HILLEBRAND, B., *Das Heer 1933-45*, 3 vols, E. S. Mittler, Darmstadt 1954.

NOLTE, E., 'Big business in German politics. A comment', *AHR*, 75, 1969, pp.71ff.

OHLSEN, M., 'Ständischer Aufbau und Monopole 1933/4', *ZGW*, 1, 1974, pp.28ff.

O'LESSKER, K., 'Who voted for Hitler? A new look at the class basis of Nazism', *American Journal of Sociology*, 74, 1968, pp.63ff.

O'NEILL, R. J., *The German Army and the Nazi Party*, Cassell, 1966.

PARSONS, T., 'Some sociological aspects of the fascist movement', *Social Forces*,

21, 1942.
PELCOVITS, N. A., 'The Social Honour Courts of Nazi Germany', *Political Science Quarterly,* 53, 1938, pp.350ff.
PETRY, C., *Studenten aufs Schafott. Die Weisse Rose und ihr Scheitern*, Piper, Munich, 1968.
PETZINA, D., Hitler und die deutsche Industrie', *GWU*, 17, 1966, pp.482ff.
PEUKERT, D., Ruhrarbeiter gegen den Faschismus, Univ. of Mannheim, 1971.
— *Inside Nazi Germany,* Batsford, 1987.
POLLOCK, J. K., An areal study of the German electorate 1930-1933', *American Political Science Review*, 38, 1944, pp.89ff.
POOL, J., POOL, S., *Who financed Hitler?* Macdonald and Janes, London, 1979.
PRINZ, M., *Vom neuen Mittelstand zum Volksgenossen. Die Entwicklung, des sozialen Status der Angestellte von der Weimarer Republik bis zur Ende der NS*, Oldenbourg, Munich, 1986.
PRITTIE, T. C., *Germans against Hitler*, Hutchinson, 1964.
RABINACH, A., 'The aesthetics of production in the Third Reich', *JCH*, 11, 1976, pp.43ff.
RECKER, M.-L. *Nationalsozialistische Sozialpolitik im Zweiten Weltkrieg*, Oldenbourg, Munich, 1985.
REPGEN, K., *Hitlers Machtergreifung und der deutsche Katholizismus*, Raueiser, Saarbrücken, 1967.
RITTER, G., *The German resistance. Carl Goerdeler's struggle against tyranny*, Praeger, N.Y., 1959.
ROGOWSKI, R., 'The Gauleiter and the social origins of fascism', *Society and History*, 19, no.4, 1977.
ROLOFF, E.-A., *Bürgertum und Nationalsozialismus. Braunschweigs Weg ins Dritte Reich*, Verlag f. Literatur und Zeitgeschehen, Hannover, 1961.
ROON, G. van, 'Hermann Kaiser und der deutsche Widerstand', *VJH*, 24, 1976, pp.259ff.
ROTH, H., 'Die nationalsozialistische Betriebszellenorganisation von der Gründung bis zur Röhm-Affäre', *JBW*, 1978, I, pp.49ff.
ROTHFELS, H., 'Zur 25 Wiederkehr des 20 Juli 1944', *VJH*, 17, 1969, p.237.
RUPP, L., *Mobilising women for war. German and American propaganda 1939-45*, Princeton U.P., 1978.
SAAGE, R. von, 'Konservatismus und Faschismus', *PVS*, 1978, 2, pp.254ff.
— 'Zum Verhältnis von Nationalsozialismus und Industrie', *Das Parlament*, Beilage 9, 1975, pp.17ff.
SALDERN, A. von, *Mittelstand im 'Dritten Reich'*, Campus Verlag, Frankfurt, 1979.
— "'Alter Mittelstand' im 'Dritten Reich'. Anmerkungen zu einer Kontroverse", *G&G*, 12, no.2, 1986, pp. 235-43.
SCHADT, J., *Verfolgung und Widerstand in Baden. Die Lageberichte der Gestapo und des Generalstaatsanwalts Karlsruhe 1933-40*, Kohlhammer, Stuttgart, 1976.
SCHELLENBERGER, B., *Katholische Jugend im Dritten Reich,* Grünewald, Mainz, 1975.
SCHMAEDEKE, J., STEINBACH, P. (eds.), *Der Widerstand gegen den Nationalsozialismus. Die deutsche Gesellschaft und der Widerstand gegen Hitler*, Piper, Munich-Zurich, 1985.
SCHMIDT, J., *Martin Niemöller im Kirchenkampf*, Leibniz Verlag, Hamburg, 1971.

SCHNABEL, T., "'Wer waehlte Hitler?'. Bemerkung zu einigen Neuerscheinungenand ueber die Endphase der Weimarer Republik", *G&G*, 8, 1982, pp. 116-33.

SCHOEN, P., *Armenfürsorge im Nationalsozialismus. Die Wohlfahrtspflege in Preussen zwischen 1933 und 1939 als Beispiel der Wirtschaftsfürsorge*, Beltz, Weinheim-Basle, 1985.

SCHOENBAUM, D., *Hitler's Social Revolution. Class and status in Nazi Germany*, Weidenfeld and Nicolson, 1966.

SCHOLDER, K., 'Die Evangelische Kirche in der Sicht der nationalsozialistischen Führung bis zum Kriegsausbruch', *VJH*, 16, 1968, pp.15ff.

— *Die Kirchen und das Dritte Reich*, Propyläen, Frankfurt-Berlin-Vienna, Vol 1, 1977.

SCHUMANN, H. G., *Die Vernichtung der deutschen Gewerkschaften und der Aufbau der DAF*, O. Goedel, Hannover, 1958.

SCHWEITZER, A., *Big business in the Third Reich*, Indiana U.P., Bloomington, 1964.

SIEGELE-WENSCHKEWITZ, L., *Nationalsozialismus und Kirchen. Religionspolitik von Partei und Staat*, Droste, Düsseldorf, 1974.

SMELSER, R., *Robert Ley. Hitler's Labour Front Leader*, Berg, Oxford-N.Y.-Hamburg, 1985.

SONTHEIMER, K., *Anti-demokratisches Denken in der Weimarer Republik*, Nymphenburger Verlagshandlung, Munich, 1968.

SPEIER, H., *Der Angestellten vor dem Nationalsozialismus*, Vandenhoeck and Ruprecht, Göttingen, 1977.

STACHURA, P. D., 'Who were the Nazis?', *ESR*, 11, 1981, pp.293-324.

STEGMANN, D., 'Zum Verhältnis von Grossindustrie und Nationalsozialismus 1930-1933. Ein Beitrag zur Geschichte der sogenannten Machtergreifung', *Archiv für Sozialgeschichte*, XIII, 1973, pp.399ff.

STEINBACH, P., 'Widerstand gegen den Nationalsozialismus', *GWU*, 37, no.8, 1986, pp.481-97.

STEINBACH, P. (ed.), *Widerstand. Ein Problem zwischen Theorie und Geschichte*, Verlag für Wissenschaft und Politik, Cologne, 1987.

STEINBERG, H. J., *Widerstand und Verfolgung in Essen 1933-45*, Friedrich Ebert Stiftung, Hannover, 1969.

STEINBERG, M. S., *Sabers and brownshirts. The German students' path and National Socialism 1918-1935*, Univ. of Chicago Press, 1977.

STEINWARZ, H., 'The amenities of Industry and labour in Germany', *International Labour Review*, 1937.

STEPHENSON, J., *Women in Nazi Society*, Croom Helm, 1976.

— 'Reichsbund der Kinerreichen. The league of large families in the population policy of Nazi Germany', *ESR*, 9, no.3, 1979, pp.351ff.

STOLTENBER, G., *Politische Strömungen in Schleswig-holsteinschen Landvolk 1918-1933*, Droste, Düsseldorf, 1962.

TILTON, T., *Nazism, neo-Nazism and the peasantry*, Indiana U.P., Bloomington, 1975.

TROEGER, W. (ed.), *Hochschule und Wissenschaft im Dritten Reich*, Campus, Frankfurt, 1984.

TURNER, H. A., 'Fritz Thyssen und "I paid Hitler", *VJH*, 19, 1971, pp.225ff.

— 'Big business and the rise of Hitler', *AHR*, 75, 1969, pp.56ff.
— 'Hitler's secret pamphlet for industrialists 1927', *JMH*, 40, 1968, pp.348ff.
— 'Emil Kirdorf and the Nazi Party', *CEH*, 4, 1968, pp.324ff.
— 'Grossunternehmertum und Nationalsozialismus 1930-33', *HZ*, 221, 1975, pp.18ff.
UHLIG, H., *Die Warenhäuser im Dritten Reich*, Opladen, Cologne, 1975.
VOGELSANG, T., *Reichswehr, Staat und NSDAP*, Stuttgart, 1962.
VOLK, L., *Das Bayerische Episikopat und der Nationalsozialismus 1930-1934*, Matthias Grünewald, Mainz, 1965.
VOLK, L. (ed.), *Akten deutscher Bischoefe ueber die Lage der Kirche 1933-1945*, vol.5, Commission for Contemporary History, Mainz, 1983.
VOLLMER, B., *Volksopposition im Polizei Staat*, Vol.2, DVA, Stuttgart, 1957.
WALKER, L. D., *Hitler Youth and Catholic Youth 1933-1936*, Catholic Univ. of America Press, Washington D.C., 1971.
WALSER, H., 'Wer stand hinter der NSDAP?', *ZG*, 7, 1979-80, pp.288ff.
WEISENBORN, G., *Der lautlose Aufstand. Bericht über die Widerstandsbewegung des deutschen Volkes 1933-1945*, Rowohlt, Hamburg, 1962.
WENGST, U., 'Der Reichsverband der deutschen Industrie in den ersten Monaten des Dritten Reiches', *VJH*, 28, 1980, pp.94ff.
WHEELER-BENNETT, J. W., *Nemesis of Power. The German Army in Politics 1918-1945*, Macmillan, 1953.
WINKLER, D., *Frauenarbeit im Dritten Reich*, Hoffmann and Campe, 1977.
WINKLER, H. A., 'Unternehmerverbände zwischen Ständeideologie und Nationalsozialismus', *VJH*, 17, 1969, pp.341ff.
— 'Extremismus der Mitte? Sozialgeschichtliche Aspekte der nationalsozialistischen Machtergreifung', *VJH*, 22, 1972, pp.175ff.
— 'From social protectionism to National Socialism', *JMH*, 1976, pp.1ff.
— 'Der entbehrliche Stand', *Archiv f. Sozialgeschichte*, 27, 1977.
— 'German society, Hitler and the illusion of restoration 1930-1933', *JCH*, 11, 1976, pp.1ff.
WOLFFSOHN, M., *Indistrie und Handwerk im Konflikt mit staatlicher Wirtschaftspolitik? Studien zur Politik der Arbeitsbeschaffung in Deutschland 1930-1934*, Duncker and Humblot, Berlin, 1977.
WULFF, B., 'The Third Reich and the Unemployed: National Socialist Work-Creation Schemes in Hamburg 1933-4' in EVANS, R.J. AND GEARY, R. (eds.), *The German Unemployed*, Croom Helm, 1987.
WUNDERLICH, F., *Farm labour in Germany 1810-1945*, Princeton U.P., 1961.
YANO, H., *Hüttenarbeiter im Dritten Reich. Die Betriebsverhältnisse und soziale Lage bei der Gutehoffnungshütte Aktienverein und der Fried. Krup A.G. 1936 bis 1939*, Steiner, Stuttgart, 1986.
ZANDTMOYER, L., von, *The Kraft durch Freude movement in Nazi Germany 1933-9*, Ann Arbor, Michigan, 1977.
ZOFKA, Z., *Die Ausbreitung des Nationalsozialismus auf dem Lande. Eine regionale Fallstudie*, Wölfle, Munich, 1979.
ZIPFEL, F., *Kirchenkampf in Deutschland, 1933-1945. Religionsverfolgung und Selbstbehauptung der Kirchen in der nationalsozialistischen Zeit*, De Gruyter, Berlin, 1965.

## 5 Foreign policy: ideology in action?


ABENDROTH, H.-H., *Hitler in der spanischen Arena. Die deutsch-spanischen Beziehungen im Spannungsfeld der europäischen Interessenpolitik vom Ausbruck des Bürgerkrieges bis zum Ausbruck des Weltkrieges*, Ferdinand Schöningh, Paderborn, 1973.

BAUM, W., WEICHOLD, E., *Der Krieg der 'Achsenmächte' im Mittelmeerraum*, Musterschmidt, Göttingen, 1973.

BAUMGART, W., 'Zur Ansprache Hitlers vor den Führern der Wehrmacht am 22 August 1939', *VJH*, 16, 1968, pp.120ff.

BELL, P. M. H., *The origins of the Second World War in Europe*, Longman, 1986.

BENZ, W., GRAML, H. (eds.), *Sommer 1939: Die Grossmächte und der europäischen Krieg*, Stuttgart, DVA, 1979.

BERNHARDT, W., *Die deutsche Aufrüstung 1934-9. Militärische und politische Konzeptionen und ihre Einschätzung durch die Allierten*, Bernard & Graefe, Frankfurt, 1969.

BERTIN, F., *L'Europe de Hitler*, 3 vols., Librairie français, 1976-7, Paris.

BLOCH, C., *Le III Reich et le Monde*, Imprimerie Nationale, Paris, 1986.

BOEDDEKER, G., *Der Untergang des Dritten Reiches. Mit den Berichten des Ober Kommando der Wehrmacht vom 6 Jan-9 Mai 1945 und einer Bilddokumentation*, Herbig, Munich, 1985.

BOTTING, D., *In the ruins of the Reich*, Allen and Unwin, London, 1985.

BRACHER, K. D., 'Das Anfangsstadium der Hitlerschen Aussenpolitik', *VJH*, 5, 1957, pp.61ff.

BRÄUTIGEM, O., *Überblick über die besetzten Ostgebiete während des zweiten Weltkrieges*, Institut f. Besatzungsfragen, Tübingen, 1954.

BREYER, R., *Das Deutsche Reich und Polen 1933-1937*, Holzner, Würzburg, 1955.

BROWN, M., 'The Third Reich's mobilisation of the German Fifth Column in Eastern Europe', *CEH*, 19, 1959, pp.128ff.

BROSZAT, M., *Nationalsozialistische Polenpolitik 1939-1945*, Fischer, Frankfurt 1965 (revised edition).

— 'Deutschland und Ungarn-Rumänien. Entwicklung und Grundfaktoren nationalsozialistische Hegemoniale-und Bündnispolitik, 1938-41', *HZ*, 206, 1968, pp.45ff.

BURDICK, C. B., 'German military planning and France 1930-1938', *World Affairs Quarterly*, 30, 1959-60, pp.299ff.

BUSSMANN, W., 'Zur Entstehung und Überlieferung der "Hossbach-Niederschrift"', *VJH*, 16, 1968, pp.373ff.

CARR, W., *Arms, autarky and aggression. A study in German foreign policy 1933-1939*, Edward Arnold, 1972.

— *Poland and Pearl Harbour. The making of the Second World War*, Edward Arnold, 1985.

COMPTON, J. W., *Hitler und die USA. Die Amerikapolitik des Dritten Reiches und die Ursprünge des Zweiten Weltkrieges*, Oldenbourg, Hamburg, 1968.

CREVELD, M., *Hitler's strategy, 1940-1*, C.U.P., 1973.

DALLIN, A., *German rule in Russia 1941-45*, Macmillan, 1957.

DEAKIN, F. W., *The brutal friendship. Mussolini, Hitler and the fall of Italian fascism*, Weidenfeld & Nicolson, 1962.

DEIST, W., MESSERSCHMIDT, M., VOLKMANN, H.-E., WETTE, W., *Ursachen und Voraussetzungen der deutschen Kriegspolitik*, DVA, Stuttgart, 1979.

DRECHSLER, K., GROEHLER, O., HASS, G., 'Politik und Strategie des faschistischen Deutschlands im zweiten Weltkrieg', *ZGW*, no.1, 1976, pp.5ff.

DÜLFFER, J., *Weimar, Hitler und die Marine: Reichspolitik und Flottenbau 1920-1939*, Droste, Düsseldorf, 1973.

— 'Politik zum Kriege! Das Deutsche Reich und die Mächte auf dem Weg in den Zweiten Weltkrieg', *NPL*, 1981, pp.42ff.

EICHHOLTZ, D., 'Grossgermanisches Reich und "Generalplan Ost"', *ZGW*, 2, 1980, pp.835ff.

— 'Wege zur Entbolschewisierung und Entrussung des Ostraumes. Empfehlungen des IG-Farben-Konzerns f. Hitler im Früjahr 1943', *JBW*, 1970, III, pp.32ff.

EICHOLTZ, D., HASS, G., 'Zu den Ursachen des Zweiten Weltkrieges und den Kriegeszielen des deutschen Imperialismus', *ZGW*, no.15, 1967, pp.1148ff.

EISENBLÄTTER, G., *Grundlinien der Politik des Reiches gegenüber dem Generalgouvernement 1939-1945*, Frankfurt, 1969.

EHRICH, E., *Die Auslandsorganisation der NSDAP*, Berlin, 1937.

FABRY, W., *Die Sowjetunion und das Dritte Reich*, Seewald, Stuttgart, 1971.

FEDERAU, F., *Der zweite Weltkrieg. Seine Finanzierung in Deutschland*, Wunderlich, Tübingen, 1962.

FENYO, M. D., *Hitler, Horthy and Hungary. German-Hungarian relations 1941-1944*, Yale U.P., 1972.

FORNDRAN, E. et al., *Innen-und Aussenpolitik unter nationalsozialistischer Bedrohung*, Westdeutscher Verlag, Düsseldorf, 1977.

FOX, J. P., *Germany and the Far Eastern Crisis 1931-1938. A study in diplomacy and ideology*, Clarendon Press, 1985.

FREYMOND, J., *Le III[e] Reich et la réorganisation de l'Europe 1940-1942*, A. W. Sijthoff, Leyden, 1974.

FRYE, A., *Nazi Germany and the American Hemisphere 1933-1941*, Yale U.P., New Haven, 1967.

FUNKE, M. (ed.), *Hitler, Deutschland und die Mächte*, Droste, Düsseldorf, 1976.

FUNKE, M., *Sanktionen und Kanonen. Hitler, Mussolini und der internationale Abessinienkonflikt, 1934-1936*, Droste, Düsseldorf, 1976.

GEHL, J., *Austria, Germany and the Anschluss*, O.U.P., 1963.

GEMZELL, C. A., *Organisation, conflict and innovation. A study of German Naval strategy and planning, 1888-1940*, Lund, 1973.

GEISS, I., JAKOBMEYER, W., *Deutsche Politik in Polen 1939-1945*, Westdeutscher Verlag, 1980.

GIBBONS, R., 'Opposition gegen "Barbarossa" im Herbst 1940', *VJH*, 23, 1975, pp.332.

— 'Allegemeine Richtlinien f. die politische und wirtschaftliche Verwaltung der besetzten Ostgebiete', *VJH*, 25, 1977, pp.252ff.

GROEHLER, O., SCHUMANN, W., 'Zu den Bündnisbeziehungen des faschistischen Deutschlands im zweiten Weltkrieg', *ZGW*, 1980, 2, pp.624ff.

GRUCHMANN, L., *Der zweite Weltkrieg*, DVA, Stuttgart, 1974, 2nd edition.

GÜTH, R., *Die Marine des Deutschen Reiches 1919-1939*, Bernard Graefe,

Frankfurt, 1972.

HARPER, G. T., *German economic policy in Spain during the Spanish Civil War 1936-9*, Mouton, The Hague, 1967.

HASS, G., SCHUMANN, W., *Anatomie der Aggression.* Deutsche Verlag der Wissenschaften, E. Berlin, 1972.

HAUSER, O., *England und das Dritte Reich*, Seewald, Stuttgart, 1972.

HEINEMANN, J. L., *Hitler's first foreign minister. Konstantin Freiherr von Neurath, diplomat and statesman*, Univ. of California Press, 1979.

HELLING, G., 'Zur Bodenpolitik des deutschen Imperialismus 1913-1945', *JBW*, 1963, 3.

HENKE, J., *England in Hitlers politischem Kalkül 1935-1939*, Harold Boldt, Boppard, 1973.

— 'Hitler und England mitte August 1939', *VJH*, 23, 1973, pp.231ff.

HERDEG, W., *Grundzüge der deutschen Besatzungsverwaltung in den west-und nordeuropäischen Ländern während des zweiten Weltkrieges*, Tübingen, 1953.

HIDEN, J. W., *Germany and Europe 1919-1939*, Longman, 1977.

— 'National Socialism and Foreign Policy 1919-1933', in P. D. STACHURA (ed.), *Hitler's Machtergreifung 1933*, Allen and Unwin, 1983.

— 'Germany, Home and Away', *HJ*, 30, no.2, 1987, pp.463-82.

HILDEBRAND, K., *Vom Reich zum Weltreich. Hitler, NSDAP und koloniale Fragen 1919-1945*, Wilhelm Fink, Munich, 1969.

— 'Hitlers "Mein Kampf": Propaganda oder Programm?', *NPL*, 1969, pp.72ff.

— 'Innenpolitische Antriebskräfte der nationalsozialistischen Aussenpolitik', *Sozialgeschichte Heute*, Göttingen, 1974.

— *The foreign policy of the Third Reich*, Batsford, 1973.

— 'Le programme et sa réalisation 1939-1942', *RGM*, 84, 1971, pp.7ff.

HILLGRUBER, A., *Deutsche Grossmacht und Weltpolitik im 19 und 20 Jahrhundert*, Droste, Düsseldorf, 1977.

— *Hitlers Strategie, Politik und Kriegsführung 1940-1*, Bernard and Graefe, Frankfurt, 1965.

— *Kontinuität und Diskontinuität in der deutschen Aussenpolitik von Bismarck bis Hitler*, Droste, Düsseldorf, 1969.

— 'Der Faktor America in Hitlers Strategie 1938-41', *Aus Politik und Zeitgeschichte. Beilage zur Wochenzeitung*, 'Das parlament', v, 11.5. 1966.

— 'Die Endlösung; das deutsche Ostimperium als Kernstück des rassenideologischen Programms des Nationalsozialismus', *VJH*, 20, 1972, pp.133ff.

— 'England's place in Hitler's plans for world dominion', *JCH*, 9, no.1, 1974, pp.5ff.

— *Probleme des Zweiten Weltkrieges*, Cologne, 1967.

— *Deutschlands Rolle in der Vorgeschichte der beiden Weltkriege*, Vandenhoeck and Ruprecht, Göttingen, 1967.

HIRSCHFELD, G. *Fremdherrschaft und Kollaboration. Die Niedelande unter deutscher Besatzung*, DVA, Stuttgart, 1984.

HOFER, W., *Die Entfesselung des Zweiten Weltkrieges*, DVA, Stuttgart, 1954.

JÄCKEL, E., *Frankreich in Hitlers Europa. Die deutsche Frankreichpolitik im zweiten Weltkrieg*, DVA, Stuttgart, 1966.

JACOBMEYER, W. (ed.), *Das Diensttagebuch des deutschen Generalgouvernors in Polen 1939-1945*, DVA, Stuttgart, 1975.

JACOBSEN, H. A., 'Krieg in Weltanschauung und Praxis des Nationalsozialismus 1919-1945, eine Skizze' in *Festschrift Ludwig Jedicka*, Niederösterr. Pressehaus, 1976.

— *Nationalsozialistische Aussenpolitik 1933-8*, Alfred Metzner, Frankfurt, 1968.

JARAUSCH, K. H., 'From Second to Third Reich. The problem of continuity in German foreign policy', *CEH*, 12, 1979, pp.68ff.

JASPER, G., 'Über die Ursachen des zweiten Weltkrieges. Zu den Büchern von A. J. P. Taylor und D. Hoggan', *VJH*, 10, 1962, pp.311ff.

JONAS, M., *The United States and Germany. A diplomatic history*, Cornell U.P., Ithaca-N.Y., 1984.

KETTENACKER, L., *Nationalsozialistische Volkstumspolitik in Elsass*, DVA, Stuttgart, 1973.

KIELMANSEGG, P., 'Die militär-politische Tragweite der "Hossbach-Besprechung"', *VJH*, 8, 1960, pp.268ff.

KLESSMANN, C., 'Der Generalgouverneur Hans Frank', *VJH*, 19, 1971, pp.245ff.

KNAPP, M., LINK, W., SCHRÖDER, H. J., SCHWABE, K., *Die USA und Deutschland 1918-1945*, C. H. Beck, Munich, 1978.

KRACHT, K., LEWIN, B., MUELLER, K. (eds.), *Japan und Deutschland im 20 Jahrhundert*, Ruhr-Universität Bochum, Wiesbaden, 1984.

KRAUSNICK, H., 'Kommissarbefehl und "Gerichtsbarkeitserlass Barbarossa" im neuer Sicht', *VJH*, 25, 1977, pp.682ff.

KROSBY, H. P., *Finland, Germany and the Soviet Union 1940-1941*, Madisan, Milwaukee, 1968.

KRUMMACHER, F. A., LANGE, E. H., *Krieg und Frieden. Geschichte der deutsch-sowjetischen Beziehungen von Brest-Litovsk zum Unternehmen Barbarossa*, Bechtle, Munich, 1970.

KUHN, A., *Hitlers aussenpolitisches Programm. Entstehung und Entwicklung 1919-1939*, Klett, Stuttgart, 1970.

KWIET, K., *Reichskommissariat Niederlands*, DVA, Stuttgart, 1968.

LANGE, K., 'Der Terminus "Lebensraum" in Hitlers "Mein Kampf"', *VJH*, 13, 1965, pp.426ff.

LEACH, B. A., *German strategy against Russia*, O.U.P., 1973.

LEVINE, H., *Hitler's Free City. A history of the Nazi Party in Danzig 1925-1939*, Chicago U.P., 1973.

LONGERICH, P., 'Joseph Goebbels und der Totale Krieg: Ein unbekannte Denkschrift des Propagandaministers vom 18 Juli 1944' *VJH*, 1987, 35, no.2, pp.289-3.

LOOCK, H. D., *Quisling, Rosenberg und Terboven*, DVA, Stuttgart, 1970.

— 'Zur "Grossgermanischen Politik" des Dritten Reiches', *VJH*, 1960, pp.37ff.

LUZA, R., *Austro-German relations in the Anschluss era*, Princeton U.P., 1976.

McMURRAY, D. D., *Deutschland und die Sowjetunion 1933-6*, Bohlau, Cologne, 1979.

MADAJCZYK, C., *Die deutsche Besatzungspolitik 1939-1945*, F. Steiner, Wiesbaden, 1967.

MARTEL, G. (ed.), *The origins of the Second World War reconsidered. The A. J. P. Taylor debate after twenty five years*. Allen and Unwin, 1986.

MARTIN, B., 'Britisch-deutsche Friedenskontakte in den ersten Monaten des zweiten Weltkrieges', *Zeitschrift f. Politik*, 19, 1972, p.206ff.

— *Friedensinitiativen und Machtpolitik im zweiten Weltkrieg 1939-1942*, Droste, Düsseldorf, 1974.

MAIER, K. et al., *Das Deutsche Reich und der zweite Weltkrieg*, DVA, Stuttgart, 1979.

MENGER, M., PETRICK, F., WILHELMUS, W., 'Nordeuropa unter der Vorherrschaft des faschistischen deutschen Imperialismus 1940-45', *ZGW*, 5, 1976, pp.516ff.

MERKES, M., *Die deutsche Politik im Spanischen Bürgerkrieg 1936-9*, Ludwig Röhrscheid, 1969, 2nd edition.

METZMACHER, H., 'Deutsch-englische Ausgleichsbemühungen im Sommer 1939', *VJH*, 14, 1966, pp.369ff.

MICHAELIS, M., 'World power status or world dominion? A survey of the literature on Hitler's plan of world dominion 1937-1970', *HJ*, 15, 2, 1972, pp.331ff.

MICHALKA, W., *Ribbentrop und die deutsche Weltpolitik 1933-40*, Wilhelm Fink, Munich, 1980.

MICHALKA, W. (ed.), *Nationalsozialistische Aussenpolitik*, Darmstadt, 1978.

MOMMSEN, W. J., KETTENACKER, L. (eds.), *The fascist challenge and the policy of appeasement*, Allen and Unwin, 1983.

MOORE, R. B., 'Refugees from Nazism. Emigration and Exile after 1933', *European History Quarterly*, 16, no.3, 1986, pp.369-77.

MULLER, K. J., 'Zur Vorgeschichte und Inhalt der Rede Himmlers vor der höheren Generalität am 13 März 1940 in Koblenz', *VJH*, 18, 1970, pp.95ff.

MÜLLER, N., *Wehrmacht und Okkupation*, Deutscher Militärverlag, Berlin, 1971.

MUELLER, R.-D., *Das Tor zur Weltmacht. Die Bedeutung der Sowjetunion für die deutsche Wirtschafts-und Rüstungspolitik zwischen den Weltkriegen*, Boldt, Boppard.

NAMIER, L.B., *Diplomatic prelude*, Macmillan, 1948.

NEUBACHER, H., *Sonderauftrag Südost 1940-45*, Musterschmidt, Berlin-Frankfurt, 1957.

NEULEN, H. W., *Europa und das Dritte Reich. Einigungsbestrebungen im deutschen Machtbereich 1939-45*, Universitas, Munich, 1987.

NICLAUSS, K., *Die Sowjetunion und Hitlers Machtergreifung*, Röhrscheid, Bonn, 1966.

NIEDHART, G. 'Weltherrschaft versus World Appeasement', *NPL*, 1978, pp.281ff.

NIEDHART, G., (ed.), *Kriegsbeginn 1939. Entfesselung oder Ausbruch des zweiten Weltkrieges, Wissenchaftliche Buchgesellschaft*, Darmstadt, 1976.

NIPPERDEY, T., '1933 und Kontinuität der deutschen Geschichte', *HZ*, 1978, pp.86ff.

OVERY, R., *The origins of the Second World War*, Longman, 1988.

OVERY, R. J., 'Hitler and air strategy', *JCH*, 1980, pp.405ff.

PETERSEN, J., *Hitler, Mussolini. Die Entstehung der Achse Berlin-Rom, 1933-6*, Niemeyer, Tübingen, 1973.

POSEN, B. R., *The sources of military doctrine. France, Britain and Germany between the World Wars*, Cornell U.P., Ithaca-London-N.Y., 1984.

PUCHERT, B., 'Die deutsch-polnische Nichtangriffserklärung von 1934 und die

Aussenwirtschaftspolitik des deutschen Imperialismus gegenüber Polen bis 1939', *Jahrbuch f. Geschichte der UdSSR und der volksdemokratischen Länder Europas*, 12, 1968, pp.339.

RATENHOF, U., *Die Chinapolitik des Deutschen Reiches 1871 bis 1945*, Boldt, Boppard, 1987.

RECKER, M.-L. (ed.), *Von der Konkurrenz zur Rivalität. Das Britisch-Deutsche Verhältnis in den Ländern der Europäischen Peripherie 1919-39*, Steiner, Stuttgart, 1986.

REINHARD, K., *Die Wende vor Moskau. Das Scheitern der Strategie Hitlers im Winter 1941-2*, DVA, Stuttgart.

RICH, N., *Hitler's war aims, vols. 1 and 2*, André Deutsch, 1973, 1974.

ROBERTSON, E. M., *Hitler's prewar policy and military plans 1933-1939*, Longmann, 1963.

— 'Hitler und die Sanktionen des Völkerbunds. Mussolini und die Besetzung des Rheinlands', *VJH*, 26, 1978, pp.237ff.

ROBERTSON, E. M. (ed.), *The origins of the Second World War. Historical interpretations*, Macmillan, 1971.

— 'Zur Wiederbesetzung des Rheinlandes 1936', *VJH*, 10, 1962, pp.178ff.

ROSS, D., *Hitler und Dollfuss. Die deutsche Oesterreichpolitik 1933-4*, Hamburg, 1966.

ROSAR, W., *Deutsche Gemeinschaft. Seyss-Inquart und der Anschluss*, Europa Verlag, Vienna-Frankfurt, 1971.

RUHL., K. J., *Spanien im zweiten Weltkrieg. Franco, die Falange und das Dritte Reich*, Hoffmann and Campe, 1975.

SALEWSKI, M., *Die deutsche Seekriegsleitung 1933-45*, 3 vols., Bernard and Graefe, Frankfurt, 1973.

SCHAUSBERGER, N., *Der Griff nach Österreich. Das Jahr 1938*, Jugend und Volk, Vienna, 1978.

SCHEIDER, W., DIPPER, C. (eds.), *Der Spanische Bürgerkrieg in der internationalen Politik*, Nymphenburger, Munich, 1976.

SCHRÖDER, H. J., *Deutschland und die Vereinigten Staaten 1933-9*, Franz Steiner, Wiesbaden, 1970.

— 'Deutsche Südosteuropapolitik 1929-1936. Zur Kontinuität deutscher Aussenpolitik in der Weltwirtschaftskrise', *G&G*, 1976, 1, pp.5ff.

SCHUBERT, G., *Anfänge nationalsozialistischer Aussenpolitik*, Verlag Wissen und Politik, Cologne, 1963.

SCHUMANN, W. et al. (eds.), *Deutschland im Zweiten Weltkrieg*, vol.5 (1984), vol.6 (1985), Pahl-Rugenstein, Cologne, 1984-5.

SCHUMANN, W., HASS, G., *Deutschland im zweiten Weltkrieg. Vorbereitung, Entfesselung und Verlauf des Krieges bis zum 22 Juni 1941*, Akad.der Wissenschaften, Berlin, 1974.

SEATON, A., *Der russisch-deutsche Krieg 1941-1945*, Bernard and Graefe, Frankfurt.

SMELSER, R. M., *The Sudeten problem 1933-8. Volkstumspolitik and the formation of Nazi foreign policy*, Dawson, Folkestone, 1975.

SOMMER, T., *Deutschland und Japan zwischen den Mächten 1935-40*, J. C. B. Mohr, Tübingen, 1962.

STEED, W., 'From Frederick the Great to Hitler. The consistency of German aims', *International Affairs*, 17, 1938.

STOAKES, G., 'More unfinished business? Some comments on the evolution of the Nazi foreign policy programme 1919-1924', *ESR*, 8, no.4, 1978, pp.425ff.

— *Hitler and the quest for World dominion. Nazi ideology and foreign policy in the 1920s*, Berg, Leamington Spa-Hamburg-N.Y., 1986.

STREIT, C., *Keine Kameraden. Die Wehrmacht und die sowjetischen Kriegsgefangenen 1941-5*, DVA, Stuttgart, 1978.

TAYLOR, A. J. P., *The origins of the Second World War*, Hamish Hamilton, 1961.

THIES, J., *Architekt der Weltherrschaft. Die 'Endziele' Hitlers*, Droste, Düsseldorf, 1976.

TOSCANO, M., *The origins of the pact of steel*, Johns Hopkins U.P., Baltimore, 1967.

TREUE, W., *'Hitlers Rede vor der deutschen Press (10 Nov 1939)'*, *VJH*, 6, 1958, p.175.

TREVOR-ROPER, H. R., 'Hitlers Kriegsziele', *VJH*, 1960, pp.121ff.

VOIGT, J. H., 'Hitler und Indien', *VJH*, 10, 1971, pp.33ff

WAGNER, G. (ed.), *Lagevorträge des Oberbefehlshabers der Kriegsmarine vor Hitler 1939-1945*, J. F. Lehmanns, Munich, 1972.

WAGNER, W., *Belgien in der deutschen Politik während des zweiten Weltkrieges*, Harold Boldt, Boppard, 1974.

WATT, D. C., 'German strategic planning and Spain 1938-9', *Army Quarterly*, LXXX, 1960, pp.220ff.

— 'Hitler's visit to Rome and the May weekend crisis; Hitler's response to external stimuli', *JCH*, 9, no.1, 1974, pp.223ff.

— 'The Rome-Berlin Axis 1936-40. Myth and reality', *Review of Politics*, XXII, 1960, pp.519ff.

— 'The Anglo-German naval agreement of 1935. An interim judgement', *JMH*, 28, 1956, pp.15ff.

— *Too serious a business. European armed forces and the approach to the Second World War*, Temple Smith, 1975.

— 'Zur Wiederbesetzung des Rheinlandes', *VJH*, 10, 1962, pp.192ff.

WEINBERG, G. L., *The foreign policy of Hitler's Germany. Diplomatic revolution in Europe 1933-6*, Univ. of Chicago Press, 1970.

— *The foreign policy of Hitler's Germany. Starting World War II, 1937-9*, Univ. of Chicago Press, 1981.

— 'Hitler's image of the United States', *AHR*, 69, 1964, pp.106ff.

— 'National Socialist organization and foreign policy aims in 1927', *JMH*, 36, 1964, pp.428ff.

WILHELMUS, W., 'Schweden und das faschistische Deutschland in zweiten Weltkrieg', *ZGW*, 7, 1973, pp.793.

WISKEMANN, E., *The Rome-Berlin Axis*, Fontana, 1966.

WOLLSTEIN, G., *Von Weimarer Revisionismus zu Hitler. Das deutsche Reich und die Grossmächte in der Anfangsphase der NS-Herrschaft*, Wiss. Archiv, Bonn, 1973.

ZIPFEL, F., *Hitlers Konzept einer Neuordnung Europas'*, in D. KURZE (ed.), *Aus Theorie und Praxis der Geschichtswissenschaft*, 1972.

## 6 The economics of Third Reich: ideology, management, planning

AUGUST, J. et al., *Herrenmenschen und Arbeitsvoelker. Ausländische Arbeiter und Deutsche 1939-1945*, Rotbuch Verlag, Berlin, 1986.

BALOGH, T., 'The national economy of Germany', *The Economic Journal*, 48, 1938.

BARKAI, A., 'Die Wirtschaftsauffassung der NSDAP', *Politik und Zeitgeschichte*, Beilage zur Wochenzeitung 'Das Parlament', 1975, pp.3ff.

— *Das Wirtschaftssystem des Nationalsozialismus. Der historische und ideologische Hintergrund 1933-6*, Berendt and Nottbeck, Cologne, 1977.

— 'Sozialdarwinismus und antiliberalismus in Hitlers Wirtschaftskonzept', *G&G*, 3, 1977, pp. 406ff.

BETTELHEIM, C., *L'économie allemande sous le nazisme. Un aspect de la décadence du capitalisme*, Bibliothèque générale d'économie politique, Paris, 1946.

BILLIG, J., *Les campes de concentration dans l'économie du Reich hitlérien*, P.U.F., Paris, 1973.

BIRKENFELD, W., *Der synthetische Treibstoff 1933-1945. Ein Beitrag zur nationalsozialistischen Wirtschafts-und Rüstungspolitik*, Musterschmidt, Göttingen, 1964.

BLEYER, W., 'Pläne der faschistischen Führung zum totalen Kreig im Sommer 1944', *ZGW*, no.10, 1969, pp.1312.

— *Staat und Monopole im totalen Kreig. Der staatmonopolistische Machtapparat und die 'totale Mobilisierung' im ersten Halbjahr 1943*, Academie Verlag, E. Berlin, 1970.

BOELCKE, W. A. (ed.), *Deutschlands Rüstung im zweiten Weltkrieg. Hitlers Konferenzen mit Albert Speer 1942-45*, Athenaion, Frankfurt, 1969.

BORKIN, J., *The crime and punishment of I. G. Farben*, Free Press, N.Y., 1978.

CARROLL, B., *Design for total war*, Mouton, The Hague, 1968.

CZOLLEK, R., EICHHOLTZ, D., 'Zur wirtschaftlichen Konzeption des deutschen Imperialismus beim Überfall auf die Sowjetunion', *JBW*, 1968, 1, pp.143ff.

DENGG, S., *Deutschlands Austritt aus dem Völkerbund und Schachts Neuer Plan. Zum Verhältnis von Aussen- und Aussenwirtschaftspolitik*, Lang, Frankfurt, 1986.

DÜLFFER. J., 'Der Beginn des Krieges 1939: Hitler, die innere Krise und das Mächtesystem', *G&G*, 4, 1976, pp.443ff.

ECONOMIST, THE, 'Dr Schacht and the Nazis', 7 December 1935.

— 'Anti-socialistic Socialists', 14 December 1935.

EICHHOLTZ, D., 'Alte und neue Konzeptionen', *JBW*, 1971, pp.231ff.

— 'Expansionrichtrung Nordeuropa. Der "Europäische Grosswirtschaftsraum" und die nordischen Länder nach dem faschistischen Überfall auf die UdSSR', *ZGW*, 1979, 1, pp.17ff.

— *Geschichte deutscher Kriegswirtschaft 1939-1945*, vol. 1, Akademie Verlag, E. Berlin, 1969.

— 'Probleme einer Wirtschaftsgeschichte des Faschismus in Deutschland', *JBW*, 1963, Pt.III, pp.97ff.

— 'Zum Anteil des IG-Farben-Konzerns an der Vorbereitung des zweiten Weltkrieges', *JBW*, 1969, Pt.II, pp.99ff.

— 'Manager des staatsmonopolitischen Kapitalismus', *JBW*, 3, 1974, pp.217ff.

EICHHOLTZ, D., SCHUMANN, W. (eds.), *Anatomie des Krieges. Neue Dokumente über die Rolle des deutschen Monopolkapitals bei der Vorbereitung und Durchführung des Zweiten Weltkrieges*, VEB, E. Berlin, 1969.

ERBE, R., *Die nationalsozialistische Wirtschaftspolitik 1933-1939 im Lichte der modernen Theorie*, Polygraphischer Verlag, Zurich, 1958.

FEAR, J., 'Die Rüstungsindustrie im Gau Schwaben 1939-1945', *VJH*, 35, no.2, 1987, pp.193-216.

FEDER, G., *Das Program der NSDAP und seine weltanschauliche Grundlage*, Franz Eher Verlag, Munich, 1974.

FISCHER, W., *Deutsche Wirtschaftspolitik*, Leske, Opladen, 1978.

FORSTMEIER, F., VOLKMANN, H. E., *Wirtschaft und Rüstung am Vorabend des zweiten Weltkrieges*, Droste, Düsseldorf, 1975.

— *Kriegswirtschaft und Rüstung 1939-1945*, Droste, Düsseldorf, 1977.

GARRATY, J. A., 'The New Deal, National Socialism and the Depression', *AHR*, 78, pp.907ff.

GILLINGHAM, J. R., *Ruhr coal, Hitler and Europe. Industry and politics in the Third Reich*, Methuen, 1985.

GREBLER, L., 'Work creation policy in Germany 1932-5', *International Labour Review*, 35, 1937, pp.329-51, 505-27.

GUILLEBAUD, C. W., *The economic recovery of Germany from 1933 to the incorporation of Austria*, Macmillan, 1939.

HAMBURGER, L., *How Nazi Germany controlled business*, Brookings Instit., Washington D.C., 1943.

HAYES, P., *Industry and Ideology. IG Farben in the Nazi Era*, C.U.P.., 1987.

HEINEMANN. J. L., 'Neurath and German policy at the London Economic Conference', *JMH*, 41, 1969, pp.161ff.

HENNING, F. W., *Probleme der Nationalsozialistishchen Wirtschaftspolitik*, Duncker and Humblot, Berlin, 1976.

HENNING, H.-J., 'Kraftfahrzeugindustrie und Autobahnbau in der Wirtschaftspolitik des Nationalsozialismus 1933-1936', *VSW*, 2, 1978, pp.217ff.

HERBERT, U., *Fremdarbeiter. Politik und Praxis des 'Ausländer Einsatzes' in der Kriegswirtschaft des Dritten Reiches*, Dietz, Bonn-Berlin, 1985.

HERBST, L., 'Die Krise des nationalsozialistischen Regimes am Vorabend des Zweiten Weltkrieges und die forcierte Aufrüstung', *VJH*, 26, 1978, pp.347ff.

HERFERTH, W., *Der Reichsnährstand—ein Instrument der Kriegspolitik des fashistischen deutschen Imperialismus*, Wissenschaftliche Zeitschrift der Universität Rostock, no.17, 1968, pp.225ff.

HEYL, J., 'Hitler's economic thought. A reappraisal', *CEH*, VI, 1973, pp.83ff.

HIGGINS, B., 'Germany's bid for agricultural self-sufficiency', *Journal of Farm Economics*, 21, 1939, pp.435ff.

HOEFT, K. D., *Zur Agrarpolitik des deutschen Imperialismus von 1933 bis zur Gegenwart*, Deutscher Landwirtschafts Verlag, E. Berlin, 1960.

— 'Die Agrarpolitik des deutschen Faschismus als Mittel zur Vorbereitung des zweiten Weltkieges', *ZGW*, 7, 1959.

HOMZE, E. L., *Arming the Luftwaffe. The Reich Air Ministry and the German aircraft industry 1919-1939*, Univ. of Nebraska Press, Lincoln, 1976.

— *Foreign Labour in Nazi Germany*, Princeton U.P., 1967.

JÄGER, J. J., *Die wirtschaftliche Abhängigkeit des Dritten Reichs vom Ausland, dargestellt am Beispiel der Stahlindustrie*, Berlin Verlag, 1969.

JOHN, J., 'Rustungsindustrie und NSDAP-Organisation in Thüringen 1933 bis 1939', *ZGW*, 4, 1974, pp.412ff.

KADRITZE, N., *Faschismus und Krise, Zum Verhältnis von Politik und Ökonomie im Nationalsozialismus*, Campus Studium, Frankfurt, 1976.

KARNER, S., 'Bemüngen zur Ausweitung der Luftrüsting im Dritten Reich 1940-1', *ZG*, 6, 1978-9, pp.318ff.

KASPER, H.-H., 'Das Erdöl in den Raubplänen des deutschen Faschimus in Vorbereitung und bei der Durchführung des zweiten Weltkrieges', *JBW*, 1976, III, pp.55ff.

KEHRL, H., *Krisenmanager im Dritten Reich*, Droste, Düsseldorf, 1973.

KLEIN, B. H., *Germany's economic preparations for war*, Harvard U.P., Cambridge, Mass., 1959.

KRAUSE, W., *Wirtschaftstheorie unter dem Hakenkreuz. Die bürgerliche politische Ökonomie in Deutschland während der faschistischen Herrschaft*, Akademie Verlag, E. Berlin, 1969.

KRÜGER, P., 'Zu Hitlers "nationalsozialistischen" Wirtschaftserkenntnissen', *G&G*, 1980, 2, pp.263ff.

KROLL, G., *Von der Weltwirtschaftskrise zur Staatskonjunktur*, Duncker and Humblot, Berlin, 1958.

LÄRMER, K., *Autobahnen in Deutschland 1933 bis 1945-Zu den Hintergründen*, Akademie Verlag, Berlin, 1975.

LEHMANN, J., *Zur Funktion des 'Bauerlichen Berufserziehungswerkes' in den Plänen der faschistischen Agrarführung während des zweiten Weltkrieges*, Wissenschaftliche Zeitschrift der Universität Rostock, no.25, 1976, pp.799ff.

LOVIN, C. R., 'Die Erzeugungsschlacht 1934-6', *ZAG*, 1974, pp.209ff.

LURIE, S., *Private investment in a controlled economy (Germany 1933-9)*, Columbia U.P., N.Y., 1947.

MANDELBAUM, K., 'Controls in the German economy 1933-1938', in *The economics of full employment. Six studies in applied economics prepared at the Oxford University Institute of Statistics*, 1967.

MARTIN, B., 'Friedensplanungen der multinationalen Grossindustrie (1932-40) als politische Krisenstrategie', *G&G*, no.1, 1976, pp.66ff.

MERLIN, S., 'Trends in German economic control since 1933', *Quarterly Journal of Economics*, 56, 1942.

MEINCK, G., *Hitler und die deutsche Aufrüstung 1933-7*, Franz Steiner, Wiesbaden, 1959.

MILWARD, A. S., *The German economy at war*, Athlone Press, 1965.

— *The fascist economy in Norway*, O.U.P., 1972.

— *The New Order and the French Economy*, O.U.P., 1970.

MUELLER, R.-D., *Das Tor zur Weltmacht. Die Bedeutung der Sowjetunion für die deutsche Wirtschafts- und Rüstungspolitik zwischen den Weltkriegen*, Boldt, Boppard, 1984.

NATHAN, O., *The Nazi economic system. Germany's mobilisation for war*, Durham, N. Carolina, 1944.

NUSSBAUM, H., ZUMPE, L., *Wirtschaft und Staat in Deutschland*, 3 vols., Berlin, 1978.

OVERY, R. J., Transport and rearmament in the Third Reich', *HJ*, XVI, 1973, 2,

pp.389ff.
— 'The German aircraft production plans 1936-9', *English Historical Review*, 1975, pp.778ff.
— 'Cars, roads and economic recovery in Germany 1932-9', *Economic History Review*, XXVIII, 3, 1975, pp.466ff.
— *The Nazi economic recovery 1932-8*, Macmillan, 1982.
— 'The conversion to total war. Germany 1939-41', in COTTRELL, P. L. (ed.), *Government, politics and the economy of Europe 1914-45*, Croom Helm, 1987.
PERREY, H.-J., *Der Russlandausschuss der Deutschen Wirtschaft. Die deutsch-sowjetischen Wirtschaftsbeziehungen der Zwischenkriegszeit*, Oldenbourg, Munich, 1985.
PETZINA, D., *Autarkiepolitik im Dritten Reich*, DVA, Stuttgart, 1968.
— 'IG-Farben und nationalsozialistische Autarkiepolitik', *Tradition*, 5, 1968.
— 'Die Mobilisierung deutscher Arbeitskräfte vor und während des zweiten Weltkrieges', *VJH*, 18, 1970, pp.443ff.
— 'Hauptprobleme der deutschen Wirtschaftspolitik 1932-33', *VJH*, 15, 1967, pp.18ff.
PFAHLMANN, H., *Fremdarbeiter und Kriegsgefangene in der deutschen Wirtschaft 1939-1945*, Wehr und Wissen Verlagsgesellschaft, Darmstadt, 1968.
PISKOL., J., 'Zur Entwicklung der aussenpolitischen Nachkriegskonzeptionen der deutschen Monopolbourgeoisie', *JBW*, 1969, Pt.II, pp.329ff.
PLUMPE, G., 'The IG Farben company 1925-1945', in LEE, W. R., (ed.), *Industrialisation and industrial growth etc*, Croom Helm, 1987.
POHL, H. (ed.), *Zur Politik und Wirksamkeit des Deutschen Industrie-und Handelstages und der Industrie-u.Handelskammern 1861-1949*, Steiner, Stuttgart, 1987.
POHL, H. et al., *Die Daimler-Benz AG in den Jahren 1933 bis 1945*, Steiner, Stuttgart, 1986.
PUCHERT, B., 'Einige überlegungen zum deutschen Kapitalexport', *JBW*, 1976, Pt.III, pp.79ff.
RADANT, H., 'Deutsche Monopole raubten polnisches Erdöl', *JBW*, 1960, Pt.II, pp.301ff.
— 'Die IG Farben Industrie und Südosteuropa bis 1938', *JBW*, 1966, Pt.III, pp.146ff, and 1938-1945, ibid., 1967.
RADKAU, J., 'Entscheidungsprozesse und Entscheidungsdefizite in der deutschen Aussenwirtschaftspolitik 1933-40', *G&G*, 1976, pp.34ff.
RAWLINS, E. C., *Economic conditions in Germany to March 1936*, HMSO, 1936.
RIEDEL, M., 'Die Rohstofflage des Deutschen Reiches im Frühjahr 1936', *Tradition*, 14, 1969, pp.31ff.
— *Eisen und Kohl für das Dritte Reich. Paul Plegiers Stellung in der national-sozialistischen Wirtschaft*, Musterschmidt, Göttingen, 1973.
RIEMENSCHNEIDER, M., *Die deutsche Wirtschaftspolitik gegenüber Ungarn 1933-44. Ein Beitrag zur Interdependenz von Wirtschaft und Politik unter dem National-sozialismus*, Europäische Hochschulschriften, Frankfurt, 1987.
SCHACHT, H., 'Germany's position in the world economy', in *Germany Speaks. By 21 leading members of Party and State*, Butterworth, 1938, pp.279ff.
SCHMELZER, J., *Dies war ein Staatsgeheimnis (Ein Blick in die Handakten des ehemaligen Direktors der IG-Farben Agfa-Betriebe)*, VEB, Filfabrik Wolfen,

1963.

SCHRÖDER, H. J., 'Südosteuropa als "Informal Empire" Deutschlands 1933-9. Das Beispiel Jugoslawien', *Jahrbücher f. Geschichte Osteuropas*, 23, 1975, pp.70ff.

— 'Nachkriegsplanungen der Reichsgruppe Industrie im Herbst 1944', *JBW*, 1972, Pt.III, pp.259ff.

— 'Die wirtschaftliche Überlebensstrategie des deutschen Imperialismus in der Endphase des zweiten Weltkreiges', *ZGW*, 5, 1979, pp.499ff.

— 'Neue Dokumente der Reichsgruppe Industrie zur Neuordnung Europas', *Jahrbuch f. Geschichte*, 5, Berlin, 1971.

SCHROETER, H.-G., *Aussenpolitik und wirtschaftsinteresse. Skandinavien im aussenwirtschaftlichen Kalkül Deutschlands und Grossbritaniens 1918-39*, Lang, Frankfurt-N.Y., 1983.

SCHWEITZER, A., 'On depression and war. Nazi phase', *Political Science Quarterly*, 62, 1947, pp.321ff.

SIEGFRIED, K.-J., *Rüstungsproduktion und Zwangsarbeit im Volkswagenwerk 1933-1945*, Campus, Frankfurt-N.Y., 1987.

SONNEMANN, R. 'Wirtschaftsgeschichte Deutschlands', *JBW*, 1975, Pt.III, pp.141ff.

STERN, W. M., 'Wehrwirtschaft. A German contribution to economics', *Economic History Review*, 1960-1, pp.271ff.

STRATMANN, F., *Chemische Industrie unter Zwang? Staatliche Einflussnahme am Beispiel der chemischen Industrie Deutschlands 1933-49*, Steiner, Stuttgart, 1985.

STUEBEL, H., Die Finanzierung der Aufrüstung im Dritten Reich' *Europa Archiv*, 6, 1951, pp.4128ff.

SWATEK, D., *Unternehmerskonzentration als Ergebnis und Mittel nationalsozialistischer Wirtschaftspolitik*, Volkswirtschaftliche Schriften, Berlin, 1972.

TEICHERT, E., *Autarkie und Grossraumwirtschaft in Deutschland 1930-39. Aussenwirtschaftliche Konzeptionen etc.*, Oldenbourg, Munich, 1984.

THOMAS, G., *Geschichte der deutschen Wehr-und Rüstungswirtschaft 1918-1943-45*, Harold Boldt, Boppard, 1966.

TREUE, W., 'Hitlers Denkschrift über den 4 Jahr Plan', *VJH*, 3, 1955, pp.184ff.

— 'Das Dritte Reich und die Westmächte auf dem Balkan. Zur struktur der Aussenhandelspolitik Deutschlands, Grossbritannien und Frankreichs 1933-9', *VJH*, 1953, pp.45ff.

— 'Die Einstellung einiger deutscher Industrieller zu Hitlers Aussenpolitik', *GWU*, 17, 1966, pp.491ff.

TREUE, W., FREDER, G. (eds.), *Wirtschaft und Politik 1933-45*, Braunschweig, Limbach, 1964 (4th edition).

TURNER, H. A., 'Hitlers Einstellung zu Wirtschaft und Gesellschaft', *G&G*, 1976, 1, pp.89ff.

ULSHÖFER, O., *Einflussnahme auf Wirtschaftsunternehmungen in den besetzten Nordwest und Südosteuropäischen Länder während des zweiten Weltkrieges*, Institut f. Besatzungsfrage, Tübingen, 1958.

VOLKER, K.-H., *Die deutsche Luftwaffe 1933-1939. Aufbau, Führung und Rüstung der Luftwaffe*, Stuttgart, 1967.

VOLKMANN. H.-E., 'Das aussenwirtschaftliche Programm der NSDAP 1930-1833', *ASG*, XVII, 1977, pp.251ff.

— 'Zurr Interdependenz von Politik, Wirtschaft und Rüstung im Nationalsozialistischen Staat', *Militärgeschichtliche Mitteilungen*, Heft 15, 1974, pp.161ff.

WAGENFÜHR, R., *Die deutsche Industrie im Kriege 1939-1945*, Duncker and Humblot, Berlin, 1954.

WOLFE, M., 'The development of Nazi monetary policy', *Journal of Economic History*, XV, 1955, pp.392ff.

WOTTOWA, D., *Protektionismus im Aussenhandel Deutschlands mit Vieh und Fleisch zwischen Reichsgründung und Beginn des Zweiten Weltkrieges*, Lang, Bern-N.Y.-Frankfurt, 1985.

ZUMPE, L., 'Weltwirtschaftslage und faschistische Aussenwirtschaftsregulierung', *JBW*, 1978, Part IV, pp.201ff.

— *Wirtschaft und Staat in Deutschland 1933 bis 1945*, Akademie Verlag, Berlin, 1980.

## 7 National Socialism: the problem of a general interpretation

a. *The Rise of National Socialism*

ABEL, T., *Why Hitler came to power*, new ed. with preface by T. Childers, Harvard U.P., Chicago, 1986.

ALLEN, W. S., *The Nazi seizure of power. The experience of a single German town 1930-1935*, Quadrangle Books, Chicago, 1965.

ARMSTRONG, H. F., *Hitler's Reich. The first phase*, Macmillan, 1933.

BECKER, J., BECKER, R. (eds.), *Hitlers Machtergreifung 1933. Vom Machtantritt Hitlers 30 Januar bis zur Besiegelung des Einparteienstaates 14 Juli 1933*, DTV, Munich, 1983.

BÖHNKE, W., *Die NSDAP im Ruhrgebiet 1920-1933*, Verlag Neue Gesellschaft, Bonn, 1974.

BONNIN, G., *Le Putsch de Hitler à Munich en 1923*, Bonnin Editeur, Les Sables-d'Olonne, 1966.

BRACHER, K. D., *Die Auflösung der Weimarer Republik*, Schwarzwald Ring Verlag, Villingen, 1964.

— 'Stufen totalitärer Gleichschaltung. Die Befestigung der nationalsozialistischen Herrschaft', *VJH*, 4, 1956, pp.30ff.

BRACHER, K. D., SAUER, W., SCHULTZ, G., *Die Nationalsozialistische Machtergreifung*, Cologne, 1960.

BRÜDIGAM, H., *Das Jahr 1933. Terrorismus an der Macht*, Röderberg, Frankfurt, 1978.

BURKHARDT, B., *Eine Stadt wird braun. Die nationalsozialistische Machterfreifung in der schwäbischen Provinz*, Hoffmann and Campe, Hamburg, 1980.

CHILDERS, T. (ed.), *The formation of the Nazi constituency, 1919-1933*, Croom Helm, 1987.

CHILDERS, T., *The Nazi voter. The social foundations of fascism in Germany 1919-1933*, Univ. of North Carolina, Chapel Hill-London, 1983.

CONWAY, J. S., 'Machtergreifung or due process of history. The historiography of Hitler's rise to power', *HJ*, VIII, 1965, pp.399ff.

DEUERLEIN, E. (ed.), *Der Aufstieg der NSDAP in Augenzeugenberichten*, Karl

Rauch, Düsseldorf, 1968.
— *Der Hitler-Putsch. Bayerische Dokumente zum 8 und 9 November 1923*, DVA, Stuttgart, 1962.
DICKMANN, F., 'Die Regierungsbildung in Thüringen als Modell der Machtergreifung', *VJH*, 14, 1966, pp.454ff.
DOUGLAS, D. M., 'The parent cell. Some computer notes on the composition of the first Nazi Party group in Munich 1919-1921', *CEH*, X, 1977, pp.55ff.
EPSTEIN, K., *Vom Kaiserreich zum Dritten Reich. Geschichte und Geschichtswissenschaft*, Ullstein, Vienna, 1972.
FALTER, J. W. et al. (eds.), *Wahlen und Abstimmungen in der Weimarer Republik. Materialen zum Wahlverhalten 1919-1933*, Beck, Munich, 1986.
FARIS, E., 'Takeoff point for the National Socialist Party. The Landtag elections in Berlin 1929', *CEH*, 1975, no.2, pp.140ff.
FARQUHARSON, J., 'The NSDAP in Hannover and Lower Saxony 1921-1926', *JCH*, 8, no.4, 1973, pp.103ff.
FENSKE, H., 'Historische Analysen deutscher Politik. Untersuchungen zur Geschichte der NSDAP', *PVS*, 1, 1976, pp.115ff.
FISCHER, C., *Stormtroopers. A social, economic and ideological analysis, 1929-35*, Allen and Unwin, London-Boston-Sydney, 1983.
GORDON, H. J., *Hitler and the Beer Hall Putsch*, Princeton U.P., New Jersey, 1972.
HAMBRECHT, R., *Der Aufstieg der NSDAP in Mittel-und Oberfranken (1925-33)*, Selbstverlag d.Stadtarchivs, Nuremberg, 1976.
HEIDEN, K., *Geburt des Dritten Reiches*, Europa Verlag, Zurich, 1934.
HENNIG, E., 'Regionale Unterscheide bei der Entstehung des deutschen Faschismus', *PVS*, 2, 1980, pp.152ff.
HENTSCHEL, V., *Weimars letzte Monate. Hitler und der Untergang der Republik*, Droste, Düsseldorf, 1978.
HEUSS, T., *Hitlers Weg. Eine Schrift aus dem Jahre 1932*, Rainer Wunderlich.
HILDEBRAND, K., 'Hitlers "Mein Kampf". Propaganda oder Programm? Zur Frühgeschichte der nationalsozialistischen Bewegung', *NPL*, 1969, pp.73ff.
HOFMANN, H. H., *Der Hitler Putsch. Krisenjahre deutscher Geschichte 1920-1924*, Nymphenburger, Munich, 1961.
HOFFMANN, H., *Im Gleichschritt in die Diktatur? Die nationalsozialistische 'Machtergreifung' in Heidelberg und Mannheim, 1930 bis 1935*, Lang, Frankfurt, 1985.
HOLBORN, H. (ed.), *Republic to Reich. The making of the Nazi Revolution*, Random House, N.Y., 1972.
HORN, W., MATTHIAS, E., *Führerideologie und Parteiorganisation in der NSDAP (1919-33)*, Droste, Düsseldorf, 1972.
HORN, W., 'Regionale Entwicklung des Nationalsozialismus', *NPL*, 1976, pp.366ff.
— 'Hitler und die NSDAP', *NPL*, 1968, pp.467ff.
HÜTTENBERGER, P., 'Die Anfänge der NSDAP im Westen', in W. FÖRST (ed.), *Zwischen Ruhrkampf und Wiederaufbau*, Kohlhammer, Cologne, 1972.
JASPER, G., *Die gescheiterte Zaehmung. Wege zur Machtergreifung Hitlers 1930-34*, Suhrkamp, Frankfurt, 1986.
JASPER, G. (ed.), *Von Weimar zu Hitler 1930-33*, Kiepenheuer & Witsch, Cologne-Berlin, 1968.
JOCHMANN, W., *Ursprung und Geschichte der NSDAP in Hamburg 1922-1933*.

Hamburg, 1963.
KATER, M. H., *The Nazi Party. A social profile of members and leaders, 1919-1945*, Basil Blackwell, Oxford, 1983.
KICH, H. W. (ed.), *Aspects of the Third Reich*, Macmillan, 1985.
KIESENKOETTER, U., *Gregor Strasser und die NSDAP*, Schriftenreihe der *VJH*, Stuttgart, 1978.
KRATZENBERG, V., *Arbeiter auf den Weg zu Hitler? Die NS Betriebszellen-Organisation Ihre Entstehung, ihre Programmatik, ihr Scheitern 1927-34*, Lang, Frankfurt, 1987.
KREBS, A., *The infancy of Nazism. The memoirs of ex-Gauleiter Krebs 1923-1933*, edited by W. S. ALLEN, Croom Helm, 1976.
LEPSIUS, M. R., *Extremer Nationalismus. Strukturbedingungen vor der nationalsozialistischen Machtergreifung*, Kohlhammer, Stuttgart, 1966.
LOEWENBERG, P., 'The psychohistorical origins of the Nazi Youth Cohort', *AHR*, LXXVII, 1971, pp.1457ff.
MANSTEIN, P., *Die Mitglieder und Wähler der NSDAP 1919-1933*, Lang, Frankfurt-Bonn-N.Y.-Paris, 1988.
MASER, W., *Die Frühgeschichte der NSDAP. Hitlers Weg bis 1924*, Athenäeum Verlag, Frankfurt-Bonn, 1965.
MATTHIAS, E., MORSEY, R., *Das Ende der Parteien 1933*, Droste, Düsseldorf, 1966.
MATZERATH, H., TURNER, H. A., 'Die Selbstfinanzierung der NSDAP 1930-1932', *Geschichte und Gesellschaft*, 3, 1977, pp.93ff.
MERKL, P., *Political violence under the Swastika. 581 early Nazis*, Princeton U.P., 1975.
— *The making of a Stormtrooper*, Princeton U.P., 1980.
MICHALKA, W. (ed.), *Die nationalsozialistische Machtergreifung*, Schöningh, Paderborn-Munich, 1984.
MOMMSEN, H., 'Der Reichstagbrand und seine politischen Folgen', *VJH*, 12, 1964, pp.351ff.
MOREAU, P., *Nationalsozialismus von Links. Die 'Kampfgemeinschaft Revolutionaerer Nationalsozialisten' und die 'Schwarze Front'*, DVA, Stuttgart, 1985.
MUEHLBERGER, D. (ed.), *The social basis of European fascist movements*, Croom Helm, 1987.
NOAKES, J., 'Conflict and development in the NSDAP 1924-7', *JCH*, 1, no.4, 1966.
— *The Nazi Party in Lower Saxony 1921-1933*, O.U.P., 1971.
NYOMARKAY, J. L., 'Factionalism in the National Socialist German Workers' Party 1925-1926', *Political Science Quarterly*, 80, 1965, pp.22ff.
ORLOW, D., 'The organizational structure of the NSDAP 1919-1923', *JMH*, 37, 1965, pp.208ff.
— *The history of the Nazi Party*, 2 vols: *I, 1919-1933*, David and Charles, 1971; *II, 1933-1945*, David and Charles, 1973.
— 'The conversion of myths into political power. The case of the Nazi Party 1925-6'. *AHR*, 72, 1966-7, pp.906ff.
PHELPS, R. H., 'Hitler and the Deutsche Arbeiterpartei', *AHR*, 68, 1962-3, pp.974ff.
PINSDORF, K., 'Nature and aims of the National Socialist German Labour Party', *American Political Science Review*, 25, 2, 1931, pp.377ff.

PLEWNIA, M., *Auf dem Weg zu Hitler. Der 'völkische' Publizist Dietrich Eckart*, Schünemann Universitätsverlag, Bremen, 1970.

PRIDHAM, G., *Hitler's rise to power. The Nazi movement in Bavaria, 1923-33*, Hart-Davis, 1973.

REHBERGER, H., *Die Gleichschaltung des Landes Baden, 1932-3*, Winter Verlag, Heidelberg, 1966.

REICHE, E. G., 'From "spontaneous" to legal terror. S.A. police and judiciary in Nuremberg, 1933-4', *ESR*, 9, no.2, 1979, pp.237ff.

SCHÖN, E., *Die Entstehung des Nationalsozialismus in Hessen*, Anton Hain, Meisenheim a. Glan, 1972.

SCHULZ, G., *Aufstieg des Nationalsozialismus. Krise und Revolution in Deutschland*, Propyläen, Frankfurt, 1975.

SCHWARZWÄLDER, H., *Die Machtergreifung der NSDAP in Bremen 1933*, Carl Schünemann, Bremen, 1966.

SPEIER, H., *German white collar workers and the rise of Hitler*, Yale U.P., New Haven, 1987.

STACHURA, P. D., 'The ideology of the Hitler Youth in the Kampfzeit', *JCH*, 1973, vol.8, no.3, pp.155ff.

— 'Der kritische Wendepunkt? Die NSDAP und die Reichstagswahlen vom 20 Mai 1928', *VJH*, 26, 1978, pp.66ff.

— *Gregor Strasser and the rise of Nazism*, Allen and Unwin, London-Boston-Sydney, 1983.

— *Nazi Youth in the Weimar Republic*, Clio Press, Santa Barbara, 1975.

— 'The National Socialist Machtergreifung and the German Youth movement', *AHR*, 77, 1975, pp.255ff.

STEGER, B., 'Der Hitlerprozess und Bayerns Verhältnis zum Reich', *VJH*, 1977. 25, pp.441ff.

TRACEY, D. R., 'The development of the National Socialist Party in Thuringia 1924-30', *CEH*, VIII, 1975, pp.23ff.

TRÖGER, A., 'Die Dolchstosslegende der Linken: "Frauen haben Hitler an die Macht gebracht"', *Frauen und Wissenschaft. Beiträge zur Sommeruniversität für Frauen*, Berlin, 1976.

TYRELL, A., 'Führergedanke und Gauleiterwechsel. Die Teilung des Gaues Rheinland der NSDAP 1931', *VJH*, 23, 1975, pp.341ff.

— *Führer-befiehl... Selbstzeugnisse aus der Kampfzeit der NSDAP*, Droste, Düsseldorf, 1969.

VOGT, M., 'Zur Finanzierung der NSDAP zwischen 1924 und 1928', *GWU*, 4, 1970, pp.234ff.

WHEATON, E. B., *Prelude to calamity. The Nazi Revolution 1933-5*, Gollancz, 1968.

WILLING, E. G., *Die Hitler Bewegung*, vol.I, R. V. Decker, Hamburg, 1962.

WISSEMANN, F., *Die Vorgeschichte der nationalsozialistischen Machtübernahme in Bayern, 1932-3*, Duncker & Humblot, Berlin, 1975.

b. *The Third Reich and general theories*

ABENDROTH, W. (ed.), *Faschismus und Kapitalismus. Theorien über die sozialen*

*Ursprünge und die Funktion des Faschismus*, Europäische Verlagsanstalt, Frankfurt/M, 1967.

ADLER, L. K., PATTERSON, T. G., 'Red facism', *AHR*, 75, 1969-70, pp.1046ff.

AGNOLI, J., BLANKE, B., LADRITZE, N. (eds.), *Alfred Sohn-Rethel: Ökonomie und Klassenstruktur des deutschen Faschismus. Aufzeichnungen und Analysen*, Suhrkamp, Frankfurt, 1973.

ALBRECHT, D., 'Zum Begriff des Totalitarismus', *GWU*, 1975, no.3, pp.135ff.

ALLARDYCE, G., 'What fascism is not. Thoughts on the deflation of a concept', *AHR*, 84, 1979, p.367.

ARENDT, H., *The origins of totalitarianism*, Allen and Unwin, 1958.

AUGENSTEIN, R. et al., *'Historikerstreit'. Die Dokumentation der Kontroverse um die einzigartigkeit der nationalsozialistischen Judenvernichtung*, Piper, Munich, 1987.

BESSON, W., 'Die Interpretation des Faschismus', *NPL*, 1968, pp.307ff.

BLANKE, B., REICHE, R., WERTH, J., 'Die Faschismus Theorie der DDR', *Das Argument*, no.7, Heft 2, 1970, pp.35ff.

BLOCH, E., *Erbschaft dieser Zeit*, Suhrkamp, Frankfurt, 1973 (original publication, 1935).

BRACHER, K. D., *The German dictatorship. The origins, structure and consequences of National Socialism*, Penguin, 1973.

— *Zeitgeschichtliche Kontroversen*, Piper, Munich, 1976.

BRADY, R., *The spirit and structure of German fascism*, Left Book Club, 1937.

BROSZAT, M. (ed.), *Bayern in der NS-Zeit*, vol.2: *Herrschaft und Gesellschaft in Konflikt*, Oldenbourg, Munich-Vienna, 1979.

BROSZAT, M., FRÖHLICH, E., WIESEMANN, F. (eds.), *Bayern in der NS-Zeit. Soziale Lage und politischen Verhaltes der Bevölkerung im Spiegel vertraulicher Berichte*, Oldenbourg, Vienna, 1977.

BROSZAT, M., *Der Staat Hitlers*, Deutscher Taschenbuch Verlag, Munich, 1969 (Eng. translation, *The Hitler State*, Longman, 1981).

— *German National Socialism*, Clio Press, Santa Barbara, California, 1961.

BRÜDIGAM, H., *Wahrheit und Fälschung. Das Dritte Reich und seine Gegner in der Literatur seit 1945*, Röderberg Verlag, Frankfurt, 1959.

BUCHHEIM, H., *Totalitäre Herrschaft: Wesen und Merkmale*, Kösel, Munich, 1962.

BULL, H. (ed.), *The challenge of the Third Reich: The Adam von Trott memorial lectures*, Clarendon Press, 1986.

CARSTEN, F., *Essays in German History*, Hambledon Press, 1985.

CARSTEN, F. L., *The rise of fascism*, Batsford, 1967.

CASINELLI, C. W., *Total revolution. A comparative study of Germany under Hitler. the Soviet Union under Stalin and China under Mao*, Clio Press, Santa Barbara, California, 1976.

CLEMENZ, M., *Gesellschaftliche Ursprünge des Faschismus*, Suhrkamp, Frankfurt, 1972.

DAHRENDORF, R., *Society and democracy in Germany*, Weidenfeld and Nicolson, 1968.

DÜLFFER, J., 'Bonapartism, Fascism and National Socialism', *JCH*, 11, no.4, 1976, pp.109ff.

— 'David Irving, der Widerstand und die Historiker', *GWU*, 11, 1979, pp.686ff.

EBENSTEIN, W., *The Nazi State*, Farrar and Rinehart, N.Y., 1934.

EICHHOLTZ, D., 'Alte und "neue" Konzeptionen. Bürgerliche Literatur zur Wirtschaftsgeschichte des Faschismus in Deutschland', *JBW*, 1971, Pt.III, pp.231ff.

EICHHOLTZ, D., GOSSWEILER, K., *Faschismus Forschung. Positionen, Probleme, Polemik*, Akademie Verlag, Berlin, 1980.

ERDMANN, K. D., 'Die Zeit der Weltkriege', in *Handbuch der deutschen Geschichte*, vol.4, Ernst Klett, Stuttgart, 1976.

— 'Nationalsozialismus, Faschismus and Totalitärismus', *GWU*, 8, 1976, pp.457ff.

EVANS, R., *Rethinking the German past. 19th Century Germany and the origins of the Third Reich*, Allen and Unwin, 1987.

FISCHER, F., *From Kaiserreich to Third Reich*, Allen and Unwin, 1986.

FOCKE, H., REIMER, U., *Alltag unterm Hakenkreuz*, Rowohlt, Reinbek bei Hamburg, 1979.

FRIEDRICH, C. J., *Totalitarianism. Proceedings of a conference held at the American Academy of Arts and Sciences*, Harvard U.P., Cambridge, 1954.

FRIEDRICH, K., 'Fascism versus totalitarianism. Ernst Nolte's views re-examined', *CEH*, 4, 1971, pp.271ff.

FROMM, E., *The fear of freedom*, Routledge and Kegan Paul, 1942.

FUNKE, M., *Totalitärismus. Eine Studien-Reader zur Herrschaftsanalyse moderner Diktaturen*, Droste, Düsseldorf, 1978.

FUNKE, M. (ed.), *Demokratie und Diktatur. Geist und Gestalt politischer Herrschaft in Deutschland und Europa*, Droste, Düsseldorf, 1987.

GLUM, F., *Der Nationalsozialismus, Werden und Vergehen*, C. H. Beck, Munich, 1962.

GÖHRING, M., *Alles oder Nichts*, J. C. B. Mohr, Tübingen, 1966.

GÖRGEN, H. P., *Düsseldorf und der Nationalsozialismus. Studie zur Geschichte einer Grosstadt im Dritten Reich*, Schwann, Düsseldorf, 1969.

GRAML, H., HENKE, K.-D. (eds.), *Nach Hitler. Der schwierige Umgang mit unserer Geschichte*, Oldenbourg, Munich, 1987.

GREBING, H., *Aktuelle Theorien über Faschismus und Konservatismus; eine Kritik*, Kohlhammer, Stuttgart, 1974.

— 'Erneuerung des Konservatismus?', *PVS*, no.3, 1978, pp.372ff.

— *Nationalsozialismus: Ursprung und Wesen*, Olzog, Munich-Vienna, 1967.

GREBING, H. et al. (eds.), *Der 'deutsche Sonderweg' in Europa 1806-1945. Eine Kritik*, Kohlhammer, Stuttgart, 1986.

GROSSER, A. (ed.), *Dix leçons sur le nazisme*; Fayard, Paris, 1976.

GROTH, A., 'The "isms" in totalitarianism', *APSR*, LVIII, 1964, pp.888ff.

GRZESINKSI, A., *Inside Germany*, E. P. Dutton, N.Y., 1939.

GUÉRIN, D., *Fascisme et grande capitale: Italie-Allemagne*, Paris, 1945.

HAFFNER, S., *Anmerkungen zu Hitler*, Kindler Verlag, Munich, 1978.

— *Jekyll and Hyde*, Secker and Warburg, 1940.

HAMILTON, A., *The appeal of fascism: A study of intellectuals and fascism 1919-1945*, Blond, London, 1971.

HANISCH, E., 'Neuere Faschismustheorien', *ZG*, no.1, 1973-4, pp.19ff.

HAYES, C. J. H., 'The novelty of totalitarianism in the history of western civilization', *Proceedings of the Amer. Philosophical Society*, 82, 1940.

HEIDEN, K., *A history of National Socialism*, Methuen, 1934.

HENNIG, E., *Bürgerliche Gesellschaft und Faschismus in Deutschland*, Suhrkamp, Zurich, 1977.

— *Thesen zur deutschen Sozial-und Wirtschaftsgeschichte 1933 bis 1938*, Suhrkamp, Frankfurt, 1973.

— *Hessen unter Hakenkreuz. Studien zur Durchsetzung der NSDAP in Hessen*, Insel-Verlag, Frankfurt, 1983.

HEUSER, B., 'The Historikerstreit: uniqueness and comparability of the Holocaust', *German History*, 6, no.1, 1988, pp. 69-78.

HEYEN, F. J. (ed.), *Nationalsozialismus im Alltag. Quellen zur Geschichte des Nationalsozialismus vornehmlich im Raum Mainz-Koblenz-Trier*, Harold Boldt, Boppard, 1967.

HILDEBRAND, K., *Das Dritte Reich*, Oldenbourg, Munich, 1979.

— 'Noch einmal: Zur Interpretation des Nationalsozialismus', *GWU*, 4, 1981, pp.199ff.

— 'Hitlers Ort in der Geschichte des preussisch-deutschen Nationalstaat', *HZ*, 217, 1973, pp.584ff.

— 'Stufen der Totalitärismusforschung', *PVS*, 9, 1968.

— *The Third Reich*, Allen and Unwin, 1984.

HILLGRUBER, A., *Zweierlei Untergang. Des Zerschlagung des deutschen Reiches und das Ende des europäischen Judentums*, Siedler, Berlin, 1987.

HOFER, W., *Der Nationalsozialismus. Dokumente 1933-45*, Fischer Taschenbuch, 1957.

— *Die Diktatur Hitlers bis zum Beginn des zweiten Weltkrieges*, Akademische Verlagsgesellschaft, Konstanz, 1960.

HURST, M., 'What is fascism?', *HJ*, XI, 1968, pp.165ff.

INSTITUT FÜR ZEITGESCHICHTE, *Alltagsgeschichte der NS-Zeit. Neue Perspektive oder Trivialisierung?* (Colloquium), Munich, 1984.

INTERNATIONAL COUNCIL FOR PHILOSOPHY AND HUMANISTIC STUDIES, *The Third Reich*, Weidenfeld and Nicolson, 1955.

IRVING, D., *Hitler's Germany 1933-9*, Michael Joseph, 1978.

KAISER, H., 'Vom "Totalitärismus zum "Mobilisierungs" Modell', *NPL*, XVIII, 1976, pp.141ff.

KEDWARD, H. R., *Fascism in Western Europe 1900-1945*, Blackie, 1969.

KERSHAW, I., *The Nazi dictatorship. Problems and perspectives of interpretation*, Edward Arnold, 1985.

KIELMANSEGG, P. G., 'Krise der Totalitärismus Theorie', *Zeitschrift für Politik*, Neue Folge, 21, 1974, pp.311ff.

KITCHEN, M., 'August Thalheimer's theory of fascism', *Journal of the History of Ideas*, XXXIV, no. 1, 1973, pp.67ff.

— *Fascism*, Macmillan, 1976.

KLOENNE, A., *Zurück zur Nation? Kontroversen zu deutschen Fragen*, Diedrichs, Cologne, 1984.

KOCH, H. W. (ed.), *Aspects of the Third Reich*, Macmillan, 1985.

KRIEGER, L., 'Nazism, highway or byway?', *CEH*, XI, 1978, pp.3ff.

KUCZYNSKI, J., *Germany under fascism 1933 to the present day*, F. Muller, 1944.

KUHN, A., *Das faschistische Herrschaftssystem und die moderne Gesellschaft*, Hoffmann & Campe, Hamburg, 1973.

KÜHNL, R., *Der deutsche Faschismus in Quellen und Dokumenten*, Pahl

Rugenstein, Cologne, 1975.
— 'Der deutsche Faschismus', *NPL*, 1970, pp.13ff.
— *Formen bürgerlicher Herrschaft. Liberalismus-Faschismus*, Rowohlt, Reinbeck bei Hamburg, 1971.
— *Faschismustheorien. Texte zur Faschismusdiskussion. Ein Leitfaden*, Rororo Aktuell, Reinbek bei Hamburg, 1979.
— 'Neuere Ergebnisse und Tendenzen in der Faschismusforschung', *PVS*, 1, 1980, pp.17ff; 2, pp.121ff.
— 'Probleme einer Theorie über den internationalen Faschismus', *PVS*, 1, 1975, pp.89ff.
— 'Der deutsche Faschismus. Nationalsozialismus und "Drittes Reich" in Einzeluntersuchungen und Gesamtdarstellungen', *NPL*, 1970, pp.13ff.
KULKA, O. D., 'Die deutsche Geschichtsschreibung über den Nationalsozialismus und die Endlösung. Tendenzen und Entwicklungsphasen 1924-84' *NPL*, 240, pp.599-640.
LASKI, H., *Reflections on the revolution of our time*, Allen and Unwin, 1943.
LASSWELL, H., 'The psychology of Hitlerism', *The Political Quarterly*, 4, 1933.
LEDERER, E., *Kapitalismus, Klassenstruktur und Probleme der Demokratie in Deutschland, 1910-1940*, edited by J. KOCKA, Vandenhoeck & Ruprecht, Göttingen, 1979.
LEUSCHNER, J., 'Der Nationalsozialismus, Hitler und das "Dritte Reich"', *NPL*, 1966, pp.241ff.
LIPSET, S. M., *Political man. The social bases of politics*, Garden City Press, N.Y., 1966.
LAQUEUR, W., *Fascism. A reader's guide*, Penguin, 1979 (2nd edition).
LOZEK, G., MEIER, H. et al. (eds.), *Unbewältigte Vergangenheit. Handbuch zur Auseinandersetzung mit der Westdeutschen bürgerlichen Geschichtsschreibung*, Akademie, E. Berlin, 1971 (2nd edition).
MALETTKE, K. (ed.), *Der Nationalsozialismus an der Macht. Aspekte nationalsozialistischer Politik und Herrschaft*, Vandenhoeck and Ruprecht, Göttingen, 1984.
MALTITZ, H. von, *The evolution of Hitler's Germany*, McGraw Hill, 1973.
MASON, T. W., 'The primacy of politics', in S. J. WOOLF (ed.), *The nature of fascism*, Weidenfeld and Nicolson, 1968.
MEINECKE, F., *The German catastrophe*, Harvard U.P., 1950.
MIERENDORFF, C., 'Gesicht und Charakter der nationalsozialistischen Bewegung', *Die Gesellschaft*, no.7, 1930, pp.489ff.
MOELLER, H., 'Die Nationalsozialistische Machtergreifung, Konterrevolution oder Revolution', *VJH*, 31, no.1, 1983 pp. 25-51.
MOSSE, G. L., *Nazism. A historical and comparative analysis of National Socialism*, Basil Blackwell, Oxford, 1979.
NEUMANN, F., *Behemoth. The structure and practice of National Socialism 1933-4*, O.U.P., 1944.
NICHOLLS, A., MATTHIAS, E. (eds.), *Germany democracy and the triumph of Hitler*, Allen and Unwin, 1971.
NOLTE, E., 'Zeitgenössische Theorien über den Faschismus', *VJH*, 15, 1967, pp.247ff.
— *Der Faschismus in seiner Epoche*, Piper, Munich, 1963.

— *Deutschland und der Kalte Krieg*, Piper, Munich, 1974.
— *Die faschistischen Bewegungen. Die Krise des liberalen Systeme*, Deutscher Taschenbuchverlag, Munich, 1973 (4th edition).
— *Theorien über den Faschismus*, Kiepenheuer & Witsch, Berlin-Cologne, 1967.
PALME-DUTT, R., *Fascism and social revolution*, International Publishers, N.Y., 1935.
PARMELEE, M., *Bolshevism, fascism and the liberal democratic state*, Chapman and Hall, 1935.
PERZ, B., SAFRIAN, H., 'Wege und Irrwege des Faschismusforschung', *ZG*, 7, 1979-80, pp.437ff.
PETZINA, D., 'Germany and the Great Depression', *JCH*, 4, no.4, 1969, pp.59ff.
PHILIPS, W. A. P., *The tragedy of Nazi Germany*, Routledge and Kegan Paul, 1974.
PLESSNER, H., *Die verspätete Nation. Über die politische Verführbarkeit bürgerlichen Geistes*, Stuttgart-Cologne-Mainz, 1959 (first published 1935).
PRIDHAM, G., NOAKES, J. (eds.), *Documents on Nazism 1919-1945*, Jonathan Cape, 1974.
RAUSCHNING, H., *Germany's revolution of destruction*, Heinemann, 1939.
RAUSHENBRUSH, S., *The march of fascism*, Yale U.P., 1939.
REMAK, J., *The Nazi Years*, Prentice Hall, Englewood Cliffs, N.J., 1969.
ROBERTS, S., *The house that Hitler built*, Methuen, 1937.
ROSENBERG, A., *Faschismus als Massenbewegung. Sein Aufstieg und seine Zerstörung*, Carlsbad, 1934.
SAAGE, R., *Faschismus Theorien*, Beck, Munich, 1976.
— 'Konservatismus und Faschismus', *PVS*, 2, 1978, pp.254ff.
SAUER, P., *Württemberg in der Zeit des Nationalsozialismus*, Süddeutsche Verlagsgesellschaft, Ulm, 1975.
SAUER, W., 'National Socialism. Totalitarianism or fascism?' *AHR*, LXXIII, 2, 1967, pp.404ff.
SCHIEDER, W. (ed.), *Faschismus als soziale Bewegung. Deutschland und Italien im Vergleich*, Hoffmann & Campe, Hamburg, 1976.
SCHREIBER, G., Hitler und seine Zeit. Bilanze, Thesen, Dokumente, *NPL*, Beiheft 3, 1986, pp.137-62.
SCHÜDDEKOPF, O. E., *Linke Leute vom Rechts*, Kohlhammer, Stuttgart, 1960.
— *Fascism*, Weidenfeld and Nicolson, 1973.
SCHULZ, G., *Faschismus. Nationalsozialismus. Versionen und theoretische Kontroversen, 1923-72*, Propyläen, Berlin, 1974.
SCHULZE, G., *Deutschland seit dem Ersten Weltkrieg 1918-1945*, Vandenhoeck and Ruprecht, Göttingen, 1985.
SEIDEL, B., JENKNER, S. (eds.), *Wege der Totalitärismusforschung*, Wissenschaftliche Buchgesellschaft, Darmstadt, 1968.
SERING, P., (R. LÖWENTHAL), *Jenseits des Kapitalismus. Ein Beitrag zur sozialistischen Neuorientierung*, Nuremberg, 1948.
SHIRER, W., *The rise and fall of the Third Reich*, Signet Books, N.Y., 1961.
STACHURA, P. D. (ed.), *The shaping of the Nazi State*, Croom Helm, 1978.
STEINERT, M. G., *L'Allemagne national-socialiste 1933-45*, Richelieu-Bordas, Univ. de Paris I, 1972.
STRACHEY, J., *The menace of fascism*, Covici Friede, N.Y., 1933.
TALMON, J. L., *The origins of totalitarian democracy*, Heinemann, 1961.

THAMER, H.-U., *Verführung und Gewalt. Deutschland 1933-45*, Siedler, Berlin, 1986.
TURNER, H. A., 'Fascism and modernisation', *World Politics*, 24, 1971-2, pp.547ff.
– *Faschismus und Kapitalismus in Deutschland*, Vandenhoeck & Ruprecht, Göttingen, 1972.
ULBRICHT, W., *Die Legende vom 'deutschen Sozialismus'. Ein Lehrbuch für das schaffende volk über das Wesen des deutschen Faschismus*, Verlag Neuer Weg, E. Berlin, 1945.
UNGER, A., *The totalitarian party. Party and people in Nazi Germany and Soviet Russia*, C.U.P., 1974.
WAITE, R. G. (ed.), *Hitler and Nazi Germany*, Rinehart and Winston, N.Y., 1965.
WEBER, E. J., *Varieties of fascism*, J. van Nostrand, Princeton, N.J., 1964.
WINKLER, H. A., *Mittelstand, Demokratie und Nationalsozialismus*. Kiepenheuer & Witsch, Cologne, 1972.
WIPPERMANN, W., *Faschismus-Theorien. Zum Stand der gegenwärtigen Diskussion*, Wissenschaftliche Buchgesellschaft, Darmstadt, 1972.
– 'The postwar German Left and fascism', *JCH*, 11, no.4, 1976, pp.185ff.
WISTRICH, R. S., 'Leon Trotsky's theory of fascism', *JCH*, 11, 1976, pp.157ff.
WOOLF, S. J., *European Fascism*, Weidenfeld and Nicolson, 1968.
WOOLF S. J. (ed.), *The nature of fascism*, Weidenfeld and Nicolson, 1968.
YAMAGUCHI, Y., 'Faschismus als Herrschaftssystem in Japan and Deutschland. Ein Versuch des Vergleichs', *GWU*, no.2, 1976, pp.89ff.
ZUMPE, L., 'Stand und Probleme der wirtschaftshistorischen Imperialismus-forschung', *ZGW*, 5, 1975, pp.495ff.

# Index